"What emerges from these well-c   ____ __ ___
understanding of competitions critical to preserving peace and promoting prosperity. Michael Auslin identifies the critical factors that will determine whether the future for free and open societies across the Indo-Pacific region remains bright or a darker future emerges in which autocratic and closed systems are ascendant. All who have a stake in that future should read and discuss *Asia's New Geopolitics*."

> —H. R. McMaster, former US national security adviser
> and author of *Battlegrounds*

"Michael Auslin is one of America's sharpest analysts of Asia's geopolitics. This collection brims with insights about the future of the world's most important region."

> —Hal Brands, coauthor of
> *The Lessons of Tragedy: Statecraft and World Order*

"Auslin's book is a must-read for anyone interested in the question of how the US can respond to China's ambitions to dominate East and South Asia."

> —James Hankins, *Claremont Review of Books*

"An extremely engaging and timely discussion of the US strategy in the Indo-Pacific in the midst of China's growing influence and the diminishing US presence in the region. With insightful analysis of the challenges faced by the United States, Auslin reminds us why we cannot remain a spectator to the reshaping of regional order. A must-read for anyone, let alone experts and policy makers, who is concerned about the future role of the United States in the region."

> —Gi-Wook Shin, the William J. Perry Professor of Contemporary Korea
> and director of the Shorenstein Asia-Pacific Research Center
> at Stanford University

"A work about the geopolitics and policies of Asia written with the depth of a true historian, Auslin's *Asia's New Geopolitics* offers a set of insightful essays about some of the key challenges in this part of the world over the next generation. I found the work engaging as an expert in the field, but also, as a professor, I found it to be an excellent teaching text for my students."

> —Victor Cha, vice dean and D.S. Song-KF Professor of Government,
> School of Foreign Service, Georgetown University,
> and former senior director for Asia, National Security Council

ASIA'S NEW GEOPOLITICS

ASIA'S NEW GEOPOLITICS

Essays on Reshaping the Indo-Pacific

Michael R. Auslin

HOOVER INSTITUTION PRESS

Stanford University | Stanford, California

With its eminent scholars and world-renowned library and archives, the Hoover Institution seeks to improve the human condition by advancing ideas that promote economic opportunity and prosperity, while securing and safeguarding peace for America and all mankind.

hoover.org

Hoover Institution Press Publication No. 706

Hoover Institution at Leland Stanford Junior University,
Stanford, California 94305-6003

Cover illustration maps: *L'Asie: dressée pour l'étude de la géographie* (Paris, 1786); *Dated Events. On To Tokyo. Map of the Pacific and the Far East* (Toronto, 1944); both courtesy of the David Rumsey Map Collection, www.davidrumsey.com. *Theater of Operations, Sino-US Littoral War of 2025* by International Mapping.

First printing 2020
First paperback printing 2021
27 26 25 24 23 22 21   9 8 7 6 5 4 3

Manufactured in the United States of America

Library of Congress Control Number: 2020931284

ISBN 978-0-8179-2324-2 (cloth)
ISBN 978-0-8179-2325-9 (pbk)
ISBN 978-0-8179-2326-6 (epub)
ISBN 978-0-8179-2327-3 (mobi)
ISBN 978-0-8179-2328-0 (PDF)

To Sachiko Kuno

CONTENTS

FOREWORD

"Whether through economic pressure, political and military intimidation, espionage, or propaganda, Beijing is actively trying to reshape the world to fit its interests, picking and choosing which Western norms it adopts and which it ignores. . . . The 'new China rules' . . . are the . . . greatest strategic challenge of the next generation."

It would be hard to improve upon this summary by Michael Auslin of the way Washington now perceives China. The point is that Auslin has been making such arguments for many years. It is only in the last two that they have become part of a new consensus.

Recall the 2015 National Security Strategy document, the last published by the administration of Barack Obama. "The scope of our cooperation with China is unprecedented," it declared. "The United States welcomes the rise of a stable, peaceful, and prosperous China. We seek to develop a constructive relationship with China that delivers benefits for our two peoples and promotes security and prosperity in Asia and around the world. We seek cooperation on shared regional and global challenges. . . . While there will be competition, we reject the inevitability of confrontation."[1]

Compare and contrast this language with the December 2017 edition, published during H. R. McMaster's tenure as President Donald Trump's national security adviser:

China seeks to displace the United States in the Indo-Pacific region, expand the reaches of its state-driven economic model, and reorder the region in its favor. . . . China gathers and exploits data on an unrivalled scale and spreads features of its authoritarian system, including corruption and the use of surveillance. It is building the most capable and well-funded military in the world, after our own. Its nuclear arsenal is growing and diversifying.[2]

The report continues, "China is using economic inducements and penalties, influence operations and implied military threats to persuade other states to heed its political and security agenda." Vice President Mike Pence used similar language in his October 2018 speech to the Hudson Institute, adding that Beijing was also "employing a whole-of-government approach, using political, economic, and military tools, as well as propaganda, to advance its influence and benefit its interests in the United States."[3]

The question is: Can the United States counter this Chinese challenge without—as Henry Kissinger, Graham Allison, and others have warned—unwittingly falling into the "Thucydides Trap," which tends to bring an incumbent power into costly, violent conflict with a rising power?[4] Few scholars are better qualified to address that question than Michael Auslin. The eight essays brought together here illustrate the breadth and depth of his Asian expertise.

Unlike some specialists, Auslin is a fox, not a hedgehog: to follow the distinction drawn by the Greek poet Archilochus, he knows not just one thing, but many. The subjects under discussion in this volume range from the safety of North Korea's nuclear arsenal to the persistent impediments to gender equality in India. Auslin started his career as a student of Japan, and there is much of interest here about that unique country, a country that can seem to foreigners (as he nicely puts it) "of the world but perhaps not fully in it." (This comes from a brilliant essay, "Japan's Eightfold Fence," which is as good an introduction to modern Japan as I have ever read.) However, the main focus of *Asia's New Geopolitics* is, as it should be, the challenge posed by China to the hegemonic position the United States has enjoyed in the Pacific region since the end of World War II.

Auslin implies a certain skepticism about the viability of treating the "Indo-Pacific" as a single strategic theater—as in the Department of Defense's 2019 *Indo-Pacific Strategy Report*—and of making (in the report's words) "a free and open Indo-Pacific" the paramount goal of American policy. This, he suggests, is too vast a battlefield. Instead, Auslin revives the concept of an "Asiatic Mediterranean"—an idea he attributes to the Dutch-born cofounder of the Yale Institute of International Studies, Nicholas J. Spykman. In his book *The Geography of the Peace* (1944), Spykman developed Halford Mackinder's thesis that, if the Eurasian landmass was the "heartland" of geopolitics, then the "rimlands" at either end of it were the likely battlegrounds for its control. According to Spykman, the three key waterways were (in Auslin's formulation) "the North Sea and the Mediterranean in Europe, the Persian Gulf and littoral waters of the western Indian Ocean in the Middle East, and the East and South China Seas, along with the Yellow Sea, in Asia." A similar argument had been made by Mackinder himself in his 1943 essay "The Round World and the Winning of the Peace."

Auslin's focus is on the last of these: the Yellow Sea, the East China Sea, and the South China Sea. As the expanse of water between China and its neighbors—Korea, Japan, the Philippines, and Indonesia—this may well be regarded as Asia's answer to the Mediterranean, but China increasingly treats all three seas as its own coastal waters. "Today," Auslin argues, "America has lost a conscious understanding of the strategic importance of the inner seas and skies, at a moment when it faces the greatest challenge to its control of them since 1945. . . . China is contesting control not of the high seas . . . but of the marginal seas and skies of Asia, even while the United States remains dominant on the high seas of the Pacific."

In addition to its own naval and air forces, since the 1950s the United States has relied for its dominance of Asia's Mediterranean on five bilateral treaties: with Australia (1951), the Philippines (1951), South Korea

(1953), Thailand (1954), and Japan (1960). The key to China's challenge to American primacy, however, is the more ambiguously situated island of Taiwan, which lies in the middle of what Chinese strategists call the "first island chain" between China and the Pacific Ocean. (The first island chain extends from the Kamchatka Peninsula to the Malay Peninsula and encompasses the Kuril Islands, Japan, the Ryukyu Islands, Taiwan, the northern Philippines, and Borneo.)

The Taiwan Relations Act of April 10, 1979, states that America will "consider any effort to determine the future of Taiwan by other than peaceful means, including by boycotts or embargoes, a threat to the peace and security of the Western Pacific area and of grave concern to the United States" and that America "will make available to Taiwan such defense articles and defense services in such quantity as may be necessary to enable Taiwan to maintain a sufficient self-defense capability."

Since Trump's election, the United States has been underlining its commitment to Taiwan in a variety of ways—for example, the Asia Reassurance Initiative Act of 2018. The Taiwan Assurance Act, passed unanimously by the US House of Representatives in May 2019, urges the United States not only to continue selling arms to Taiwan but also to support Taiwan's participation in international organizations (in other words, to resist Beijing's efforts to freeze Taiwan out of all such organizations). (At the time of writing, January 2020, the bill has yet to be put before the Senate.) In 2019 Washington authorized two major arms sales to Taiwan: M1 Abrams tanks and F-16 Viper jets.

This flies in the face of the Chinese government's ambition to integrate Taiwan into the People's Republic of China (PRC), ending its de facto autonomy. As a recent report from the Australian Lowy Institute put it:

> For Xi's China, annexing Taiwan is core to achieving national redemption and the "Chinese dream"—Xi's agenda for "the great rejuvenation of the Chinese nation in the new era." In theory,

China has time on its side, as the deadline set by Xi for achieving the Chinese dream is 2049; in reality, Xi's China is becoming more and more impatient to regain control over the island. . . . Xi himself has potentially set the clock ticking on unification, stating in a speech early in 2019 that the Taiwan problem could not be passed down from "generation to generation." . . . In a landmark speech in January 2019, Xi lauded the "one country, two systems" model used in Hong Kong for Taiwan.[5]

Yet only ten percent of Taiwanese support unification with the mainland, according to opinion polls, and that share is largely accounted for by PRC-born residents. A paradoxical feature of the past decade has been the fact that, contrary to Beijing's expectations, "the closer the two economies grew, the more people identified as Taiwanese rather than Chinese, and the less open they have become to rule from Beijing."[6] The storm of protest unleashed in Hong Kong by an ill-advised extradition bill, and the response of the government in Beijing, has only increased the antipathy of Taiwanese voters to the idea of submitting to a status equivalent to Hong Kong's.

Auslin's most explosive chapter is his last. "The Sino-American Littoral War of 2025: A Future History" imagines the dire consequences of what he sees as the American failure to maintain a proper alignment between ends and means in the Asian Mediterranean. In this speculative scenario, which is evidently informed by recent Department of Defense war games, Auslin imagines an escalation of the Sino-American antagonism into a full-scale conventional naval war, culminating in the sinking of the USS *Gerald R. Ford*, the newest and biggest of American aircraft carriers, which was formally commissioned by President Trump in July 2017.

In this vision, it is the first year of a new Democratic administration. Nothing in (by implication) the second Trump term has reduced the antagonism between Beijing and Washington. When President Newsom—who would certainly not be the first governor of California to make it to the White House at a time of international tension—and Defense Secretary Flournoy find themselves called on to support a new Filipino government in its attempts to counter China's annexation of the Scarborough Shoal, things rapidly escalate from midair and surface collisions to the biggest naval clashes since World War II.

Although both sides pull back from the brink of committing ground forces or firing nuclear missiles, the net result of the conflict is a decisive shift in the balance of regional power to the advantage of China.

The key point of this hypothetical exercise is that, although American air power is still superior to Chinese, the US Navy no longer has the relative strength to win such a war against its Chinese counterpart in a theater so far from the United States and so near to China. Nor, Auslin suggests, are the relationships with Taiwan, South Korea, or the Philippines strong enough for the United States to be able to count on them in a showdown with China. In his war scenario, all three defect from the US side to protect themselves.

Such future histories only rarely come to pass. But that is sometimes because they achieve their objective of making contemporary strategists think again. No one who reads this book will put it down content with the state of American strategy in the so-called Indo-Pacific region. They may even conclude that the very concept of an Indo-Pacific strategy is misconceived. If nothing else, they will be compelled by Auslin's argument that it is control of the "rimlands" that will determine which of the two superpowers wins the unfolding struggle for mastery in East Asia.

This admiring reader could only wonder how the United States could possibly cope with a coordinated challenge in all three of the key maritime theaters identified by Spykman. The great merit of this kind of historically informed writing about contemporary geopolitics is precisely that it raises such new and deeply troubling questions.

Niall Ferguson
Hoover Institution, Stanford
January 2020

Notes

1. White House, National Security Strategy, February 2015 (Washington, DC), 24.
2. White House, National Security Strategy of the United States of America, December 2017 (Washington, DC), 25, 46.
3. Hudson Institute, "Remarks by Vice President Pence on the Administration's Policy Toward China," October 4, 2018, https://china.usembassy -china.org.cn/remarks-by-vice-president-pence-on-the-administrations -policy-toward-china.
4. Graham Allison, *Destined for War: Can America and China Escape Thucydides's Trap?* (New York: Houghton Mifflin Harcourt, 2017).
5. Natasha Kassam and Richard McGregor, "Taiwan's 2020 Elections," Lowy Institute, January 7, 2020, https://www.lowyinstitute.org/publications /taiwan-s-2020-elections.
6. Kassam and McGregor, "Taiwan's 2020 Elections."

INTRODUCTION

The essays contained in this volume were written over half a decade, though most appeared between 2016 and 2018. Although penned separately, collectively they paint a portrait of geopolitics in the Indo-Pacific region, impressionistic in some cases and far from comprehensive to be sure, but a broad-based view nonetheless of how the region is changing, how it is not, and what are the key trends shaping Asia. Having spent much of the period from 2010 to 2017 focused on researching and writing my book *The End of the Asian Century* and penning regular columns for the *Wall Street Journal*, as well as publishing numerous opinion pieces for *National Review*, *Politico*, *The Atlantic*, and other outlets, the occasional opportunity to strike a middle ground between writing a monograph and an op-ed became increasingly attractive. Being able to tackle more speculative ideas or interpretations of what I was seeing on my travels seemed, as well, a welcome alternative to the more direct policy pieces I was writing.

The following essays, most of them expanded and updated from their original form, deal with individual nations, including China, Japan, India, and North Korea; bilateral relations between Japan and China; and American strategy in the Indo-Pacific. The collection starts out with an argument to bring back the idea of the "Asiatic Mediterranean," expressed in the geopolitical thought of Nicholas Spykman during the 1940s. The great power struggles in the long twentieth century (starting with the Sino-Japanese War of 1894) centered more on control of the inner seas and littoral rimlands than on the heartland of Halford Mackinder's more famous formulation. To see Asia as an integrated strategic space may offer new avenues for maintaining stability and understanding the scope of China's bid for regional hegemony.

That discussion is followed by a piece laying out what I call the "new China rules," by which Beijing hopes to deal with the world, including pervasive espionage, stealing of intellectual property, intimidation, and further shutting off of China from the outside, all policies being pushed by Chinese president Xi Jinping. The third essay argues that the greatest threat from a nuclear North Korea is not that Kim Jong-un or his successors will one day decide to nuke San Francisco, but rather that maintaining a nuclear arsenal is an extraordinarily difficult job, one in which the risk of accidents and miscalculations is frighteningly high, as attested by the history of the American nuclear arms program. If the world does not succeed in denuclearizing North Korea, then it will have to trust Pyongyang to know how to keep its nuclear weapons safe from malfunction, accidental launch, and the like.

The next two chapters are largely focused on domestic affairs in India and Japan. I wrote "India's Missing Women" from a journalistic standpoint, based on interviews I conducted in New Delhi and Chennai a few years ago. Though India is steadily increasing its global role, social attitudes at home continue to change too slowly to benefit millions of educated women, who often continue to be forced into arranged marriages and who have to give up their professional careers. Until India taps into the skills and talents of these women, it will continue to lag in development. In a similar vein, "Japan's Eightfold Fence" is a sweeping reconsideration of how Japan has embraced "modernity" and how that has shaped its response to a generation of economic stagnation. In looking over the past twenty-five years of Japanese history, the essay argues that the Japanese have consciously made a choice to maintain certain barriers against the world so as to preserve social stability and harmony. Though ignored or disparaged for its supposedly ossified society, Japan continues to do extraordinarily well on international measures of education, health, crime, and the like.

The last three pieces return to the great power struggle for mastery in the Indo-Pacific. Though shelves of books have been written on the recent Sino-American competition, from treatises claiming that China will effortlessly supplant the United States to those darkly predicting war, the much older and arguably more important battle between Japan and China has been all but overlooked, which is the subject of "China versus Japan." For Asian nations, the great historical question is not whether they will choose the outsider America over China, but rather which Asian model to follow, that of Tokyo or Beijing. It was but a few years ago that Japan seemed dominant; now it is China. This competition comprises everything from visions of civil society to economic development models and will continue long after the United States is no longer a major player in the region.

Yet America is not leaving Asia anytime soon, and the following essay takes a long historical look at US strategy in the Indo-Pacific from the beginning of the republic to today. The goal for America remains the same as it has been since 1945—namely, to maintain a balance of power in the Indo-Pacific region while supporting liberal nations that are attempting to create ever more accepted norms and durable links. Such a strategy should not be waylaid by an unwise attempt to contain China, but rather should focus on American strengths and Washington's deep relationships to create meaningful communities of interest on everything from trade to maritime security. Such will do more to blunt China's rise than a frantic attempt to counter every move Beijing makes, and this approach is more sustainable for the long run.

It is the once unimaginable specter of military conflict between China and the United States that drives much of the contemporary commentary on the future of the Indo-Pacific. The final chapter in this volume takes a speculative look from a future historian's perspective at a fictional war between Beijing and Washington, focusing on what precipitated the armed clash and how the conflict unfolded. An era of mistrust and worsening of working relations falls victim to circumstance and accident on the high seas and skies of Asia, a fictional scenario that unfortunately is backed up by plenty of historical precedent. The geopolitical implications of a Sino-US clash are the ultimate focus of this what-if essay.

The prospects for continued stability and growth in Asia look dimmer today than they have for years. Politicians can, and often do, make dangerously misguided choices, and given the continuing legacy of historical distrust in Asia combined with stubborn territorial disputes, there are numerous paths by which conflict could erupt. Despite such worrisome signs of trouble, however, the region remains vibrant and far more integrated than in the past. The shadow of nationalism competes with better-educated middle classes that hope to pass on to their children the gains they have made, while China's mercantilist policies face pushback from nations looking to more open and fairer trading networks. An America that remains engaged in the Indo-Pacific, and which works with partners to help preserve stability, is acting in its own interests as well as contributing to the common good.

I am grateful to the following individuals who either published or commissioned the original essays: David Berkey, Ryan Evans, Freddy Gray, Victor Davis Hanson, Jacob Heilbrunn, Julius Krein, Rich Lowry, Siddhartha Mahanta, Lara Prendergast, Matt Seaton, and Nick Schulz. In addition, Niall Ferguson, H. R. McMaster, Admiral (ret.) Cecil Haney, Lt. General (ret.) James Kowalski, Dick Samuels, Ted Bromund, Toshi Yoshihara, Jim Holmes, Hal Brands, Jim Fannell, Olivia Morello, Howard Wang, Robert Girrier, and several individuals who wish to remain anonymous offered suggestions, support, research assistance, or feedback. I would also like to acknowledge the support of Tom Gilligan, director of the Hoover Institution. At the Hoover Press, Chris Dauer, Barbara Arellano, Danica Hodge, Elizabeth Berg, and Alison Law provided a truly enjoyable publishing experience.

As with the original publications, any errors of fact are mine alone.

Michael R. Auslin
Hoover Institution, Stanford
January 2020

1

ASIA'S MEDITERRANEAN

Strategy, Geopolitics, and Risk in the Seas of the Indo-Pacific

I.

"I believe China seeks hegemony in East Asia."[1]

The statement, delivered in congressional testimony by the then commander of US Pacific Command in February 2016, was shockingly blunt by official standards.[2] US policy toward China since the opening of bilateral relations in the 1970s has been predicated on incorporating China into the liberal global order and creating a cooperative relationship of trust between the two nations. For years, media reports, books, and scholarly studies had approvingly talked about China's unprecedented modernization, while high-level US government officials repeated their hopes that Beijing would eventually become a pillar of the international order, sharing with America the burden of maintaining the post–World War II system.

This essay is adapted from "Asia's Mediterranean: Strategy, Geopolitics, and Risk in the Seas of the Indo-Pacific," *War on the Rocks*, February 29, 2016, https://warontherocks.com/2016/02/asias-mediterranean-strategy-geopolitics -and-risk-in-the-seas-of-the-indo-pacific.

Yet by the time Admiral Harry Harris made his claim, the nature of the US-China relationship was shifting steadily from cooperation toward confrontation. Years of bilateral engagement over political, economic, and security issues appeared irrelevant in the face of China's massive growth in power and influence, much of which seemed aimed squarely at reducing America's role in the Indo-Pacific region. Watching the slowly gathering storm clouds were Asian nations large and small, some of which were US allies, most of which had ties with the United States, and all of which viewed China's rise with a mixture of opportunism and wariness.

Hegemony, however, was a particularly loaded term. The goal of US security policy since 1945 has been to prevent the rise of an aggressive hegemon in either Asia or Europe. To label China as such was tantamount to declaring it a threat to US interests and regional stability alike. For its part, Beijing had for years denied any hegemonic ambitions, imputing such aims instead to the United States; to be so called out by America's senior military leader in the Indo-Pacific revealed the dawn of a new era in relations between the two nations.

Until Harris's statement, US officials had more often than not downplayed China's increasingly assertive military tendencies during the second decade of the twenty-first century. Such an approach was not new in Sino-American relations. In similar ways, American policy makers had quietly moved to restore relations that were briefly interrupted after the 1989 Tiananmen Square massacre, had largely ignored credible evidence that China had stolen top-secret nuclear missile technology from the United States during the 1990s, and had no response to China's rampant industrial espionage in the 2000s and beyond.[3] The default position of the US government for decades had been to try and ignore offensive or threatening Chinese behavior and instead redouble its efforts to reach accommodation with Beijing.

By the time of Harris's testimony, the question of whether decades of US military dominance in the Indo-Pacific region would continue was openly being discussed by allies and antagonists alike. Not merely had China embarked on a long military modernization program, but it had steadily begun to increase its military presence in the South and East China Seas, as well as venturing into the Indian Ocean and western Pacific. It had also begun to use its military to back up its various territorial claims in some of those same waters. But what caught regional attention in particular was China's dramatic land reclamation and island-building campaign among reefs and atolls in disputed waters in the Spratly and Paracel Islands in the South China Sea during the mid-2010s. It seemed Beijing was actively, even physically, changing the balance of power in the region, discarding international law and postwar norms, and ignoring the claims of smaller Southeast Asian nations to some of the same territory. It was, perhaps, the "Sputnik moment" for America's Asia policy.

Starting in 2014 or so, publicly available satellite photography dramatically showed that what had been largely underwaters reefs just a few years prior were now islands.[4] Moreover, the nearly three thousand acres of reclaimed land on China's new territory were being fortified with airfields, hangars, radars, and other support buildings. Admiral Harris called this China's "great wall of sand," even as Beijing repeatedly asserted that the islands would not be used for military purposes. Evidence soon emerged that the People's Liberation Army (PLA) had landed advanced fighter jets and strategic bombers, and emplaced surface-to-air missiles, on Woody Island in the disputed Paracel island chain. Subsequent months revealed the fortification of Fiery Cross Reef and other Chinese-claimed isles in the South China Sea.[5] As Harris testified, "You'd have to believe in a flat Earth" not to see that China was indeed militarizing the South China Sea.[6] China's rapid and assertive building up of its military capabilities in one of the world's most vital waterways stoked wide-ranging concerns about the balance of power, Beijing's intentions, and America's ability to remain the predominant power in the Indo-Pacific region.

Washington was not blind to the implications of Beijing's actions. Starting in the early 2010s, a prolonged American debate began on how to respond to China's moves in the South China Sea, stretching over both the Obama and Trump administrations. The positions ranged from a legalistic stance based on accepted international law to calls for limited military activity, including freedom of navigation operations (ambiguously twinned with claims of "innocent passage")[7] by US Navy ships and occasionally flyovers by US planes around China's claimed territories. Plans for multination maritime patrols in the South China Sea were discussed while observers totaled up the acreage of China's reclaimed islands and observed the ongoing construction of military-use facilities on the former reefs.[8]

Yet this intense interest in the South China Sea, however justified, occluded a larger picture of the strategic environment in East Asia, even as it revealed fears about America's position within it. There often seems to be a serial quality to Washington's concern and response. It traditionally appears to prefer focusing, or is able to focus, on only one subregion at a time. Thus, at a given moment, the Spratlys occupy its analysis while it ignores the Paracels in the same sea. Only a few years ago, the Obama administration concentrated on the growing risk of a clash between Japan and China over the Senkaku Islands (Ch. Diaoyutai) in the East China Sea while doing little about the South China Sea. Washington is thus taken by surprise each time a new challenge to the status quo appears. Meanwhile, the Chinese steadily attempt to encroach throughout the Indo-Pacific, linking maritime and land trade routes under the umbrella of the One Belt One Road (OBOR) initiative, while expanding the operational capabilities of the PLA Navy and Air Force in waters and skies far from China's shores.

Chinese strategy in the region has long been guided by the desire to control the maritime and air space within the so-called first- and second-island chains. These "chains" encompass firstly the East and South China Seas, linking up with Beijing's "nine-dash line" claim to the South China Sea. The second island chain is far broader in scope, encompassing Japanese territory and reaching far into the western Pacific, all the way to the US territory of Guam in the Marianas.

Moving westward, China has also sought to expand its influence through what some call the "string of pearls" throughout the Indian Ocean, namely ports and access points ringing the Indian subcontinent and reaching all the way to Africa and the Persian Gulf region.[9] All this has been integrated with the overarching OBOR initiative, as access to strategic bases increasingly follows in lockstep with growing Chinese trade routes and economic agreements. When looked at in totality, the Chinese challenge is political, economic, and military, as well as region-wide; so must be America's response.

Effectively responding to China's challenge requires adopting a larger geostrategic picture of the entire Indo-Pacific region and America's position in it. Drawing such a picture is the stated goal of the 2019 Department of Defense *Indo-Pacific Strategy Report*, which is the first such official US strategy document for the Pacific since 1998.[10] The report opens by stating that the "Indo-Pacific is the Department of Defense's priority theater," which is an explicit reori-entation of US defense strategy away from the Atlantic and Middle East. To ensure the continuation of what the Trump administration has called the "free and open" Indo-Pacific, the Pentagon's strategy is built around "preparedness, partnerships, and the promotion of a net-worked region."

As articulate as the Defense Department's approach is, the demands of acting throughout the vast Indo-Pacific region, thousands of miles from the continental United States, often strain even the best-considered strategy. It is easy to get mired in the tactical and nudge aside the truly strategic. To bring the two approaches into sync, it may be useful to exhume a concept discussed briefly during the 1940s: that of the integrated strategic space of East Asia's "inner seas," or what was called the Asiatic Mediterranean.[11] The utility of this concept will make clear that the geopolitical challenge the United States and its allies and partners face is an emerging struggle for control of the entire common maritime/air space of East Asia. It is helpful to briefly review the evo-lution of geopolitical thought in relation to this region.

II.

The academic field of geopolitics began with Halford Mackinder and his oft-quoted, oft-misunderstood "heartland" thesis. Mackinder's famous 1904 article, "The Geographical Pivot of History," in fact discussed only briefly the idea of the heartland, essentially steppe Eurasia, as the ultimate goal of any world power.[12] Mackinder may have written that "whoever controls the heartland controls the world," but his real insight was into the struggle over the "rimlands," which both guard and give access to the heartland. The rimlands properly include the European peninsula of the Eurasian landmass, as well as the littoral areas of Asia and the Middle East. The great struggles for world power that followed on the heels of Mackinder's article in fact took place in the rimlands, and over the course of the twentieth century, the greatest economic growth took place in those same rimlands. In the second decade of the twenty-first century they have once again become areas of competition. As Wess Mitchell and Jakub Grygiel wrote, it is the rimlands that both revanchist Russia under Vladimir Putin and revisionist China seem to be trying to contest.[13]

Four decades after Mackinder's original thesis, during the darkest days of World War II, the Yale geopolitical thinker Nicholas John Spykman returned to the rimland thesis and further modified it to take into account recent great-power warfare in the twentieth century. In a posthumously published book titled *The Geography of the Peace* (1944), Spykman provided the insight that it is in the rimlands that the real struggle for mastery has taken place.[14] More importantly, he argued that attaining control of the "marginal" or "inner" seas adjacent to the rimlands, bordered by the offshore "outer crescent" of island nations like Great Britain and Japan, was the prerequisite to dominating the rimlands. Thus, according to Spykman, the most crucial waterways for global power were the North Sea and the Mediterranean in Europe, the Persian Gulf and littoral waters of the western Indian Ocean in the Middle East, and the East and South China Seas, along with the Yellow Sea, in Asia.

Spykman's claims challenged Alfred Thayer Mahan's famous assertion in *The Influence of Seapower upon History* that control of the high
seas rightly was the great goal of the maritime powers.[15] Instead of
looking at the vast global maritime highway, as Mahan did, Spykman
instead concentrated on the areas where most of the global population
lived, where production was most concentrated, and where trade was
most intensely conducted. In a 1943 *Foreign Affairs* article, "The Round
World and the Winning of the Peace," Mackinder himself had joined
Spykman, modifying his earlier position.[16] Mackinder, like Spykman,
now emphasized the importance of the rimlands and their marginal
seas. The great naval battles of World War II, except for the Battle of
the Atlantic, the Coral Sea, and Midway, were indeed fought largely in
the inner seas of Europe and Asia.

Control of the inner seas was not a new military concept. It explains
the decades-long war waged by the British Royal Navy against
Napoleon's ships in the English Channel and French littoral waters, as
well as the Imperial Japanese Navy's reduction of the Chinese and
Russian fleets in the Yellow Sea in both 1894 and 1904, giving it control
over access to Korea and China. As both these examples also point out,
the struggle for control of the inner seas is often the first step to a larger
contest over the rimlands, and this maritime-based competition can
last years before a move is made on land or the issue is decided by
opposing armies.

Technological advances since the Great War had come fully to frui-
tion by the 1940s, and Spykman struggled to expand his thesis to incor-
porate the most modern type of combat: aerial warfare. Command of
the skies and the ability to effect devastating results on the ground from
the air only became a feasible military capability in World War II. The
ferocious aerial warfare of the Battle of Britain was one example of the
struggle for the inner seas being expanded to the realm of aerospace.
Indeed, due to the limitations of 1940s-era aircraft, aerial warfare was
almost wholly restricted to the littoral and rimlands regions. The objective, however, remained the same: control the maritime/aerial commons that give access to the rimlands.

Yet World War II was the last major war where command of the ocean, whether the high or inner seas, was a strategic necessity. In the post–World War II era, the United States dominated the oceans and most of the skies, except over the Soviet bloc. The new era required a new geopolitical concept, and Spykman's thesis was modified by the Harvard political scientist Samuel Huntington. Prior Eurasian struggles for mastery had taken place among Eurasian powers. Now, with the balance of global military might held by a nation in a different hemisphere, how could the idea of maintaining geopolitical control fit traditional models?

Huntington provided an answer in his well-known 1954 article in the US Naval Institute's *Proceedings*. "National Policy and the Trans-oceanic Navy" recapped the eras of US naval strategy and argued that in the modern era the power of the US Navy would be employed over transoceanic range but for the same goals.[17] Huntington presciently saw that naval power in the post–World War II era would be used almost solely for effecting land-based struggles in the rimland (and he could have made the same argument about the US Air Force). Huntington's insight helped explain MacArthur's landing at Inchon in 1950, US carrier-based air operations against North Vietnam, the air and amphibious operations of the 1991 Gulf War, and the Iraq War two decades later. No longer was naval power concerned with command of the sea, since the United States held it uncontested, except perhaps in the submarine race with the Soviets during the Cold War. Transcontinental air power also removed limitations on US bombers, though tactical fighters were still employed to defend the "marginal skies" of the American homeland, just as the Soviets planned to counter the US Air Force over the inner skies of Europe. While the geostrategic chessboard had expanded, the military objectives were little altered.

III.

Today America has lost a conscious understanding of the strategic importance of the inner seas and skies, at a moment when it faces the greatest challenge to its control of them since 1945. Washington should acknowledge bluntly that China is contesting control not of the high seas, like Germany in World War I or Japan in World War II, but of the marginal seas and skies of Asia, even while the United States remains dominant on the high seas of the Pacific. Indeed, it is arguable that the Chinese military already can assert control over the waters and skies of the first island chain—in other words, the marginal seas and skies of eastern Asia. This control will make it difficult, perhaps impossible, to fight back into the region if US forces are dislodged or preemptively choose a posture of offshore balancing.

Recognizing this fact not only clarifies our understanding of Chinese military activity in the region but also maps out the area under risk and the geopolitical pivot of the Indo-Pacific: the Asiatic Mediterranean. The integrated waters of the Sea of Japan, the Yellow Sea, and the East and South China Seas are as vital to the history, identity, and trade of eastern Asia as the Mediterranean is to Europe. While it is geographically a stretch to connect the Asiatic Mediterranean to the Indian Ocean, the passageways between the two remain among the world's most vital waterways, through which one-third of global trade passes, in the form of over seventy thousand ships per year moving into the Asiatic Mediterranean.[18] The great factories and workshops of China, Japan, South Korea, Taiwan, Vietnam, and others, on which the global trading network depends, are located along the littoral of the Asiatic Mediterranean. It forms the hinge between maritime Eurasia and the entire Western Hemisphere. To return to Spykman's formulation, control of the Asiatic Mediterranean means control of Asia.

The challenge posed by China is thus twofold. It threatens the maritime and aerospace freedom of the Asiatic Mediterranean, and thus ultimately of Asia's productive and trading capacities. It also is positioning China to have a preponderance of power that can be brought against the Indo-Pacific's rimlands, as well as against what Spykman called the "outer crescent," which, in Asia, includes Japan, the Philippines, Indonesia, and Australia. These rimlands and the outer crescent, it should be remembered, are uniquely composed of continental, peninsular, and archipelagic landforms. Japan's control of Korea and Formosa (now Taiwan) in the 1930s facilitated its invasion of China, which found its greatest success in the rimland and only became bogged down when it attempted to extend into China's heartland or out into the trackless Pacific. China today is attaining the capability to threaten Japan and Southeast Asia, not solely from the homeland but from its expeditionary bases in the inner seas. From this perspective, the air defense identification zone (ADIZ) that Beijing established in the East China Sea in November 2013 is another element in its attempt to establish control over the inner skies of Asia. An Asiatic Mediterranean dominated by China would severely limit America's global strategic freedom, and potentially threaten our nation's economic well-being.

IV.

What is to be done?

First, the United States must consciously redraw its mental map to adopt the idea of the Asiatic Mediterranean. Stretching from Kamchatka in the north to the Strait of Malacca in the south, its interconnected waters form the soft underbelly of Asia. Washington must then accept that its goal is to ensure that no aggressive power gains control over the Asiatic Mediterranean and thereby threatens the region's stability. This policy is a combination of maintaining the balance of power and asserting America's ability to control the waters, skies, and cyber networks of East Asia's inner seas, if necessary.

This requires several policy adaptations. First, US Indo-Pacific Command must ensure its planning and operations seamlessly cover the entire space and can maintain control when called upon, particularly at strategic checkpoints. The ability to overwhelmingly target Chinese ships in the early stages of a conflict, operate in the face of cyberattacks, and maintain control of the skies throughout the inner sea area is vital. This will help ensure that the Pentagon's goal of "preparedness" described in the *Indo-Pacific Strategy Report* is not merely a checklist of to-do items, but is an approach leading to the ability to act in a holistic fashion throughout Asia's littorals. The Allied Powers in World War II would never have accepted losing the eastern Mediterranean while keeping open the western half, nor should the Pentagon disassociate the South and East China Seas. That objective requires a sufficient forward-based force able to respond to multiple Chinese offensives at the same time, while ensuring credible defense of both allies and strategic nodes such as Taiwan and the Malacca Strait. Though potentially politically risky for Asian nations, given their economic dependence on China, the Pentagon should attempt to coordinate regular peacetime freedom of navigation operations with willing allies and partners throughout the region, while wartime planning should prepare for keeping the entire region a zone of maneuver and control by allied forces.

Second, intelligence, surveillance, and reconnaissance (ISR) activities should be strengthened to provide a holistic risk assessment of the Asiatic Mediterranean for both peacetime preparedness and wartime operations. The United States needs robust, survivable ISR coverage of the Asiatic Mediterranean, especially its choke points, and the ISR capabilities of allies and partners should be developed with US help.

Third, the Department of Defense should deepen discussions with both allies and partners on how it can cooperate specifically to help maintain stability, corresponding to the goal of a "networked" region in the *Indo-Pacific Strategy Report*. "Gray zone" incidents short of clear aggression, which often include paramilitary forces, have been increasing between China and its neighbors in recent years, and effective regional responses should be explored that can scale up during times of open conflict. This may include formalizing joint patrols, agreements over nonlethal support, greater sharing of intelligence, and the like. In addition, working with more capable partners like Japan, the US military should consider how to cooperate more effectively on both defensive and offensive cyber operations in the region.

Making promises to try to maintain stability in the Indo-Pacific should not be taken lightly. As Walter Lippmann admonished in *U.S.*

Foreign Policy: Shield of the Republic (1943), foreign commitments must be brought into balance with national power.[19] Writing, like Spykman, during the dark days of World War II, he asserted that a strategic imbalance was a direct cause of war. He scathingly faulted US foreign policy in the Pacific from 1899 to 1942 for failing to recognize the imbalance between US commitments and its power in relation to the rise of Japan, which America was unable to deter and unprepared to stop. Since 1945, however, except for a limited challenge by the Soviet Union, America has not had a credible challenger in the Pacific. Not since Vietnam nearly a half century ago—which was the last time it brought localized power to bear on the Asiatic rimland—has Washington had to ensure that its Asian commitments and its power were in balance.

Unlike when Huntington was writing what might be considered the urtext of offshore balancing, America now faces in China a credible challenger for local control. Beijing has identified control of the Asiatic Mediterranean as its goal and is acting to permanently change the geopolitical balance by deploying low-tech weapons swarms alongside high-tech weaponry, and through such initiatives as the island-building campaign. Washington thus risks failing to meet this challenge in two respects: not ensuring that its commitments and its power in the region are in balance and not appropriately recognizing the full scope of the challenge and its holistic nature. Any moves toward an offshore balancing posture as a way to reduce potential friction with China will further weaken America's ability to maintain stability and bring to bear military power when and where necessary.

The recent concern in Washington over China's capabilities and intentions is a belated recognition of these facts. Policy makers are now increasingly worried that American power is not commensurate with US commitments, especially if the commitment is understood as the continued stability of the marginal seas and ensuring that no one power controls them. From that perspective, Washington's alliance structures ironically may be secondary to the primacy of control of the marginal seas; losing that control would make fulfilling alliance commitments even more difficult or costly.

Recovering our appreciation of the strategic importance of Asia's inner seas and rimlands is necessary if America is to devise a realistic strategy to preserve both its power and its influence in the Indo-Pacific. Losing one part of the Asiatic Mediterranean will certainly cause allies and partners in other parts to consider either severing ties with the United States or declaring neutrality so as to preserve their own freedom of action. A geopolitically isolated United States is an operationally weakened United States. Being pushed out of one sea will require the US military to expend national treasure to fight its way back in during a crisis. The better course of action is to keep the Asiatic Mediterranean whole, balanced, and stable. Only then can America be certain that the vital rimlands of Asia will remain free from conflict. To paraphrase Benjamin Franklin, the Asiatic Mediterranean must certainly hang together, or it might very well hang separately.

Notes

1. Associated Press, "China Seeks to Control East Asia, US Commander Tells Senators," *The Guardian*, February 23, 2016, https://www.theguard ian.com/world/2016/feb/23/south-china-sea-east-asia-control-us -military.
2. US Pacific Command was renamed US Indo-Pacific Command in May 2018.
3. Shirley A. Kan, *China: Suspected Acquisition of U.S. Nuclear Weapon Secrets*, RL30143 (Washington, DC: US Library of Congress, Congressional Research Service, 2006), https://fas.org/sgp/crs/nuke/RL30143.pdf.
4. See, for example, Edward Wong and Jonathan Ansfield, "To Bolster Its Claims, China Plants Islands in Disputed Waters," *New York Times*, June 16, 2014, https://www.nytimes.com/2014/06/17/world/asia/spratly -archipelago-china-trying-to-bolster-its-claims-plants-islands-in-dis puted-waters.html.

5. Zack Cooper, "Saving Ourselves from Water Torture in the South China Sea," *War on the Rocks*, February 23, 2016, https://warontherocks.com/2016/02/saving-ourselves-from-water-torture-in-the-south-china-sea.

6. David B. Larter, "Pacific Command Chief Urges New Capabilities as Tensions Mount with China," *Navy Times*, February 23, 2016, https://www.navytimes.com/news/your-navy/2016/02/23/pacific-command-chief-urges-new-capabilities-as-tensions-mount-with-china.

7. Euan Graham, "Innocent Passage: Did the U.S. Just Fumble Its South China Sea Strategy?," *National Interest*, November 4, 2015, https://nationalinterest.org/blog/the-buzz/innocent-passage-did-the-us-just-fumble-its-south-china-sea-14253.

8. Sanjeev Miglani, "Exclusive: U.S. and India Consider Joint Patrols in South China Sea—U.S. Official," *Reuters*, February 10, 2016, https://www.reuters.com/article/us-southchinasea-india-usa-idUSKCN0VJ0AA.

9. Liu Zhen, "What's China's 'Nine-Dash Line' and Why Has It Created So Much Tension in the South China Sea?," *South China Morning Post*, updated September 18, 2018, https://www.scmp.com/news/china/diplomacy-defence/article/1988596/whats-chinas-nine-dash-line-and-why-has-it-created-so.

10. Department of Defense, *Indo-Pacific Strategy Report: Preparedness, Partnerships, and Promoting a Networked Region* (Washington, DC, 2019), https://media.defense.gov/2019/Jul/01/2002152311/-1/-1/1/DEPARTMENT-OF-DEFENSE-INDO-PACIFIC-STRATEGY-REPORT-2019.PDF.

11. Nicholas J. Spykman, *America's Strategy in World Politics: The United States and the Balance of Power* (New York: Harcourt, Brace, 1942), 132, available at https://books.google.com/books?id=rsIwxKfuHwIC&pg=PA132&dq=asiatic%20mediterranean&pg=PA132#V=onepage&q=asiatic%20mediterranean&f=true.

12. Halford J. Mackinder, "The Geographical Pivot of History," *Geographical Journal* (1904): 421–37, DOI 10.2307/1775498, https://www.jstor.org/stable/1775498?seq=1#metadata_info_tab_contents.

13. A. Wess Mitchell and Jakub Grygiel, "Predators on the Frontier," *American Interest* 11, no. 5 (February 12, 2016), https://www.the-american-interest.com/2016/02/12/predators-on-the-frontier.

14. Nicholas Spykman, *The Geography of Peace* (New York: Harcourt, Brace, 1944).
15. Alfred Thayer Mahan, *The Influence of Sea Power Upon History, 1660–1783* (New York: Dover, 1987).
16. Halford J. Mackinder, "The Round World and the Winning Peace," *Foreign Affairs*, July 1943, https://www.foreignaffairs.com/articles/1943 -07-01/round-world-and-winning-peace.
17. Samuel P. Huntington, "National Policy and the Transoceanic Navy," *U.S. Naval Institute Proceedings Magazine*, May 1954, https://www.usni .org/magazines/proceedings/1954-05/national-policy-and-trans oceanic-navy.
18. United Nations Conference on Trade and Development, *Review of Maritime Transport 2016*, https://unctad.org/en/PublicationsLibrary/rmt 2016_en.pdf.
19. Walter Lippmann, *U.S. Foreign Policy: Shield of the Republic* (Boston: Little, Brown, 1943).

2

THE NEW CHINA RULES

The Sources of Chinese Behavior

In July 2018, Palau Pacific Airways shuttered its doors. The small airline found itself collateral damage in a spat between its archipelago of 21,000 persons and China. It might seem odd for the world's largest country to care much what a tiny island nation does, but Palau is one of only eighteen countries to maintain diplomatic relations with Taiwan. As a result, the Chinese government banned all tour groups to Palau, imposing fines on those who defied the edict and crushing revenue for Palau Pacific Airways.[1]

That same month, four US airline companies bowed to Chinese pressure and removed all references to Taiwan as an independent nation from their websites. They followed forty other global airlines, all of whom months earlier had accepted Chinese demands to list Taipei, Taiwan's capital, as part of China. Even so, the US carriers' action was deemed insufficient by Beijing, as they had tried various ways to include Taipei without acknowledging it was part of China. As a result, Beijing

Parts of this essay first appeared as "The New China Rules," *National Review* 70, no. 19 (October 15, 2018) and "China v. America: The Espionage Story of Our Time," *The Spectator*, January 29, 2018, https://blogs.spectator.co.uk/2018/01 /china-vs-america-the-espionage-story-of-our-time.

warned of consequences to the airlines' credit ratings and other actions to force complete compliance.[2] Like Palau Pacific Airways, the large US companies found themselves caught in the middle of a geopolitical struggle between China and the rest of the world.

The power play was only the most recent example of China's increasingly aggressive foreign policy, and the American airlines were just the latest Western corporations to feel Beijing's wrath by not immediately capitulating to China's political agenda. Whether through economic pressure, political and military intimidation, espionage, or propaganda, Beijing is actively trying to reshape the world to fit its interests, picking and choosing which Western norms it adopts and which it ignores. Worse, while publicly proclaiming its support for global governance, Beijing appears actively antagonistic to many of the values that created the post-1945 world. As the commander of US Indo-Pacific Command, Admiral Phil Davidson, stated in July 2019, "The international order is now under assault by China."[3] China increasingly expects the world to bend to its wishes, and it has adopted a set of behaviors to ensure it gets the outcomes it wants. Call it the "new China rules." These new rules are the sources of Chinese behavior and pose the greatest strategic challenge of the next generation.

America's China Dreams

When US president Richard Nixon toasted Chinese premier Zhou Enlai during his historic visit to Peking (as it was then known) in February 1972, the veteran cold warrior had few illusions about the nature of the Chinese Communist Party (CCP) and its system. He proposed a relationship based on common interests, namely the balancing of the Soviet Union, in which Washington and Peking would pursue "different roads leading to the same goal, the goal of building a world structure of peace and justice." In reply, Zhou made clear that Peking was as wary of its potential new partner as it was of its erstwhile ally, Moscow, reaffirming that he and Mao Zedong were most concerned with ensuring Washington's commitment to "mutual respect for sovereignty and territorial integrity [and] noninterference in each other's internal affairs."[4] In other words, give China what it needed to thrive but otherwise leave it alone.

Nixon's successors, while being careful not to stray too far from his guarded rhetoric, over time found it almost impossible to rein in their expectations about China, which were largely economic, while downplaying the obvious political and ideological differences between the countries. Successive American administrations dismissed warnings about China's potential strategic challenge in Asia and beyond, preferring to focus instead on a vision of Sino-American relations that was shared only by one side.[5] Not even the June 1989 Tiananmen Square massacre could significantly derail Washington's engagement with China, as the George H. W. Bush administration quickly moved to reopen high-level channels of communications after imposing limited sanctions and banning senior exchanges. Pundits and commentators followed the politicians' lead over the decades, making overly optimistic assumptions about how China would develop at home and act abroad.[6] These assumptions even now retain their tenacity, despite mountains of evidence that undermine them. Yet for the past several years, and not coincidentally since the election of Donald Trump as US president, the United States and the rest of the world are in the midst of a painful reconsideration of their relations with China. That reconsideration should begin with a clear understanding of how they came by their China dream.

A particular confluence of global factors abetted these rising American and global hopes in the decades after Nixon's visit. The first factor was the collapse of the Soviet Union in 1991 and the end of the Cold War, which seemed to many Americans proof of the final victory of liberal capitalist democracy. For many commentators, particularly conservative ones such as Charles Krauthammer and Francis Fukuyama, it was logical, if not inevitable, that other nations would adopt the Western model of social, political, and economic organization, what some called the "Washington consensus."[7] It would only make sense for governments around the world to cooperate in expanding trading links and to invest in their own development, instead of pursuing ruinous military budgets. US policy makers considered China, as the world's most populous nation, crucial for ensuring the success of both global economic liberalization and peaceful cooperation.

A second factor favoring China's emergence in the American mind was the popping of the Japanese economic bubble in 1989. Japan's economic miracle had elevated the country from a ruined and defeated aggressor in 1945 to the world's second-largest economy by 1972. Democratization had taken firm hold in Japan, holding open the prospect of broader liberalization in Asia. During the 1980s, Americans had warily watched Japan's rise to seeming economic dominance, and many assumed it would soon begin flexing its political and even military muscle. Dark warnings about a coming clash between America and Japan soured relations, as did charges of unfair trading practices.[8] With the collapse of the Japanese property and stock bubbles at the end of 1989, the country's economic growth leveled off and largely stagnated for a generation, thus removing American worry about being overtaken by the vaunted Japanese business model and Japan's consensus-oriented, high-achieving society. Japan's sudden slowdown not only caught America by surprise but served both to remove a potential competitor for global power and to open up a spot, so to speak, for another rising power to grab Washington's attention.

A final factor that inflated American expectations for China was the beginning of China's own economic spurt, widely dated from then-paramount leader Deng Xiaoping's legendary "southern tour" in 1992, which restarted the economic reforms he initially promulgated in 1979. Deng's famous exhortations to create capitalism with Chinese characteristics, perhaps best summed up in the apocryphal slogan "To get rich is glorious," seemed to offer validation that Western-style capitalism was the wave of the present. Deng's policies also served as assurance that China would not fall back into the isolation and madness of Mao's era, where the Great Leap Forward and the Cultural Revolution had largely destroyed a generation of Chinese growth and scarred its population. Two decades after Nixon and Mao first established ties between their two countries, it seemed as though China's historical development indeed would make it an increasingly important economic partner of the United States. Bill Clinton's shepherding of China into the World Trade Organization at the end of his administration served as an official endorsement of the hopes placed on Beijing and its normalization into the world order.

Few, however, could have foreseen just how quickly China would develop and how powerful a role it would play in the global economy, far eclipsing even Japan at its height. From a bit player, Chinese manufacturing dominated dozens of consumer sectors by the 2000s, and the country overtook Japan to become the world's second-largest economy by 2011. From steel to consumer electronics, and from textiles to solar panels Chinese manufacturers took over entire industries. The flag followed trade, so to speak, and just as had happened with Japan several decades previously, American policy makers, analysts, and pundits soon began to tout China as the next great world power. It seemed natural, to Americans at least, that the world's most populous nation would also become one of its leading political powers. With that power, Americans assumed, Beijing (as now spelled, in the phonetic system preferred by the Chinese government) would accept global responsibility, helping to support the system instituted by the Western victors after World War II. As such, Washington and Beijing no longer would simply be engaged in a transactional relationship; the two instead would be the pillars of a post–Cold War order, a "G-2" that could shape global economic, political, and strategic issues.

The George W. Bush administration created several mechanisms in conjunction with the Chinese to elevate top-level official exchanges that would reflect Beijing's new prominence. The Senior Dialogue began in the summer of 2005, followed by the Strategic Economic Dialogue in December 2006. The goal, as expressed in a speech by then deputy secretary of state Robert Zoellick, who also represented the United States at the Senior Dialogue, was to make China a "responsible stakeholder" in the international system.[9] The same desire was shared by the Obama administration, which combined and upgraded the two sets of talks into the Strategic and Economic Dialogue starting in 2009. With Obama himself addressing the gathering, and with the Americans represented by Obama's secretaries of state and the treasury, the highest-level imprimatur was placed on the annual meeting.

Just as importantly—perhaps even more so—America's leaders assumed in the flush of post–Cold War triumphalism that a China that was increasingly treated as a near peer of the United States and pulled into the global system would eventually, if fitfully, begin to manifest liberal tendencies. Harking back to dreams shared by Christian missionaries in the nineteenth century, US policy makers and business leaders believed that positive reinforcement in the form of diplomatic respect, earnest attempts at cooperation, and avoidance of topics like human rights would eventually catalyze an evolution in China's socioeconomic-political system. The benefits of following a liberal course were so self-evident, American leaders believed, that even authoritarian Chinese leaders would be forced to grant more power to their middle class, if only to keep it supportive, and to further open their society, since development ultimately depended on cultural changes that ensured a fertile field for further capitalist-style modes of organization. They could, they believed, change China. It was the bet of the century.

The Chinese Behemoth

China has indeed been changed over the past four decades, far beyond the dreams of Nixon and his successors. It is a dominant, if not the dominant, global power by a host of measures: industrial production, export of finished goods, provision of foreign aid, size of urban areas, military strength, and diplomatic activity, to name some of the more prominent. For most observers, it is China's massive economic growth that makes it a great power. By purchasing power parity (PPP) measurement, it is the world's largest economy, at \$25.3 trillion in 2018, compared to $20.5 trillion for the United States.[10] With $2.2 trillion of exports in 2017, it is the world's largest export economy.[11] It has become the largest, second-largest, or third-largest trading partner of nearly every country in the world.[12] In 2015, China overtook Canada to become America's largest trade partner, with an astonishing $737 billion two-way trade in goods and services in 2018, and an equally massive $378.6 billion trade deficit.[13] From 2005 to 2017, Chinese firms invested approximately $170 billion in the United States.[14] With its heralded One Belt One Road (OBOR) initiative, supported by financial institutions like the new Asian Infrastructure Investment Bank and with $1 trillion in promised infrastructure investment across Eurasia, Beijing is bidding to reshape global trade and investment relations. Chinese giants like Baidu, Alibaba, and Tencent are now among the largest technology companies on earth, competing with Apple and Facebook, while Sinopec and China National Petroleum rank as the world's third- and fourth-largest corporations.[15]

All this economic wealth has not merely transformed life in China, it also has translated into usable national power. The People's Liberation Army (PLA), China's military, which includes its navy and air force, is now widely considered to be the second most powerful in the world, after the US armed forces. From a technologically inferior, largely defensive force in the 1980s, the PLA has become an increasingly high-tech military that is learning to project power far from its borders, primarily through its navy. It is also developing significant air power, space, and cyber capabilities. Chinese diplomacy complements its military influence, with Beijing hosting major international gatherings, participating more vocally in global institutions, and playing a role in high-profile diplomatic initiatives, such as the Six Party Talks, over North Korea's nuclear program. Chinese citizens are a now-common sight around the world, as Chinese students and researchers flood Western, especially American, universities. In the United States alone, over 350,000 Chinese enrolled in US institutions in 2016–17, accounting for over a third of all foreign students.[16] Just as ubiquitous are Chinese tourists, who have become a major factor in the global tourism industry, spending $261 billion in 2016.[17] From nearly every perspective, America's China bet paid off in spades: China, the "middle country," sits firmly at the center of today's globalized world.

Perhaps having been transfixed by their own beliefs, liberal nations are now disappointed and surprised that a China that has reached the heights of global power is increasingly refusing to play by the global script expected of it. While Beijing has eagerly taken advantage of access to the global economy and the prestige of sitting at the leading diplomatic tables, it has resolutely pursued its own interests, regardless of the impact on other nations, and shown far less concern for becoming a steward of the system that enriched it. It is becoming increasingly clear that American policy makers undervalued the resiliency of China's national interests and the power of the CCP, misunderstood Chinese history, and underestimated Beijing's intention to become not merely a leading but a dominant global power, an aspiration that now concerns Washington as much as did Japan's far less comprehensive challenge in the 1980s.

More realistic international observers are not surprised that as China has become more powerful it has shown increasing dissatisfaction with the rules and structures of the very international system that allowed it to rise, undermining norms and attempting to change some of the practices of global governance. At the same time, it shows no qualms in either invoking or disregarding international law to buttress its trade policies or claims over disputed territory in areas such as the South China Sea. Washington and other liberal capitals misjudged Beijing's determination to maintain, protect, and even expand its authoritarian tendencies and mercantilist policies. Far from liberalizing, as Western policy makers and pundits hoped and assumed, the CCP at the end of the second decade of the twenty-first century is increasing its tight control of civil society and freedom of association and expression at home, while at the same time engaging intensively and often overbearingly with the outside world.

After two decades of opening up under Deng Xiaoping and Jiang Zemin, marked most notably by significant economic reform and the slow separation of government administration from the CCP, China began a return to what the sinologist David Shambaugh calls "hard authoritarianism" in 2009, during the leadership of Hu Jintao.[18] Hu's successor, current CCP general secretary and Chinese president Xi Jinping, accelerated Beijing's adversarial and repressive policies on taking power in late 2012, responding to a sense of crisis within the CCP over corruption, lack of ideological clarity, and too much liberalization.[19] Xi's repeated invocations of the "Chinese Dream" being the "great rejuvenation of the Chinese people" draw freely on concepts of Han nationalism, including references to Confucianism. Yet these overlay a very traditional legalist approach to society, in which hierarchy is underpinned by strict state control.[20]

Alternative visions of Chinese society, such as those offered by the student activists of the 1919 May Fourth Movement or the 1989 Tiananmen Square democracy demonstrations, are thoroughly suppressed. In foreign affairs, "Xi Jinping Thought on Diplomacy," which was unveiled in 2018, sets the guidelines for the country's overseas relations, in which China's "major-country diplomacy . . . is tasked with realizing the rejuvenation of the Chinese nation."[21] As this entails diplomacy "based on the focal points of the work of the party and the country," according to leading diplomat Yang Jiechi, Chinese diplomacy is thus subordinated to CCP goals of ensuring the triumph of Chinese socialism over the capitalist system.[22] In other words, despite platitudes that Beijing is committed to global development and progress, diplomacy is about strengthening China.

The China that has emerged after nearly a half century of engagement with the West is more suspicious, less satisfied, less cooperative, and less liberal than its eager American interlocutors hoped it would be. Americans and others are finally accepting this reality, disappointed though they might be and as split as they are on how to deal with China going forward, not least among the China-watching community.[23] No longer is Beijing portrayed in Washington as a "responsible stakeholder," nor do many hold out hope that an effective G-2 might yet emerge. Indeed, the specter of a second Cold War increasingly shapes

Western commentary, even as other commentators urge a return to traditional engagement as practiced until Donald Trump's presidency.[24] Regardless of what approach they advocate, most observers agree that rather than converging, Chinese values are increasingly diverging from those of the West, and that the two systems appear more incompatible than many believed just a decade ago.

China seems to be on a confrontational course with its neighbors and other leading powers, primarily the United States. Often bristling at what it considers condescending attitudes in Washington, Tokyo, and other capitals, and resentful of attempts to force it to play by global rules not of its own design, Beijing is more willing to probe and push the limits of antagonistic behavior, combining military intimidation with diplomatic browbeating and economic blackmail. Given the continued dependence of countries around the world on Chinese-produced goods and access to China's tantalizing market, Beijing has found few capitals willing to stand up to its provocative behavior. Though some writers, mimicking the hyperbolic anti-Japan warnings of the 1980s, darkly intimate of a coming war that can only be avoided by American accommodation of China, a period of intensified competition and antagonistic relations between Beijing and Washington seems almost assured.[25]

The New China Rules: Enforcing Global Compliance

After a long period of biding its time, Beijing has come up with its own way to ensure that its interests are not merely respected but enforced. These are the "new China rules." In addition to outright pressure campaigns against global corporations and national governments, the rules include endemic, aggressive theft of intellectual property (IP) from around the world; pervasive espionage against its so-called international partners; widespread influence campaigns targeting media, politicians, think tanks, and educational institutions; and an unceasing military buildup and extension of Chinese military presence in strategic regions, primarily in Asia. These are complemented by the smothering of domestic liberal trends and prevention of the further growth of civil society inside China, all to forestall any domestic liberalization, such as threatened the CCP in 1989. These rules threaten to poison relations between China and the wider world, leading to further trade wars, propaganda battles, and possibly even military clashes. If unchecked, the effects on the global economy and peace in Asia could be truly destabilizing.

The new rules begin with bolstering China's economy by any means. Focused on investment profits and cheaper consumer goods, Western nations long ignored the ways in which China undercut domestic producers around the world, leading to the exodus of manufacturing jobs from advanced countries. Its mercantilist policies led it to conquer sectors like textiles or solar panels, and drive out all competition from the marketplace. By some estimates, up to 3.4 million American jobs were lost due to Chinese competition between 2001, when China entered the World Trade Organization, and 2015.[26] Observers long credited low wages paid to Chinese workers, state subsidies, and outright dumping as leading ways in which Chinese companies outmaneuvered Western competitors.

Only in recent years, however, has attention been focused on the scale and scope of China's technological and industrial espionage as an element in its economic growth. For decades, the world was willing to turn a blind eye to Chinese theft of intellectual property, all in the hopes of gaining access to the country's vast market. Yet untold billions, probably trillions, of dollars of proprietary information has been pilfered by Chinese hackers and more traditional spies. The US-based Commission on the Theft of American Intellectual Property estimates the annual cost to the US economy of IP theft could be as high as $600 billion and not less than $200 billion.[27] The US Office of the Director of National Intelligence has calculated the cost of economic espionage by hacking to be $400 billion a year.[28] By far the majority of that stealing is done by China, much of it directed by the PLA, which has developed dedicated cyber espionage units, such as Unit 61398, which was exposed in February 2013 by the Mandiant Corporation.[29] Everything from purses and CDs to solar panels and software has been illegally copied by the Chinese, who have taken petabytes of information illegally over the past decade. Similarly, official Chinese policies such as "indigenous innovation" are meant to transfer intellectual property from Western businesses to their Chinese partners, some of which are government owned.[30] The world may never fully know the degree to which America and other advanced nations unknowingly subsidized the growth of the Chinese economy.

Nor does Chinese spying stop at consumer goods and trade secrets; rather, it is employed as a primary tool of Chinese statecraft. Beijing spies in sweeping, indiscriminate ways on a broad range of American interests and citizens. In 2015, it was revealed that Chinese hackers stole from the US government the confidential personal information of more than 22 million Americans, many of whom held security clearances, as well as their spouses and family members.[31] At the same time, newspapers reported that Chinese actors were breaking into private corporations such as insurance companies, further stealing information on millions of Americans, all with the goal of building massive databases to identify potential targets of blackmail.[32] Seemingly good-faith aid by the Chinese government also can hide espionage activities. After Beijing financed and built the new African Union's headquarters in Addis Ababa, Ethiopia, in 2012, the building's computer servers sent sensitive data to Shanghai every night, while hidden microphones were discovered in subsequent security sweeps.[33]

China's recent telecommunications dominance raises fears of sophisticated espionage operations against private companies and individuals, as well as governments. Although it has become the world's largest telecom systems provider, Huawei has long been dogged by allegations of hidden backdoors and sloppy security protocols in its systems, which can lead to the planned or inadvertent siphoning off of data from users of Huawei equipment.[34] Huawei and other Chinese telecoms firms also undermine good governance and gain support of corrupt elites, particularly in developing areas of the world. For example,

Huawei plays a dominant role in African telecommunications systems, and the company's employees have been reported to have helped repressive governments in Uganda and Zambia track political opponents, including by intercepting their communications.[35]

Uncertainty about the extent of Huawei's ties to the PLA and Chinese intelligence services has further raised suspicions about its use by official Chinese actors. China's 2017 National Intelligence Law also requires Chinese companies and individuals "to provide access, cooperation, or support for Beijing's intelligence-gathering activities," as recounted by one report.[36] Given such concerns, the Trump administration banned the company from participating in the building of America's 5G networks, while governments ranging from Canada to Japan and New Zealand similarly blocked Huawei's 5G technology. Others, however, including many in Europe, either decided to allow Huawei access to their 5G networks or postponed decisions while balancing Chinese pressure with security concerns.

China's military has similarly benefited from Beijing's traditional and cyber espionage. When the PLA Air Force made a surprise maiden flight of the country's first stealth fighter, the J-20, during the visit of then secretary of defense Robert Gates to Beijing in January 2011, the diplomatic awkwardness was paralleled by the commentary on the uncanny similarities between the Chinese prototype and the American-made F-22 Raptor.[37] Two years after pictures of the J-20 were revealed, the US Defense Department acknowledged that nearly every American military weapons development program had been infiltrated by Chinese hackers, thus helping to explain why Chinese advanced fighters and drones looked like copies of American versions.[38] Such defense industrial espionage means that US taxpayers are in essence subsidizing the development of the Chinese military.

Despite promises by Chinese president Xi Jinping to Barack Obama in 2015 to halt such predatory practices against American companies and citizens, there has been no letup in Chinese cyber aggressiveness. Such unprecedented attacks on private individuals of another nation go far beyond the type of cyber influence campaigns run by Russia that so attract the attention of the Western media. China's spying in America is so pervasive and endemic that current FBI director Christopher Wray has called it the most significant long-term threat the country faces, stating that Beijing has placed spies in scores of American universities and research institutes across the country.[39]

Economic and political espionage are just part of China's global strategy. Much of China's newfound wealth, whether gained lawfully or illicitly, has been poured into the gleaming, futuristic cities that now dot its landscape, and into the pockets of its political and economic elites, who buy up prime property in Los Angeles, New York, and Hong Kong. Yet just as much wealth has gone into increasing China's national power and dramatically modernizing its military. Just a few decades ago, China's army was based on 1950s weaponry, while its navy was a coastal patrol force and its air force was far outclassed by that of tiny Taiwan. Today, in terms of both quantity and quality, the PLA is second only to the armed forces of the United States. That military, and how Beijing is using it, comprises another of the new rules by which the country is protecting its interests, often at the expense of other nations.

Perhaps more important than building bigger, more powerful armed forces, which all nations do when they have the money, is the type of armed forces Beijing is building. From hypersonic weapons to aircraft carriers, and from antisatellite capabilities to nuclear missiles and cyberattack capabilities, China has invested in a military that far outstrips those of any of its neighbors. Specifically, the modernized PLA appears designed to target the strengths of US forces in Asia. Beijing has used stolen information on the US Air Force's F-22 and F-35 stealth fighters to build copycat versions that can outduel planes of neighboring states and challenge older US aircraft such as the F-15 and F-16. It also has invested heavily in attack submarines and Asia's largest surface combatant vessels, and its new aircraft carrier, along with three other currently planned carriers, will one day be able to project Chinese power throughout the waters of the Indo-Pacific region. The Chinese navy now has approximately 400 vessels and could reach as many as

530 by 2030, as compared with just 288 US Navy ships in 2019. While many of its naval ships are smaller, new and powerful cruisers and guided missile destroyers, such as the Type 055, are being built at a rapid pace (nearly double the rate of US ships being put to sea), and the Chinese outclass their US counterparts in advanced antiship missiles.[40] Despite the world welcoming China's rise and doing all it can to integrate it into global economic and political systems, Beijing sees enemies all around it and believes it needs an overwhelming military capability to deal with a world intent on containing it. This is traceable directly to the worldview and ideology of the CCP, which must assume a permanent counterrevolutionary vigilance to root out those at home and abroad who would destroy the communist system.[41]

This feeling of insecurity and frustration with the restrictions of international law have led China to rely on its military capability to undermine or slowly chip away at the positions of countries with which it has disputes. As Beijing has gained power, it has threatened and intimidated its neighbors and begun to act assertively, even aggressively, in the waters of East Asia so as to ensure outcomes to its liking. Its primary goal is to prevent the erosion of what it considers its territorial integrity, regardless of geopolitical complexities and questions of sovereignty or independence. The greatest threat to the CCP's sense of China's integrity is the shadow of Taiwanese independence. The Chinese government has increased its propaganda and interference operations during Taiwanese elections and in its media, and has directly threatened a military response should the island even hold a referendum on independence.[42] It continues to steadily peel away Taiwan's few remaining diplomatic partners, usually through lavish aid packages and other monetary inducements. All this is designed to isolate Taiwan and make it a de facto province of the mainland. It is par for the course for Beijing to condemn US sales of defense equipment to Taiwan as a violation of the 1970s-era "one China" principle. As relations between Washington and Beijing have worsened, however, the Chinese government ratcheted up the pressure, announcing in July 2019 that it would sanction US companies that participate in such military sales, specifically new F-16 fighters approved by the Trump administration.[43]

Other potential breakaway regions and disputed territories pose a similar danger, in Beijing's thinking. Despite promises in the 1984 Basic Framework agreed with Great Britain to respect Hong Kong's unique political status, China has steadily eroded Hong Kong's freedoms, particularly by meddling with the city's elected legislature and pressuring its courts. The Beijing-orchestrated kidnapping of a number of Hong Kong publishers (at least one of whom held a UK passport) in late 2015 further violated international law and underscored the city's vulnerability to the mainland. A proposed Hong Kong extradition law that would allow transfer to the mainland of those charged with crimes sparked massive demonstrations in the former British colony in July 2019, with up to two million protestors in the streets at times, and resulting in running battles between police and demonstrators that destroyed property and even led to the brief takeover of the Hong Kong Legislative Council building. Months of protests led Beijing to stage People's Armed Police units in Shenzhen, across from the island, and intimate that it would intervene if the Hong Kong government was not able to control protestors. This was a message not lost on Taiwanese, Tibetans, and others who saw in Hong Kong a proxy for many of their own problems with China.

China has put pressure on governments even away from areas it has traditionally claimed as its own. In the East China Sea, Beijing regularly uses private fishermen and maritime patrol vessels to challenge Japanese administrative control over the contested Senkaku/Diaoyu Islands, and it attempts to intimidate both Japan and Taiwan with naval flotillas, as well as by flying bombers near the airspace of both countries. Nor are its energies turned solely toward the oceans. Chinese forces have been in a face-off with Indian army troops high in the Himalayas over a disputed border with Bhutan.[44]

Perhaps most threateningly to the region, China has systematically moved to position itself as the dominant power in the South China Sea. For the past several years, Chinese naval vessels have attempted to intimidate the ships of other nations, from the Philippines and Vietnam to India, as they pass through waters where China contests the sovereignty of the Spratly and Paracel Island groups with a half dozen other Southeast Asian nations. It has militarized its possessions in those waters since the mid-2010s, and in doing so, it has shifted the balance of power in one of the world's most vital seas, through which passes nearly 70 percent of global trade, and which links the western Pacific to the Indian Ocean and routes to Europe. Beijing has turned once-submerged reefs into full island bases through a massive reclamation project, dredging up three thousand acres of reef bed to make islands and then outfitting them with airstrips, radar installations, weapons bunkers, and antiaircraft missile systems.[45] This militarization of Fiery Cross Reef, Mischief Reef, and Subi Reef, among others, was undertaken despite Chinese promises not to do so.[46]

Despite a weak American response during the Obama administration, which agonized over doing more frequent and publicized freedom of navigation operations, Chinese media darkly warned of war should Washington try to force Beijing to stop or reverse its island-building campaign. To smaller Southeast Asian nations, China's aggressive militarization of artificial islands represents a significant destabilization of the region's power equilibrium, yet almost all feel unable to do anything to materially counter Beijing's policy. This in turn raises questions about their sovereignty and the extent to which they (and the United States) can defend their interests. Learning to live with a newly assertive Chinese military is the major security challenge facing Asian nations in the twenty-first century.

A similar dynamic is taking place in both regional and global economies. Whereas China's rise has often created new trade and investment opportunities, the policies being put into place by Xi Jinping are raising analogous questions in Asia and beyond about economic sovereignty and the ability to resist China's swelling economic reach. Much of the concern focuses on Xi's bold bid to radically reshape trade and investment in Eurasia. He has pledged $1 trillion to his flagship One Belt One Road (OBOR) policy. The main focus of OBOR is infrastructure building across all of Eurasia, designed to link land- and sea-based trade routes, running from east to west and north to south, all centered on China. Even publicity stunts are designed to strengthen images of China's economic juggernaut, exemplified by the inaugural journey of a freight train from eastern China to the United Kingdom in January 2017, which traveled twelve thousand kilometers and arrived in London to worldwide media attention.

More substantively, Chinese companies have purchased ports in Belgium, Spain, Italy, and Greece, underscoring Beijing's growing European interests. China's grasp reaches across the oceans to Africa, where it is the major builder of infrastructure and extractor of natural resources, as well as to Latin America and the Arctic. In early 2018, Beijing published its first official Arctic white paper, in which it identified itself as a "near-Arctic state," despite being no closer to the Arctic than Poland. The paper set out to identify how the Arctic region should be governed and how the OBOR initiative could be used to construct a "Polar Silk Road" linking China and Europe.[47]

Beijing's interests, however, go far beyond just the trade elements of the OBOR. Instead, it is seen as a strategic policy to expand Chinese interests abroad, gain access to strategic ports, and use trade to foster military ties. At the core of this global expansion is the country's construction industry, which builds infrastructure on every continent. In Africa and throughout Central Asia, Chinese companies are becoming increasingly ubiquitous, erecting apartment blocks, paving roads, or building port facilities. Beijing furthers its national interests by linking a military component to its development programs, in what is sometimes referred to as "debt-trap diplomacy." In Djibouti, in the Horn of Africa, for example, China has combined development aid with building its first overseas military base, which opened in July 2017. This cost of doing business with China or of accepting Chinese foreign aid often emerges only after deals have been struck, increasingly to the benefit of China's military. Sri Lanka learned this the hard way in late 2017, when it was forced to hand over control of its largest port, Hambantota, to China after it could not pay off bills to Chinese firms.[48] This gave

Beijing a strategic outpost in the Indian Ocean, where its naval ships routinely transit. China similarly took a 70 percent stake in an equally useful port in Myanmar the same year. While all of this helps China's OBOR initiative, it also gives the Chinese navy vital access to important waterways. Beijing now appears to be setting its sights on the South Pacific, extending aid to island nations in a bid to reduce American, Australian, and Japanese influence.

These attempts to buy influence or force accommodation to China's wishes are complemented by another of the new China rules: a propaganda and influence campaign to squelch any criticism of the country or its policies. Western observers often underestimate the importance the CCP puts on the ideological competition with the rest of the world. In his first year in power, Xi Jinping released a "Communiqué on the Current State of the Ideological Sphere," colloquially known as Document 9.[49] The communiqué made clear the CCP's view of the "complicated, intense struggle" with the West over "false ideological trends." The party and Chinese society were enjoined to defend themselves from the concept of "Western constitutional democracy" and to avoid the promotion of "universal values," "civil society," and "neoliberalism," all of which threatened the party and socialism with Chinese characteristics. As much as the defense of the CCP and its system lay at home, the ideological struggle also would be waged abroad, through a global propaganda apparatus and widespread influence operations.

Here, Beijing has found all-too-willing counterparts in both foreign businesses and governments, all of whom find it easier to buckle under increasingly outrageous Chinese demands than to risk losing their economic access by taking a critical stand. Their fear is based on China's undeniable economic prowess. In just twenty years, from 1997 to 2016, China's exports exploded from $211 billion to an astonishing $2 trillion—a tenfold increase—making money for Chinese and Westerners alike while reducing consumer prices around the globe.[50] But with China's new strength has come a bare-knuckle abusiveness, often combined with an unexpected sense of insecurity, and it seems increasingly clear that Beijing expects the West to change how it thinks and acts, engage in self-censorship, and even punish our own workers for offending China.

When British prime minister Theresa May lauded the current "golden era of UK-China relations" on a visit to Beijing in January 2018, she was simply repeating what every national leader says in the face of China's economic clout.[51] Though the West has long known that a significant part of China's success has come through stealing intellectual property and pressuring foreign companies to give up their trade secrets, it has looked the other way in the name of profits and affordable goods. Now Beijing is raising the price of doing business in China, demanding that its foreign partners surrender Western values and openly espouse China's worldview for continued access to its markets.

One might expect only smaller companies, like Palau Pacific Airways, not major multinationals, to heed Chinese wishes, but such is not the case. Even international corporations are willing to kowtow to China. In February 2018, German car giant Daimler-Benz ran afoul of Beijing after committing the sin of quoting the exiled Tibetan spiritual leader the Dalai Lama in a social media ad—an ad not even run in China. The company abjectly apologized in the face of Chinese demands not once but twice "to the Chinese people." Soberly noting the "seriousness of the situation," the company solemnly averred that it offers "no support, assistance, aid or help to anyone who intentionally subverts or attempts to subvert China's sovereignty and territorial integrity."[52] That a twelve-word ad caused such an extraordinary display of corporate groveling not only revealed Beijing's insecurities, but also made clear that China now knows it can get away with bringing corporate titans to their public knees. Just over a year later, in August 2019, heralded Hong Kong airline Cathay Pacific fired its CEO after Beijing pressured the company over employees' participation in the massive prodemocracy demonstrations in Hong Kong. Chinese officials further demanded that Cathay flight crew members who took part in demonstrations be barred from flying to China.[53] The airline's new CEO agreed to the demands.

Other companies have faced similar intimidation. In January 2018, in the face of Beijing's pressure, hotel giant Marriott shut down its websites in China for a week, after one of its online questionnaires listed Tibet, Taiwan, Macao, and Hong Kong as independent countries. Once again, the company made public penance, and its CEO sounded more like a foreign minister than a corporate executive, publicly announcing that Marriott "respects and supports Chinese sovereignty and its territorial integrity." Even more Orwellian, in a separate incident Marriott fired an employee who "liked" a post by a Tibetan independence group on one of the company's social media sites.[54] It appears that international corporations are willing to let Beijing determine how they manage internal employment issues when their trade in China appears at risk. In addition to Marriott and the forty global airlines who caved to China's demand to flush Taiwan down the memory hole, car maker Audi, clothes chain Zara, medical instrument maker Medtronic, and others have fallen afoul of Beijing's outrage machine. Each has apologized for some perceived infraction or has altered company practices to suit Beijing's demands, in essence supporting Beijing's foreign policy goals.

How long such pressure tactics will continue to be successful, however, is being tested the more brazen that China gets. After the general manager of the National Basketball Association's Houston Rockets tweeted in support of Hong Kong's prodemocracy demonstrations in October 2019, the Chinese government and business punished the NBA, threatening its multibillion-dollar business in China. Chinese stores pulled the team's merchandise from stores, and broadcasters stopped showing Rockets games and threatened to cancel the league's China appearances. Following the usual script, the NBA and some of its biggest stars responded by publicly apologizing, yet this time their cravenness sparked an enormous political backlash in the United States over free-speech rights.[55]

It is not merely international business that finds itself kowtowing to Beijing. Moving from intimidation to seduction, China's global propaganda campaign has become a major element of its foreign policy. The world is just beginning to wake up to the scope of Beijing's propaganda activities. Its influence operations span the globe, ranging from covert attempts to influence policy makers and opinion leaders to overt actions designed to overwhelm opposition to China's policies. An August 2018 report by the US-China Economic and Security Review Commission documented the overseas propaganda and influence activities of the CCP, specifically the role played by the party's United Front Work Department (UFWD).

The UFWD was created in 1939 by Mao Zedong to combat both the Japanese and the Nationalist government, while pretending to work with the Nationalists. This approach has marked United Front activities throughout the decades. The United Front's goal, noted the US-China Commission report, is "to co-opt and neutralize sources of potential opposition to the policies and authority" of the CCP.[56] Under Xi Jinping, the UFWD has been rejuvenated and its influence increased. A "leading small group"—a key institutional mechanism for coordinating policy on important issues—was established in 2015 for United Front work, drawing in top officials and over two dozen government agencies. The UFWD also appears to have "growing links" with China's security service, and has been given "unified management" over religious groups and overseas Chinese affairs.[57]

Much United Front and other overseas government work is focused on finding sympathetic allies in countries where Beijing hopes to increase its influence. Official groups such as the Chinese People's Association for Friendship with Foreign Countries and the China Overseas Friendship Association are used to reach out to foreign government officials, business leaders, academics, and media leaders. These are paired with numerous diplomatic initiatives such as the Boao Forum for Asia, the Forum on China-Africa Cooperation, and the Shanghai Cooperation Organization. Billions of dollars in aid have gone to local elites throughout Eurasia and the Pacific, as well as Africa and Latin America, directly or indirectly, causing them to espouse political support for China in international forums.[58]

A report from the Europe-based Global Public Policy Institute and the Mercator Institute for China Studies detailed the degree to which Beijing's growing political influence and intimidation tactics, combined with its economic presence, are changing how Europeans deal with China. "Political elites [in Europe] have started to embrace Chinese rhetoric and interests, including where they contradict national or European interests," wrote the report's authors.[59] After Chinese investments in Greece and the Czech Republic, for example, Athens refused to support EU condemnations of Chinese human rights abuses or its predatory South China Sea actions, while Prague turned a cold shoulder to Chinese dissidents, reversing a position taken under former president Václav Havel. The influence operation in the Czech Republic was linked to the activities of both Huawei and CEFC China Energy, which forged strong ties with Czech president Milos Zeman as well as the Czech Communist Party leader.[60] On the other side of the globe, Australian politics have been rocked in recent years by allegations of massive Chinese donations to politicians, leading to legislation to limit the influx of third-country influence operations and Chinese funds to officeholders.[61] Such "elite capture" by Beijing is a growing concern in countries around the world.

Meanwhile, China's relentless propaganda campaign is spearheaded not only by the state-controlled CCTV global television news network but by a network of over five hundred Confucius Institutes on foreign university campuses and in major cities. The Confucius Institutes are sponsored in part by a division of the Ministry of Education, the awkwardly translated "Office of Chinese Language Council International" (Hanban). Academics and administrators charge that the Confucius Institutes stifle views critical of China, particularly on college campuses, in part by threatening the withdrawal of funds for programs featuring critics of Beijing.[62] The publication of contracts between Hanban and several Australian universities revealed that the Chinese office had final say over what was taught by Confucius Institutes on those campuses as well as assessments of the teaching quality of the individual centers, seeming to confirm claims of censorship and Chinese control over academic activities within the institutes.[63]

Connected to this university activism are the ways in which Chinese students studying at overseas universities not only are monitored by Beijing to ensure that they don't engage in anti-Chinese activities but are organized in countries like Australia to serve as pressure groups drowning out negative images of China.[64] The Chinese Students and Scholars Association keeps tabs on Chinese studying or researching abroad, mobilizing them when need be. Clashes between anti-Chinese and pro-Chinese students have roiled campuses in Australia, while a Chinese student at the University of Maryland in the United States suffered online harassment in China after a graduation speech in which she praised the environment of freedom she encountered in America.[65] Nor do agents of the Chinese government hesitate to target foreign scholars who expose its interference abroad. The New Zealand academic Anne-Marie Brady charged Beijing with a physical intimidation campaign designed to stop her from publishing accounts of covert Chinese actions in her country.[66] All this threatens to make censorship of anti-Chinese views on campuses around the world the norm, thus threatening academic freedom.

Thanks to China's intimidation campaigns, as well as its propaganda work and influence operations, governments, think tanks, and universities around the globe have become used to treating China with kid gloves, affording it a deference rarely given to any other country. They regularly avoid contentious yet crucial topics such as human rights, labor issues, environmental devastation, or military threat. To give but one example, on the thirtieth anniversary of the Tiananmen Square massacre, in June 2019, only one think tank in Washington, DC, held a symposium on its legacy and influence on contemporary Chinese society.[67]

Yet China's reach extends beyond the academic and policy worlds, to Western popular culture as well, serving the same goal of suppressing criticism and burying negative views of the country. Chinese interests now own or are powerful partners in major US entertainment companies, including Legendary Entertainment Group and AMC

Theaters, while the Chinese box office provides a huge part of Hollywood's profits.[68] Negative portrayals of China are almost entirely absent from US movies, a far cry from dark portrayals of Nazis, Soviets, or rapacious Japanese businessmen in the past. Indeed, a remake in 2012 of the iconic 1980s film *Red Dawn* digitally changed the invading Chinese soldiers into North Koreans in post-production, to avoid offending Chinese sensibilities. Other plots that are never likely to appear in US movies include China's worldwide espionage operations, oppression of Tibet or the incarceration of a million Uighurs in far western Xinjiang in "reeducation camps," suppression of religion, its massive prison system, forced abortions, or its military challenge to US power in Asia. Instead, Chinese are often portrayed as magnanimous statesmen, as in the 2016 science fiction thriller *Arrival*, where the wisdom of a Chinese PLA general prevents a global war. Just as noticeably, when trailers for the sequel to Tom Cruise's 1986 smash hit *Top Gun* were released in the summer of 2019, observant fans noticed that Japanese and Taiwanese flag patches had been replaced on Cruise's character's flight jacket. It was subsequently reported that the Chinese internet conglomerate Tencent helped cofinance the movie, sparking charges of Chinese demands to remove the offending patches or that producer Paramount Pictures self-censored to avoid fallout with Chinese audiences that could hurt ticket sales.[69]

These benign messages sent out on college campuses and by Hollywood undoubtedly help serve broader national purposes. They dovetail perfectly with Chinese president Xi Jinping's global PR push and bolster the attractiveness of bold Chinese plans like the One Belt One Road initiative, eliding questions about the risks of doing business with China, and dampening worries in the United States about China becoming a strategic competitor. Taken together, the new China rules are designed to sweep aside opposition to Beijing's preferred policies, to marginalize and discredit criticism of China, and to portray China's rise as inexorable.

In some ways, Beijing is merely doing what all nations do—namely, promote its interests. Yet no country can compare to China's size and the scale of its rapid expansion overseas, leading to correspondingly oversize effects. Indeed, perhaps little of this would matter if China were evolving into a more liberal society, with an accountable government and more cooperative foreign policy. When Richard Nixon and the rest of world embraced China's turn from isolationism in the 1970s, they bet that the country's rise would be peaceful and that it eventually would begin to liberalize at home, adopting liberal norms of behavior. Instead, the reality is that China is a rising power dissatisfied with the contours of the current global order, suspicious of nations around it, and thus willing to test and weaken global norms in its favor. Just as concerningly, the CCP is becoming more authoritarian, and the power of the state is increasing inside society. Much of this can be laid at the feet of Xi Jinping, who took power in 2012 and has become the most powerful Chinese leader since Mao Zedong himself. Xi has scrapped the ten-year limit on presidential terms, has made himself the ideological center (or "core") of the Party, is increasingly moving toward one-man rule, and likely will remain at the head of the Chinese party-state for years to come.

Through Xi's anticorruption campaign, Beijing has reversed the separation of Party and state pursued by former leaders Deng Xiaoping and Jiang Zemin, steadily cracked down on civil society, increased domestic propaganda, muzzled alternative media, and tried to control the internet. It is also taking major steps toward becoming an authoritarian surveillance state unparalleled in recent history. Beijing has installed over one hundred million surveillance cameras and aims at having more than a half-billion over the next decade. It is investing heavily in facial and voice recognition technologies and boasts that it can find a wanted suspect anywhere in the country in minutes.[70] It is introducing a "social credit" system whereby citizens are ranked according to their social productiveness, docility, and observance of laws.[71] The government now requires the establishment of CCP cells in almost all business and social enterprises with more than three party members, thus deepening the party's reach throughout society.[72] Underpinning all this, Xi is instituting a revitalization of Communist thought in China while demonizing the West and its values.[73] In addition, Beijing continues a policy of severe repression in both Tibet and Xinjiang, paralleling its hardening line on Hong Kong. The China of coming decades will be a more tightly controlled and surveilled society, in which even elites will be uncertain of their position.

China's hard line at home is being replicated abroad to a worrying degree. The very fact of China's brazen arrogance in making ideological demands on countries, corporations, universities, and media over issues like Taiwan or Xinjiang points to both deep insecurity and a disturbing aggressiveness. No other major trading country's government, not even Japan's at the height of its power in the 1980s, has intimidated and threatened foreign governments or businesses for perceived issues of national interest. Yet perhaps worse, Western corporations, political leaders, academics, and opinion leaders are all too often susceptible to the new China rules. Whether cravenly begging forgiveness or helping to whitewash Chinese behavior, Western self-censorship is both self-defeating and dangerous. Little by little, as reports such as those from the US-China Commission and European think tanks show, Western attitudes and behaviors have been shifting to accommodate the Chinese.

Some Western corporate leaders are trying to make the case that running away from China makes no sense. "We believe in engaging with governments even when we disagree," stated Apple's Tim Cook when discussing Chinese control over the internet inside the country.[74] But engagement is a two-way street, and Beijing has shown no willingness to accommodate. Instead, the expected growth of China's consumer sector means that it will remain a magnet for Western businesses for years to come, while its growing military strength will give it an outsize voice in political and security issues both throughout the Indo-Pacific region and globally. Its intimidation tactics thus may not abate anytime soon. Over time, an ingrained Western acquiescence to subordination to Chinese national interests and purported national feelings will further embolden Beijing's abusive behavior. Either the West will lose the will to speak truth to power or relations will reach a breaking point, spilling over into the political sphere and causing further strain. By not standing up to Chinese intimidation now, the costs of doing so later on will certainly be much higher.

All of this bodes ill for the future. The world will have to deal with a far stronger and more aggressive China that appears bent on undermining or ignoring global norms of conduct, even as it continues to nurture a sense of grievance that foreign nations are scheming against it. At home, trade with the West has enriched a Communist leadership that is intent on further subjugating its people and serving as a model of illiberal rule. Abroad, instead of building bonds of trust with its neighbors and major partners, Beijing bullies and regularly steals from them, while proclaiming its innocence and asserting that it, too, is a victim. The West should have known there was a downside to the bet it made on China nearly a half century ago. How well the world deals with the new China rules may in part determine the global balance of power over the next generation.

Notes

1. "China Has Forced a Pacific Airline to Close Down Because of Diplomatic Ties with Taiwan," *Business Insider*, July 18, 2018, https://www.businessinsider.com/palau-airline-closes-over-anger-from-china-about-taiwan-ties-2018-7.
2. Sul-Lee Wee, "Giving In to China, U.S. Airlines Drop Taiwan (in Name at Least)," *New York Times*, July 25, 2018, https://www.nytimes.com/2018/07/25/business/taiwan-american-airlines-china.html.
3. James Kitfield, "Admiral Davidson: China Assaults International Order," *Breaking Defense*, July 18, 2019, https://breakingdefense.com/2019/07/adm-davidson-china-assaults-international-order.
4. Toasts of Richard Nixon and Zhou Enlai, February 21, 1972, available at http://www.presidency.ucsb.edu/ws/?pid=3748. For an overview of Washington's China policy from the 1970s through the 1990s, see James Mann, *About Face: A History of America's Curious Relationship with China, from Nixon to Clinton* (New York: Vintage, 2000).

5. See, for example, then CIA director George Tenet's 1997 congressional testimony on current and projected national security threats to the United States, https://fas.org/irp/congress/1997_hr/s970205t.htm.

6. See, for example, Martin Jacques, *When China Rules the World: The End of the Western World and the Birth of a New Global Order*, 2nd ed. (New York: Penguin, 2012); Kishore Mahbubani, *The New Asian Hemisphere: The Irresistible Shift of Global Power to the East* (New York: PublicAffairs, 2009); Gideon Rachman, *Easternization: Asia's Rise and America's Decline from Obama to Trump and Beyond* (New York: Other Press, 2017).

7. See, for example, Charles Krauthammer, "The Unipolar Moment," *Foreign Affairs* 70, no. 1 (1990), https://www.foreignaffairs.com/articles/1991 -02-01/unipolar-moment; Francis Fukuyama, "The End of History?," *National Interest*, Summer 1989, https://www.embl.de/aboutus/science _society/discussion/discussion_2006/ref1-22june06.pdf. On the Washington consensus, see John Williamson, "The Washington Consensus as Policy Prescription for Development," Institute for International Economics, 2004, https://piie.com/publications/papers/williamson0204.pdf.

8. See, for example, George Friedman, *The Coming War with Japan* (New York: St. Martins Press, 1991).

9. Robert B. Zoellick, "Whither China: From Membership to Responsibility?," archived at https://2001-2009.state.gov/s/d/former/zoellick/rem /53682.htm.

10. "GDP Ranking, PPP Based," World Bank, https://datacatalog.worldbank .org/dataset/gdp-ranking-ppp-based.

11. CIA World Factbook, https://www.cia.gov/library/publications/the-world -factbook/geos/ch.html; see also the MIT study at the Observatory of Economic Complexity website, China page, https://atlas.media.mit.edu /en/profile/country/chn.

12. For an overview of China's trade policies, see "Is China the World's Top Trader?," China Power website, https://chinapower.csis.org/trade -partner.

13. "The People's Republic of China: U.S.-China Trade Facts," website of the Office of the United States Trade Representative, https://ustr.gov /countries-regions/china-mongolia-taiwan/peoples-republic-china.

14. See the China Global Investment Tracker at American Enterprise Institute website, http://www.aei.org/china-global-investment-tracker.

15. Global 500 list, *Fortune Magazine*, http://fortune.com/global500.
16. Alice Shen, "Chinese Students Still Drawn to U.S. Universities, but Growth Rate Slowing," *South China Morning Post*, November 14, 2017, https://www.scmp.com/news/china/society/article/2119903/chinese -students-still-drawn-us-universities-growth-rate-slowing.
17. Oliver Matthew, "Chinese Outbound Tourists—New 2017 Report," CLSA, July 19, 2017, https://www.clsa.com/idea/chinese-tourists-expand -their-horizons. CLSA predicts Chinese tourist spending will reach $429 billion by 2021.
18. David Shambaugh, "Contemplating China's Future," *Washington Quarterly* 39, no. 3 (Fall 2016): 121–30.
19. For a review of the pressures behind Xi's accession, see Joseph Fewsmith, "The 19th Party Congress: Ringing in Xi Jinping's New Age," *China Leadership Monitor* 55 (Winter 2018), https://www.hoover.org/research /19th-party-congress-ringing-xi-jinpings-new-age.
20. See, for example, "Xi Urges China's Youth to Embrace Nationalism on Key Anniversary," *Bloomberg*, April 29, 2019, https://www.bloomberg .com/news/articles/2019-04-30/xi-urges-china-s-youth-to-embrace -nationalism-on-key-anniversary; Sam Crane, "Why Xi Jinping's China Is Legalist, Not Confucian," *Los Angeles Review of Books*, June 29, 2018, https://chinachannel.org/2018/06/29/legalism.
21. Yang Jiechi, "Following the Guidance of Xi Jinping Thought on Diplomacy to Advance Diplomatic Work in the New Era," *Quishi Journal*, October–December 2018, http://english.qstheory.cn/2018-12/21/c_112 3801028.htm.
22. Yang, "Following the Guidance."
23. A public debate erupted in mid-2019 among China watchers, pitting those arguing for a continuation of traditional engagement policies against those applauding Donald Trump's harder line. For the former, see M. Taylor Fravel et al., "China Is Not an Enemy," *Washington Post*, July 3, 2019, https://www.washingtonpost.com/opinions/making-china -a-us-enemy-is-counterproductive/2019/07/02/647d49d0-9bfa-11e9-b27f -ed2942f73d70_story.html?utm_term=.38b40a70ebeb; for the latter, James Fanell et al., "Stay the Course on China: An Open Letter to President Trump," *Journal of Political Risk*, July 18, 2019, http://www.jpolrisk .com/stay-the-course-on-china-an-open-letter-to-president-trump.

24. See, for example, Niall Ferguson, "Cold War II," *Boston Globe*, March 11, 2019, https://www.bostonglobe.com/opinion/2019/03/11/cold-war/4Ebxs JrCdgBbATFwoQkwOK/story.html.

25. See Graham Allison, *Destined for War: Can America and China Escape the Thucydides Trap?* (New York: Houghton Mifflin Harcourt, 2017).

26. Robert E. Scott, "Growth in U.S.-China Trade Deficit between 2001 and 2015 Cost 3.4 Million Jobs," Economic Policy Institute, January 31, 2017, https://www.epi.org/publication/growth-in-u-s-china-trade-deficit -between-2001-and-2015-cost-3-4-million-jobs-heres-how-to-rebalance -trade-and-rebuild-american-manufacturing.

27. See the commission's report at http://www.ipcommission.org/report/IP _Commission_Report_Update_2017.pdf.

28. Chris Strohm, "No Sign China Has Stopped Hacking U.S. Companies, Official Says," *Bloomberg*, November 18, 2015, https://www.bloomberg .com/news/articles/2015-11-18/no-sign-china-has-stopped-hacking-u-s -companies-official-says. The full report from the Office of the Director of National Intelligence is available from the IP Commission website at http://www.ipcommission.org/report/Evolving_Cyber_Tactics_in _ Stealing_US_Economic_Secrets_ODNI_Report.jpg.

29. *APT1: Exposing One of China's Cyberespionage Units*, https://www .fireeye.com/content/dam/fireeye-www/services/pdfs/mandiant-apt1 -report.pdf.

30. James McGregor, *China's Drive for 'Indigenous Innovation': A Web of Industrial Policies* (US Chamber of Commerce, 2010), https://www .uschamber.com/sites/default/files/legacy/reports/100728china report_0.pdf.

31. Ellen Nakashima, "Hacks of OPM Databases Compromised 22.1 Million People, Federal Authorities Say," *Washington Post*, July 9, 2015, https:// www.washingtonpost.com/news/federal-eye/wp/2015/07/09/hack-of -security-clearance-system-affected-21-5-million-people-federal-autho rities-say/?utm_term=.b795b6b2c101.

32. Ellen Nakashima, "With a Series of Major Hacks, China Builds a Data-base on Americans," *Washington Post*, June 5, 2015, https://www.washing tonpost.com/world/national-security/in-a-series-of-hacks-china-appears -to-building-a-database-on-americans/2015/06/05/d2af51fa-0ba3-11e5 -95fd-d580f1c5d44e_story.html?utm_term=.723bc5e1d3a0.

33. John Aglionby, "African Union Accuses China of Hacking Headquarters," *Financial Times*, January 29, 2018, https://www.ft.com/content/c26a9214-04f2-11e8-9650-9c0ad2d7c5b5.

34. Jack Stubbs, "Huawei Needs 3–5 Years to Resolve British Security Fears," *Reuters*, February 6, 2019, https://www.reuters.com/article/us-huawei-europe-britain-exclusive/exclusive-huawei-needs-3-5-years-to-resolve-british-security-fears-letter-idUSKCN1PV1CG.

35. Joe Parkinson et al., "Huawei Technicians Helped African Governments Spy on Political Opponents," *Wall Street Journal*, August 15, 2019, https://www.wsj.com/articles/huawei-technicians-helped-african-governments-spy-on-political-opponents-11565793017.

36. Murray Scot Tanner, "Beijing's New National Intelligence Law: From Defense to Offense," *Lawfare*, July 20, 2017, https://www.lawfareblog.com/beijings-new-national-intelligence-law-defense-offense.

37. Elizabeth Bumiller and Michael Wines, "Test of Stealth Fighter Clouds Gates Visit to China," *New York Times*, January 11, 2001, https://www.nytimes.com/2011/01/12/world/asia/12fighter.html.

38. Ellen Nakashima, "Confidential Report Lists U.S. Weapons System Designs Compromised by Chinese Cyberspies," *Washington Post*, May 27, 2013, https://www.washingtonpost.com/world/national-security/confidential-report-lists-us-weapons-system-designs-compromised-by-chinese-cyberspies/2013/05/27/a42c3e1c-c2dd-11e2-8c3b-0b5e9247e8ca_story.html?noredirect=on&utm_term=.4eb5d510b17a.

39. "FBI Chief Says Chinese Operatives Have Infiltrated Scores of 'Naive' U.S. Universities," *South China Morning Post*, February 14, 2018, https://www.scmp.com/news/world/united-states-canada/article/2133274/fbi-chief-says-chinese-operatives-have-infiltrated.

40. Among other sources, see "China Naval Modernization: Implications for U.S. Navy Capabilities—Background and Issues for Congress," Congressional Research Service, August 1, 2018, https://www.everycrsreport.com/files/20180801_RL33153_1036f8edb5271519e9bd80690adce95f6e5b cbc6.pdf; David Lague and Benjamin Kang Lim, "The China Challenge: China's Vast Fleet Is Tipping the Balance in the Pacific," *Reuters*, April 30, 2019, https://www.reuters.com/investigates/special-report/china-army-navy.

41. See, for example, John Garnaut, "Engineers of the Soul: Ideology in Xi Jinping's China," https://sinocism.com/p/engineers-of-the-soul -ideology-in.

42. Yimou Lee, "Taiwan Says China Has Stepped Up Infiltration Efforts," *Reuters*, May 9, 2019, https://www.reuters.com/article/us-china-taiwan /taiwan-says-china-has-stepped-up-infiltration-efforts-idUSKCN 1SG08F.

43. Kristin Huang, "China Repeats Threat to Sanction US Companies over Taiwan Arms Sales," *South China Morning Post*, July 15, 2019, https:// www.scmp.com/news/china/diplomacy/article/3018691/china-repeats -threat-sanction-us-companies-over-taiwan-arms.

44. Steven Lee Myers, Ellen Barry, and Max Fisher, "How India and China Have Come to the Brink over a Remote Mountain Pass," *New York Times*, July 26, 2017, https://www.nytimes.com/2017/07/26/world/asia/dolam -plateau-china-india-bhutan.html.

45. Office of the United States Secretary of Defense, Department of Defense, *Annual Report to Congress: Military and Security Developments Involving the People's Republic of China 2017*, p. 12, https://dod.defense.gov /Portals/1/Documents/pubs/2017_China_Military_Power_Report.PDF.

46. Xi Jinping's remarks alongside then president Barack Obama in the White House Rose Garden, "Relevant Construction Activity That China Is Undertaking in the Nansha (Spratly) Islands Does Not Target or Impact Any Country and There Is No Intention to Militarize," September 25, 2015.

47. See translation of the white paper at http://www.xinhuanet.com/english /2018-01/26/c_136926498.htm.

48. Maria Abi-Habib, "How China Got Sri Lanka to Cough Up a Port," *New York Times*, June 25, 2018, https://www.nytimes.com/2018/06/25/world /asia/china-sri-lanka-port.html.

49. A translation can be found on the *ChinaFile* website, at http://www.china file.com/document-9-chinafile-translation; see also Garnaut, "Engineers of the Soul."

50. Erica Pandey, "Mapped: Chinese Exports Take Over the World," *Axios*, February 9, 2018, https://www.axios.com/chinas-takeover-as-the-world -top-exporter-180c8514-b38d-4388-b126-b40912720fca.html.

51. "Theresa May Unveils Education Deal at Start of China Visit," *BBC News*, January 30, 2018, https://www.bbc.com/news/amp/uk-politics-42865133.

52. "Germany's Daimler Issues 'Full Apology' to China over Dalai Lama," *BBC News*, February 8, 2018, https://www.bbc.com/news/world-asia-china-42986679.

53. Raymond Zhong and Ezra Cheung, "Cathay Pacific CEO's Resignation Shows China's Looming Power over Hong Kong Unrest," *New York Times*, August 16, 2019, https://www.nytimes.com/2019/08/16/business/cathay-pacific-ceo-resigns-rupert-hogg.html.

54. Wayne Ma, "Marriott Employee Roy Jones Hit 'Like': Then China Got Mad," *Wall Street Journal*, March 3, 2018, https://www.wsj.com/articles/marriott-employee-roy-jones-hit-like-then-china-got-mad-1520094910.

55. Eben Novy-Williams, "NBA China Woes Threaten Billions of Dollars, Decades' Work," *Bloomberg*, October 7, 2019, https://www.bloomberg.com/news/articles/2019-10-07/nba-china-crisis-threatens-billions-of-dollars-decades-of-work.

56. Alexander Bowe, *China's Overseas United Front Work: Background and Implications for the United States* (Washington, DC: US-China Economic and Security Review Commission, 2018), https://www.uscc.gov/sites/default/files/Research/China%27s%20Overseas%20United%20Front%20Work%20-%20Background%20and%20Implications%20for%20US_final_0.pdf. See also Larry Diamond and Orville Schell, eds., *Chinese Influence and American Interests: Promoting Constructive Vigilance* (Stanford, CA: Hoover Institution Press, 2018).

57. Alex Joske, "The Central United Front Work Leading Small Group," *Sinopsis*, July 23, 2019, https://sinopsis.cz/en/joske-united-front-work-lsg.

58. See David Shullman, ed., *Chinese Malign Influence and the Corrosion of Democracy*, International Republican Institute, July 2019, https://www.iri.org/sites/default/files/chinese_malign_influence_report.pdf.

59. Thorsten Benner et al., *Authoritarian Advance: Responding to China's Growing Political Influence in Europe*, GPPi and MERICS, February 5, 2018. https://www.gppi.net/2018/02/05/authoritarian-advance-responding-to-chinas-growing-political-influence-in-europe.

60. Martin Hala and Jicheng Lulu, "Lost in Translation: 'Economic Diplomacy' with Chinese Characteristics," *Sinopsis*, March 11, 2019, https://

sinopsis.cz/en/lost-in-translation-economic-diplomacy-with-chinese
-characteristics.

61. John Garnaut, "Australia's China Reset," *The Monthly*, August 2018, https://www.themonthly.com.au/issue/2018/august/1533045600/john -garnaut/australia-s-china-reset.

62. See, in particular, *Outsourced to China: Confucius Institutes and Soft-power in American Higher Education* (National Association of Scholars, 2017), https://www.nas.org/projects/confucius_institutes/the_report; Ethan Epstein, "How China Infiltrated U.S. Classrooms," *Politico*, January 16, 2018, https://www.politico.com/magazine/story/2018/01/16/how -china-infiltrated-us-classrooms-216327?cid=apn.

63. Fergus Hunter, "Universities Must Accept China's Directives on Confucius Institutes, Contracts Reveal," *The Age*, July 25, 2019, https://www .theage.com.au/politics/federal/universities-must-accept-china-s-direct ives-on-confucius-institutes-contracts-reveal-20190724-p52ab9.html.

64. Stephanie Saul, "On Campuses Far from China, Still under Beijing's Watchful Eye," *New York Times*, May 4, 2017, https://www.nytimes .com/2017/05/04/us/chinese-students-western-campuses-china-influ ence.html.

65. Mike Ives, "Chinese Student in Maryland Is Criticized at Home for Praising U.S.," *New York Times*, May 23, 2017, https://sinopsis.cz/en/the -ccps-model-of-social-control-goes-global.

66. "Chinese Interference: Anne-Marie Brady's Full Submission," *Newsroom*, May 11, 2019, https://www.newsroom.co.nz/2019/05/08/575479 /anne-marie-bradys-full-submission#. See also Martin Hala and Jicheng Lulu, "The CCP's Model of Social Control Goes Global," *Sinopsis*, December 20, 2018, https://sinopsis.cz/en/the-ccps-model-of-social-con trol-goes-global.

67. The symposium was organized by this author and was held at the Hoover Institution offices in Washington.

68. Ana Swanson, "China's Influence over Hollywood Grows," *Washington Post*, September 24, 2016, https://www.washingtonpost.com/news/wonk /wp/2016/09/24/chinas-influence-over-hollywood-grows/?utm_term= .ac92da304d62.

69. Patrick Brzeski, "'Top Gun: Maverick' Trailer Sparks Controversy," *Hollywood Reporter*, July 22, 2019, https://www.hollywoodreporter.com/heat

-vision/top-gun-maverick-trailer-sparks-controversy-tom-cruise-jacket -1225993.

70. Paul Mozer, "Inside China's Dystopian Dreams: A.I., Shame, and Lots of Cameras," *New York Times*, July 8, 2018, https://www.nytimes.com /2018/07/08/business/china-surveillance-technology.html.

71. Charles Rollet, "The Odd Reality of Life under China's All-Seeing Credit Score System," *Wired*, June 5, 2018, https://www.wired.co.uk/article/china -social-credit.

72. Catherine Tai, "China's Private Sector Is under Siege," *The Diplomat*, December 22, 2018, https://thediplomat.com/2018/12/chinas-private -sector-is-under-siege.

73. Jamil Anderlini, "'Western Values' Forbidden in Chinese Universities," *Financial Times* (Beijing), January 30, 2015, https://www.ft.com/content /95f3f866-a87e-11e4-bd17-00144feab7de.

74. Tim Cook, statement during Apple's August 2017 quarterly earnings call.

3

CAN KIM JONG-UN CONTROL HIS NUKES?

Nuclear Safety, Accident, and the Specter of North Korea's Atomic Arsenal

I.

There probably weren't many global travelers waiting for flights out of Pyongyang International Airport on August 29, 2017, but if there were, their early morning reveries were undoubtedly startled by the spectacle of a North Korean intermediate-range missile blasting off only a few miles beyond the runways. Just before six in the morning, a Hwasong-12 missile, also known as the KN-17, with a purported range of nearly four thousand miles, arced northeastward over North Korea and the Sea of Japan.[1] Eight minutes later, it passed over Hokkaido, the northernmost of Japan's four home islands. Roughly six minutes after that, approximately 730 miles east of Hokkaido, it broke apart and fell into the Pacific Ocean. If the trajectory of the KN-17 had

---

Parts of this essay originally appeared as "Can Kim Jong-un Control His Nukes?," *New York Review of Books*, October 27, 2017, https://www.nybooks .com/daily/2017/10/27/can-kim-jong-un-control-his-nukes, and "Trump Should Help North Korea Keep Its Nukes Safe," *The Atlantic*, November 5, 2017, https:// www.theatlantic.com/international/archive/2017/11/trump-help-nuclear -north-korea/544664.

been a little more northerly and had it broken up a few minutes earlier, it could have rained rocket debris down on Sapporo, Japan's fifth-
largest city, with a population of two million.

Like many North Korean rocket tests, this one ended in structural
failure, a reminder that, despite its boasts, Pyongyang has not yet perfected its missile technology. While that may give temporary solace to
those worrying about North Korea's nuclear capability, it serves as a
warning about perhaps the most serious threat posed by Kim Jong-un's
nuclear and ballistic missile arsenal: its safety.

The images of the unprecedented June 2018 Singapore summit
between Donald Trump and Kim raised hopes that a new era was
dawning between Washington and Pyongyang. Yet subsequent meetings of the two leaders in Hanoi and at the Demilitarized Zone along
the border between the two Koreas revealed just how difficult it remains
to achieve North Korean denuclearization. As negotiations inch along,
as they have for more than a quarter century, Pyongyang continues to
control and add to a nuclear arsenal of unknown size and effectiveness.
Yet given how little is known about Kim's nuclear and ballistic missile
capability, perhaps the world should worry less about the threat of a
North Korean–instigated nuclear war and more about the risk of a
nuclear accident. The most frightening question raised by Kim Jong-un's
pursuit of the ultimate weapon is also the simplest: Can he control his
nukes?

II.

It is the ultimate status symbol, the guarantor of national survival and
the ability to inflict unimaginable destruction on an enemy. Since the
first atomic fireball lit up the predawn New Mexico desert in 1945, only
a handful of nations have even attempted to become nuclear powers.
Once they did so, all took seriously the awesome responsibility of man-
aging their nuclear arsenals. Now a new member is joining the club,
one whose track record of recklessness, aggression, and inscrutability

can only make terrifying the idea that it, too, will now possess the ultimate weapon. Yet the real worry with North Korea becoming a nuclear power is one the headlines, and US officials, have so far ignored.

From new negotiations to war planning, the American foreign policy community is approaching North Korea as it has for the past quarter century, as a problem to be solved. Yet assuming Donald Trump (and his successors) and Kim Jong-un neither achieve denuclearization nor blunder into war, the real question is whether Kim will respect the power of his nukes enough to make sure they are safe and safely controlled. In other words, the world needs to worry less about the risk of a North Korean nuclear war than a nuclear accident. Soon enough, Kim will learn that it's not easy being a nuclear power. All he has to do is ask the Americans or the Russians.

On the evening of September 18, 1980, at the height of the Cold War, an overworked and exhausted US Air Force technician dropped an eight-pound socket eighty feet down the silo of a Titan II intercontinental ballistic missile (ICBM) in Damascus, Arkansas. The socket pierced the thin aluminum skin of the missile, releasing a jet of highly flammable missile fuel. The crew had no way of stopping the leaking fuel. Nine hours later, before an air force major crisis response team could reach the site, the missile exploded. The 740-ton concrete and steel silo door was blown off by the explosion, and the nuclear warhead itself was hurled dozens of meters beyond the silo complex. Only the warhead's safety mechanisms prevented a nine-megaton detonation barely fifty miles from Little Rock, where then US vice president Walter Mondale happened to be visiting. This accident, while one of the most potentially devastating in the history of the US nuclear operations, is just one of dozens that have occurred since America and Russia began their nuclear arms race nearly three-quarters of a century ago.

That the world has not experienced a nuclear detonation since Nagasaki, other than planned tests, or suffered a civilian catastrophe due to a military accident is due not only to the extraordinary seriousness with which the nuclear powers took their responsibilities but also to luck during potential crises. Betting on whether the world will remain so lucky will become increasingly risky once North Korea becomes a fully capable nuclear weapons state.

Unlike a conventional military, where tanks, trucks, and even fighter planes are relatively simple instruments of war, operating nuclear weapons is a huge, expensive, and complex responsibility. Warheads must be specially maintained, as must the missiles that deliver them. Launch procedures are—or should be—complicated enough that no weapon can be fired on a whim, yet reliable enough that a national leader has confidence his nukes are ready when he is. Given the terrible responsibilities involved, nuclear personnel need to be carefully chosen and trained, since the most mundane procedures have the potential to turn into unimaginable catastrophes.

The warhead that detonates over a target is but one part of a complex system. The US government calls the warheads, missiles, launchers, communications networks, satellites, production and maintenance facilities, trucks, guards, bunkers, and the like—in other words, the entire system—the "nuclear enterprise." Having confidence in that enterprise—that the weapons are safe, are in place when needed, will work as desired and (as important) will *not* work when *not* desired, and that crews are fully trained—is known as "nuclear surety."

In conversations with former nuclear weapons officers, from the previous commander of US Strategic Command down to a retired US Air Force Minuteman III launch officer, each asserted that nuclear surety was the single most important thing they thought about, trained for, and responded to, day in and day out, every minute that they were on patrol, in the silo, or making national-level decisions about America's nuclear force. Nuclear surety, in other words, *is* the business of nuclear weapons.

"I focused on four main areas," noted retired US Navy admiral Cecil Haney, former commander of US Strategic Command (Stratcom) from 2013 to 2016, during which time he was the senior nuclear warfighting officer in the US military. "Those were manning, training, equipment, and certification. How did I select the right individuals, get them trained as highly as possible, and make sure my systems were certified and tested?" A Washington, DC, native who graduated from the US Naval Academy, Haney is a quiet, lanky submariner who commanded US Pacific Fleet before assuming control of America's nuclear arsenal. "We have a culture of asking, 'What aren't we doing right?' to try and avoid mistakes," Haney said. He then paused and asked, "Will North Korea make shortcuts in a very expensive enterprise?"[2]

Nuclear weapons command and safety is a far less sexy topic than nuclear warfighting, though senior US officials such as former secretary of state George Shultz and secretaries of defense William J. Perry and Ash Carter have spent decades exploring nuclear stability and warning about the dangers of complacency.[3] It was the specter of inevitable nuclear mistakes and accidents that spawned the greatest nightmares of the Cold War, dystopic visions in books and movies such as *Fail Safe* and *Dr. Strangelove* of a world incinerated by an atomic fireball (or nearly so) due to a madman, a blown fuse, a garbled message, or a simple computer game. And the public had good reason to worry, which is why the specter of a North Korean nuclear arsenal should terrify even those who firmly believe Kim is not so suicidal as to launch an unprovoked nuclear attack. In a North Korean nuclear world, we have to be sure not only of Kim's rationality but also that the command and control system he puts into place will not break down due to mechanical or human error, that his weapons won't explode due to a glitch or poor maintenance and won't be launched accidentally. Yet when dealing with nuclear surety in North Korea, we enter a world composed almost entirely of "known unknowns."

III.

The risks of a nuclear program start with the very act of building a bomb. At the dawn of the atomic age that process was often shockingly lax compared to what it became a few decades later. Though no one knows for sure, it is unlikely that North Korean scientists work in the primitive conditions in which two American scientists died from radiation poisoning after mishandling bare plutonium cores in 1945 and 1946.[4] However, while American and foreign visitors had access to North Korea's Yongbyon nuclear reactor, plutonium reprocessing plant, and nuclear centrifuges for most of the period from 1995 through 2009, none have seen the actual factories where the North's bombs are ostensibly made, and thus few informed guesses can be made about North Korea's safety protocols in its nuclear production process. Any accident inside these confines would be a worrisome signal that Pyongyang was sacrificing safety for results.[5]

While we may never know about any North Korean accidents in laboratories or assembly plants, an accident like the September 1957 explosion at a nuclear waste processing and storage plant in Chelyabinsk, Russia, potentially could pose the first type of crisis the world may face with Pyongyang's nuclear program. Depending on its size, location, and prevailing wind patterns, a major release of nuclear material could wind up spreading radioactivity to South Korea, China, or Japan. (Figure 1 shows the locations of North Korea's nuclear facilities.) While the regional response would be focused on preventing civilian contamination, it would cause a diplomatic crisis. In response, Pyongyang might well try to deflect blame, claiming that sabotage was the cause, and even using that manufactured excuse to "retaliate" in turn.

The danger of potentially lax standards is compounded by normal wear and tear on nuclear systems. It's not surprising that the more nuclear systems are used, such as flying bombers, sailing submarines, or moving around missiles, the more likely accidents are to occur. During the Cold War, the relentless pace of constant American nuclear alerts led to numerous mishaps. In Operation Chrome Dome, for example, US Air Force B-52s carrying thermonuclear bombs were kept constantly in the air, flying to predetermined points around the Soviet Union, for eight full years, from 1960 to 1968. During that period, five major accidents occurred, ultimately leading to the cancellation of the program.

Nuclear weapons accidents such as these, called "broken arrows," nearly turned into catastrophe more than once. In late January 1961, a B-52 participating in Operation Chrome Dome flying out of Goldsboro,

North Carolina, developed a leak during its airborne refueling. Before the bomber could make it back to base, the crew was forced to eject, and the plane broke apart in midair, releasing two live nuclear bombs. When one of the bombs hit the ground, the concussion caused an electrical spark that sent a firing signal. The four-megaton weapon did not detonate only because its fifth and last safety switch held in place, the other four fifty-cent safety switches having failed when they smashed on impact. Had the last safety switch similarly failed, the bomb would have been fully armed, and the firing signal would have set off a thermonuclear explosion on American territory.

North Korea almost certainly won't have nuclear bombers, but the bulk of its ground-based force will likely be dispersed onto mobile launchers, which pose their own set of problems. These road-mobile transporter erector launchers (TELs) are fitted onto large trucks that

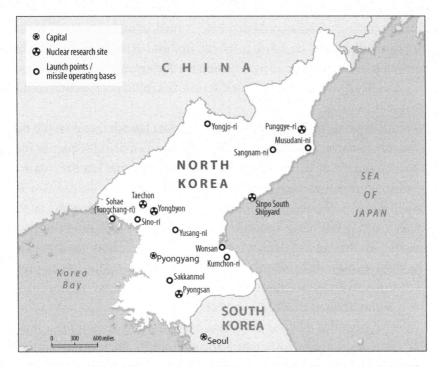

Figure 1. North Korea's Nuclear Facilities. *Note: North Korea also deploys mobile-launched missiles and is developing submarine launches as well.*

roam the countryside, making them difficult for enemies to target and destroy, unlike fixed missile silos. Yet the very nature of such a decentralized force also means a localized response to any problems.

Though some of North Korea's missiles are apparently solid-fueled, most use less stable liquid fuel with an engine designed during the Soviet era. Even the comparatively more stable liquid propellants used today are among the most toxic substances on earth, and transfer accidents have been a hazard of the job.[6] In August 1978, in one of the worst instances, a fuel line failed during a propellant transfer at a Titan II missile silo at McConnell Air Force Base in Kansas, releasing over thirteen thousand gallons of rocket fuel (dinitrogen tetroxide) and sending a "thundercloud" of orange vapor spewing out of the silo, killing one airman.[7] If North Korea has had similar accidents, we don't yet know, but in the worst-case scenario a fuel accident could cause the explosion of a missile, as in the 1980 Damascus incident. It is unlikely but conceivable that a warhead jettisoned from a missile that explodes due to a fueling mistake could detonate. A nuclear detonation on North Korean soil would be hard to cover up, and Kim Jong-un would undoubtedly deflect blame by accusing the Americans, South Koreans, or Japanese of sabotage or an attack, sparking a military crisis that could be uncontrollable.

Similarly, only on-site North Korean nuclear launch teams would be available to correct an electrical glitch that starts a firing sequence for a loaded missile or to repair a faulty missile or one that has been damaged in some other way while being transported. We don't know if North Korea will have nuclear crisis teams, but even if they do, such expertise may not reach a mobile launcher with a problem in time. In the 1980 Damascus accident, it took the US Air Force hours to dispatch the right teams to the remote silo, by which time it was too late to prevent the missile from exploding. And those were some of America's most highly trained disaster response teams.

We have no idea if Pyongyang is even planning on developing a similar crisis response infrastructure throughout its nuclear enterprise, since to do so would be to call into question the reliability of Kim's arsenal. It is hard enough to expect nuclear transparency within democratic systems, given the high level of classification required by even the most routine nuclear missions. It may well be that Kim cannot risk instituting anything near the level of America's nuclear safety regime, since dictators rule by instilling fear, not trust. Equally, Kim may feel there is no need to do so, since he has undoubtedly been assured of the program's unquestioned success.

All this raises the question of accountability. As retired air force lieutenant general James Kowalski, a B-52 pilot and the former deputy commander of US Strategic Command, put it, "Who is going to be the guy who goes to Kim Jong-un and tells him he has a problem with his nukes?"[8] Absolute trust is required between leaders and those charged with maintaining and operating nuclear weapons. It is hard to imagine such trust existing among Kim's circle of terrified sycophants.

IV.

Let's assume for the moment that Kim Jong-un's technicians and maintainers manage to keep his missiles safe and operationally reliable. The next major piece of the nuclear surety puzzle is people. Not surprisingly, dealing with the world's most powerful weapons requires an extraordinarily highly qualified cadre of specialists and some of the most rigorous training of any military specialty. Even so, US military personnel have made grave errors, including a 2007 incident when six nuclear-tipped cruise missiles were mistakenly loaded onto a B-52 that flew from Minot Air Force Base in North Dakota to Barksdale Air Force Base in Louisiana and sat unprotected on the runway at Barksdale for thirty-six hours.[9]

Operational mistakes by nuclear personnel are not the only dangers facing the nuclear enterprise. "We are continuously moving towards zero mistakes," Kowalski noted, acknowledging that even minor accidents in the nuclear enterprise can be catastrophic. Yet others have argued that the pressure to make no mistakes leads unintentionally to shortcuts, cheating, and even more stress on the human element of the nuclear force. Indeed, from 2014 to 2016, the US Air Force was rocked by a number of scandals in the nuclear community, including massive cheating among Minuteman III missile launch operators on their nuclear certification tests.[10] As a result, highly publicized investigations forced the revamp of training and testing of missile crews. Further highlighting the pressure felt by even senior nuclear commanders, the two-star air force general in charge of all Minutemen missiles was relieved of his command of the 20th Air Force in 2013 after reports of heavy drinking and unprofessional behavior during an official trip to Russia.[11]

How the North Koreans will recruit and test their nuclear personnel, ensuring their stability and reliability, is unknown. Whether they will instill a culture of zero mistakes and how often they will test their people and critically assess their system's weak points is also unknown. Clearly fear will be a major incentive not to err, as officers who make mistakes or lose Kim Jong-un's trust are more likely to be shot than reprimanded or retired. Yet fear can easily become counterproductive, forcing more errors, especially during times of crisis. North Korea might well wind up with a system that buries mistakes (and those who make them), thereby failing to learn to do things better and more safely. That, in turn, makes even more serious mistakes far more likely, some of which could one day start a nuclear war.

V.

During the Cold War, the most harrowing specter of error hung over the command and control of nuclear weapons.[12] Command and control (C2), often paired with communications and intelligence and referred to as C3I, is the acme of nuclear surety. From storage and assembly of nuclear-capable delivery systems to clear channels of authority and decision making, to early warning and launch operations, C2 can be thought of as the pointy end of the nuclear spear.

Establishing a cohesive and coherent command and control system commanded enormous attention on the part of US and Soviet political leaders and military planners throughout the Cold War and after.

The dangers of an unreliable or insufficient C2 system in North Korea are chilling to contemplate. The decision to use American nuclear weapons is initiated solely by the president, with orders confirmed and transmitted through the secretary of defense and chairman of the Joint Chiefs of Staff, and there is little reason to assume that Kim Jong-un would allow anything less. But the chain of authority in the US system is clear, from the president to the secretary of defense and chairman of the Joint Chiefs, and then through the National Military Command Center to the commander of Stratcom. How or if Kim will delegate authority down his chain remains unknown. Kowalski, the former deputy commander of Stratcom, asks, "Who [in North Korea] will have authority to order a warhead mated onto a missile? Who has authority to target? Arm it? Launch it?"

Even before launch orders are issued, each stage of getting a nuclear weapon ready for use, from taking the warhead out of the bunker, to mating it to the missile, to targeting and launching, is fraught with the potential for miscommunication and mechanical accident of the kind described earlier. The more launch systems on alert or fully armed and fueled, the higher the probability for some kind of error over time. As former Stratcom commander Haney asks, "How do you know that nuclear weapons will be taken out only when you want them to be, or that you have a trusted teamwork approach?"

The use of nuclear weapons, whether authorized or unauthorized, begins with arming a missile and making it ready for launch. Except for the small number of weapons on alert, US missiles are kept separate from their nuclear warheads, and an order must be given to move the warheads out of secured storage bunkers to be matched with the delivery systems. Given that a good part of Kim's arsenal involves road-mobile missiles, the time required to move them to safe launching locations may push the North Koreans to keep more warheads outside secured storage, either regularly mated to missiles or quickly accessible nearby.

Just as vitally, will North Korean nukes be armed and ready for detonation as soon as they are mated to missiles? In the US case, nuclear weapons can be enabled only by entering a twelve-digit code, known as the permissive action link (PAL), into the weapon itself.[13] Without the PAL, the weapon remains in safe mode, thus providing yet another layer of negative control preventing the unauthorized use of nuclear weapons. There is as yet no indication that North Korea has instituted a PAL system, and unless Pyongyang decides to tell us, we may never know whether it has enabled such a system.

At the heart of the nuclear enterprise is the turning of the launch key. No one yet knows what North Korea's nuclear release procedures will be. While Kim Jong-un likely will keep all control over nuclear weapons in his hands, he won't physically fire the missile, so he must delegate that authority in some way. Will Kim have the equivalent of the American president's nuclear "football," with its menu of launch options? Once Kim has decided what he wants to do, will the order go from him solely to the commander of the Strategic Rocket Forces, the military unit that presumably controls North Korea's nuclear ballistic missiles? Or will Kim want to give orders directly to the field units, which, in addition to the mobile launchers, comprise fixed launch pads and possibly an underground silo complex, not unlike the US Minuteman III force?

Nor do we know how North Korea's launch orders will be electronically or physically transmitted. Moviegoers remember scenes of US nuclear launch officers cracking open the thin red "wafers" holding the alphanumeric codes in movies such as *War Games* and *Crimson Tide*. Will North Korean missile officers receive similar electronic "emergency action messages" that are confirmed by opening "sealed authenticator envelopes" containing the unique codes for launch, thus ensuring that only proper commands are received? Perhaps a simple telephone call from Pyongyang will suffice to launch nuclear weapons, but that is less secure and possibly more vulnerable to misinterpretation during a crisis or third-party interference.

As Stratcom commander, Cecil Haney focused extensively on the nexus of personnel and release procedures, and in conversation worries about how a dictatorship will structure its nuclear enterprise. Will North Korea institute the inviolable two-person rule adopted by the United States, whereby no single individual has launch authority, or even the ability to be alone at any time with a nuclear weapon? In the case of US missile silo crews, not only must both launch officers turn their launch keys at exactly the same time, but a second two-man crew in a separate complex must also do so at the same instant, thereby launching together all the missiles under the control of the two groups. Will Kim trust two officers to work together, or does he believe fear is enough to keep a single officer with launch authority in line?

Even more opaque is the question of who will have ultimate launch authority at individual sites. It is hard to imagine the dictator of one of the world's most ruthless and hierarchical states allowing subordinate officers the autonomy to launch nuclear missiles. Yet if Kim fears a "decapitation strike" by US or South Korean forces, he might issue orders that delegate launch authority to dispersed units. One can envision a scenario during a crisis in which a panicky junior officer loses communication with upper-level commanders and decides that he needs to launch before he is attacked or because he believes a first strike has taken out Kim.

If Pyongyang does not have reliable communications with its nuclear launch systems and personnel, then the uncertainty in nuclear operations increases dramatically. This in turn will put pressure on US commanders who are trying to decide how North Korea may respond to any American action. "If they did something and we responded," Kowalski said, describing one of his greatest concerns, "we have to be careful to understand their command and control system and not interfere. You don't want to put into motion an automatic delegation system where a junior officer has launch authority."

Here is where the third C, communications, becomes vital. The stress of maintaining the required level of training and proficiency, not to mention ensuring operational readiness of nuclear weapons, is all-consuming. The last thing any launch officer needs to worry about is making any autonomous decisions about when to use his nukes. That means having absolute confidence in the communications system that tells him what to do. A former US Navy ballistic missile submarine commander who requested anonymity due to his current job recalled that his number one priority was to stay in constant communication with shore-based nuclear authorities. That is obviously of critical importance in the seaborne submarine fleet, but it is hardly less important on land. Dropped phone calls and network interruptions are an annoyance at normal times, but during a crisis, such failures could inadvertently unleash a nuclear strike. However Kim decides to send the orders for strategic operations, a former senior US nuclear commander notes, they likely would come through communications systems including the country's fiber optics network, as well as occasional line-of-sight radio transmitters to the road-mobile launchers. But how reliable will such systems be?

And all these uncertainties are magnified a dozenfold when talking about sea-based nuclear systems. Perhaps tempting the nuclear gods, Pyongyang apparently desires to develop an indigenous ballistic missile submarine, which is one of the most technologically complex weapons systems in existence.[14] While it remains years away from having such a capability, operating missile submarines would tax North Korea's untested command and control systems in even more acute ways, not least in the absolute confidence in the stability and reliability of the submarine's senior officers.

VI.

Outside of Moscow, in May 2017, Stanislav Petrov died at the age of seventy-seven.[15] Largely unknown to the world, Petrov may have single-handedly averted a nuclear war between the Soviet Union and the United States. As a lieutenant colonel in Soviet air defense headquarters,

Petrov was the ranking duty officer on September 26, 1983. Just past midnight, the early warning radar alarm sounded, and Petrov looked up to see a single US ballistic missile being tracked inbound toward the Soviet Union. Petrov had just fifteen minutes to decide whether the attack was real—fifteen minutes after that, the first warhead would detonate over Soviet soil. A few minutes later, another alarm sounded, and the screens warned that four more US ICBMs were rocketing toward Russia. Once Petrov confirmed that a nuclear attack was imminent, Soviet leaders would almost certainly order an equally devastating counterstrike on US and European territory.

Despite unimaginable pressure and the near panic of those around him, Petrov did not believe the attack was real. Based on what Soviet nuclear officers thought they understood about US nuclear doctrine, a surprise first strike would be massive, designed to destroy the USSR's retaliatory capability. Unlike a "first use" attack, in which one country that is feeling threatened with nuclear attack by an adversary during a crisis decides to launch nuclear missiles preemptively, a first strike could come out of the blue, in overwhelming force. On that early September morning in 1983, just five US missiles did not make sense to Petrov. But if he was wrong, then not only would the Soviet Union soon suffer at least five thermonuclear detonations but there might not be enough time to retaliate if the Soviet leadership or key command and control nodes were destroyed.

Petrov decided the alarm was a false one. With bated breath, he and his subordinates waited to see if he had made the wrong call. When no reports came in of warheads detonating on Soviet soil, they could breathe again, shaken to the core by the realization that they had come to within perhaps minutes of a global thermonuclear exchange. A later investigation to determine why the false alarm occurred concluded that Soviet early warning satellites had incorrectly identified sunlight glinting off cloud tops as the flashes of US ICBMs being launched.

North Korea will not have any early warning satellites, at least that we know of, but it will face the same question of correctly identifying perceived threats and deciding how to respond, whether during periods of relative quiescence on the peninsula or at moments of extreme tension. Because Kim will not have the multiple forms of early warning that the United States has, he may well be more likely to interpret bits of intelligence and raw analysis in the most negative light. In fact, it makes sense for him to do so, since the risk of missing the signals of an impending US attack may be existential for him and his regime. It may be not only a panicked nuclear launch officer who misinterprets a B-2 show of force, say, as an imminent attack. Forward observers, North Korean spies, and possibly even hacks into foreign satellite systems all may give incomplete information that lead Kim's senior military officials to urge him to launch a preemptive attack of his own. Fear that the United States, along with its allies, may be able to target and destroy C2 nodes could be enough justification to start a preemptive North Korean attack, as any destruction of Kim's military capability might be seen by him and his inner circle as an existential threat.

This is as much a political question as a technical one, and what can be called "national warning" is where the human and technical elements come together closest to the decision-making process. Even after the Cold War, when the ideological passions of that struggle had abated, Russia and the United States came perilously close to nuclear war. In late January 1995, then Russian president Boris Yeltsin unlocked his nuclear football and gave orders to Russian ballistic missile submarines to prepare for a nuclear retaliatory strike. Just minutes earlier, he had been advised that Russian early warning radars had picked up what looked like an incoming submarine-launched US ballistic missile.

Unlike in 1983, the radars were not malfunctioning. A real rocket was shooting through a narrow air corridor that could lead to Moscow. And even though it was only a single missile, the Russians thought it might be designed for an electro-magnetic pulse (EMP) attack. Detonated high in the atmosphere, the gamma rays of a thermonuclear explosion can cause a massive overload on a country's electrical networks, shutting down military and civilian systems alike, including radars vital to air defense.[16] The Russians feared that an EMP would be a precursor to a larger US attack crippling the nation's command and control capabilities.

Yeltsin's senior officers had ten minutes to decide if the missile was real and headed toward Moscow. If they couldn't determine the trajectory with confidence, they would have to make a recommendation, and Yeltsin, whose nuclear briefcase was open and ready, would have had to make the ultimate decision. It took eight minutes before the air defense officials decided the missile was headed out to open sea rather than to the Russian capital. Within hours, they discovered that the missile was a joint Norwegian-US scientific mission to study the aurora borealis. The United States had properly notified Moscow of the test, but that information had not been passed down to the Russian radar operators.[17]

If loyalty to or fear of Kim is as strong as most outside observers believe it to be, nuance during a crisis is likely to be lost on Kim's senior officers. Instead, there is every reason to suspect that a combination of self-preservation, ideological fervor, and even true loyalty would predispose Kim's officers to nuclear aggressiveness. The fate of Asia may rest on whether North Korea has its own Stanislav Petrov.

VII.

Safety for the North Korean nuclear arsenal will rest primarily with Kim Jong-un and his officers. One can only hope they have studied, or at least are aware of, the accidents that plagued the United States and Russia. If they adopt a cavalier attitude or are focused on avoiding responsibility and redirecting any blame, then standards, confidence, and professionalism will be the first casualty. As Haney noted, it all comes down to their perceptions of the importance of the mission. Will Kim and his lieutenants take seriously the responsibility of nuclear surety, or will each be focused on his own political reputation?

Living in this new environment will demand new, perhaps radical thinking on the part of the United States government. Though bizarre to consider, it may wind up being in America's interest to help make North Korea's nukes safer. While most US strategists must draw up plans to deter and, if necessary, defeat a nuclear-armed North Korea, others should consider unorthodox ways of ensuring a safer North Korean nuclear arsenal.

Squaring that aim with credible deterrence will be difficult. For example, to make sure that Kim has constant communications with his nuclear units so that he does not fear losing contact with them, would Washington assure him that it will not sabotage North Korea's command and control capabilities, whether through cyber warfare or other means? This was suggested by a former senior US nuclear weapons officer in private conversations. Such a promise might reduce pressure on Kim and his senior officers in a crisis. Could the United States ever propose nuclear stability steps like establishing a hotline between Washington and Pyongyang? Given North Korea's closed and hostile system, such cooperation may seem impossible, but the alternative—constant suspicion and hair-trigger reactions—is more daunting.

If any nation has a possibility, no matter how small, of helping Kim keep his nukes safe, it is China, North Korea's only official ally and its major supporter. Beijing remains the only actor close enough to Pyongyang to even try to instill some nuclear responsibility, or perhaps the only one that could try to pressure the North Koreans into accepting some "best practices" in nuclear guardianship. Given how little the United States currently understands about Chinese nuclear doctrine, it is a little like trusting the fox to guard the coyotes, but Washington has few palatable options for dealing with an established North Korean nuclear state. The question is whether Beijing has any interest in helping ensure a stable nuclear operating environment in North Korea, or whether it sees ongoing US–North Korean nuclear enmity as a means of exercising greater influence over the region.

As crazy as it sounds, the Trump administration or its successors might consider reaching out to the Chinese to encourage them to offer some friendly advice to Kim. Kim undoubtedly wants to keep the details of his program as secret as possible, but Chinese president Xi

Jinping might offer some basic technical assistance on issues like launch authentication or setting up permissive action links (PAL). Helping train missile technicians in damage control and critical repair of launch systems might add another layer of certainty to the daily maintenance of nuclear weapons. And despite the distaste for accepting Pyongyang as a nuclear power, considering some US–North Korean confidence-building mechanisms, perhaps even midwifed by Beijing, may come to be seen as a necessary evil in the new nuclear world.

VIII.

Of course, the moment that war breaks out on the Korean Peninsula, all these attempts at maintaining North Korean nuclear surety will be blown away, figuratively or literally. When that happens, the US military undoubtedly will immediately attempt to destroy North Korea's command and control network so as to make it difficult if not impossible for Kim to use his nukes. It would also most likely attempt a quick decapitation strike and would target as many of Kim's fixed and mobile nuclear assets as possible, trying to destroy them on the ground.

The outbreak of war along the Demilitarized Zone would of course represent the failure of US security policy on the Korean Peninsula. Yet ironically, if Washington is successful in avoiding war but fails to denuclearize North Korea, then Asia and the world will be condemned to a perpetual, if cold, nuclear peace with Pyongyang. Years of nuclear brinksmanship, bluffing, and threats may also ensue, at least as long as Kim Jong-un and his regime remain in power. In the absence of denuclearization, the supreme task of policy makers will be to prevent North Korea from ever using its nuclear force. That will require new thinking about deterrence and containment, but a major part of that will come down to how well the North Koreans manage their nuclear forces, keeping them safe, reliable, and under control at all times. Like the 1940s naval theorist Bernard Brodie, who wrote upon hearing about the atomic bombing of Hiroshima that everything he'd written was obsolete, our thinking similarly has to change as radically, focusing as much on North Korean nuclear stability as on how or when Kim Jong-un will launch a nuclear war.

If Donald Trump or his successors fail in persuading Kim Jong-un to give up his nuclear weapons, and if the nearly seven-decades-long stalemate on the Korean Peninsula continues without slipping into war, the world will settle down to the long-term challenge of learning to live with Pyongyang's nuclear weapons. Washington may decide never to acknowledge that North Korea is a nuclear weapons state, in a bid to keep global nonproliferation aims alive, but it will need to figure out how to ensure that the nuclear accidents and miscalculations of the Cold War are not repeated in North Korea with catastrophic consequences.

Notes

1. "Hwasong-12," *CSIS Missile Defense Project*, last modified June 15, 2018, https://missilethreat.csis.org/missile/hwasong-12.
2. Interview with Admiral (ret.) Cecil Haney, US Navy, August 2017.
3. William J. Perry and Ash Carter, "Preventive Defense," *Hoover Digest*, no. 4, October 30, 1999, https://www.hoover.org/research/preventive -defense.
4. For a recent history of the US nuclear enterprise and the accidents involved, see Eric Schlosser, *Command and Control: Nuclear Weapons, the Damascus Accident, and the Illusion of Safety* (New York: Penguin, 2014). See also Scott D. Sagan, *The Limits of Safety: Organizations, Accidents, and Nuclear Weapons* (Princeton, NJ: Princeton University Press, 1993).
5. Sigfried Hecker, former head of the Los Alamos National Laboratory and one of the few Americans who has been granted access to most of the Yongbyon nuclear facility, has noted that the North Koreans have avoided a major nuclear production accident over the past fifty years, even in the absence of Western standards. Personal conversation with author, December 2018.

6. Brian Nufer, "A Summary of NASA and USAF Hypergolic Propellant Related Spills and Fires," paper presented at Space Transportation and Safety conference, Huntsville, AL, April 25–30, 2010, available at https:// ntrs.nasa.gov/archive/nasa/casi.ntrs.nasa.gov/20100038321.pdf.

7. Associated Press, "Thunderhead of Lethal Vapor Kills Airman at Missile Silo," *Lakeland Ledger*, August 25, 1978, available at https://news .google.com/newspapers?id=lsUSAAAAIBAJ&sjid=CfsDAAAAIBAJ &pg=5959%2C7675769.

8. Interview with Lieutenant General (ret.) James Kowalski, US Air Force, August 2017.

9. An official 2008 Department of Defense report on the incident is Defense Science Board Permanent Task Force on Nuclear Weapons Surety, *Report on the Unauthorized Movement of Nuclear Weapons*, February 2008, https://www.bits.de/NRANEU/docs/2008-02-Nuclear_Weapons _Surety.pdf, while an interesting NASA analysis of the systemic causes of the accident can be found in "Strayed Spears," *System Failure Case Studies* 5, no. 5 (May 2011), https://sma.nasa.gov/docs/default-source /safety-messages/safetymessage-2011-05-02-unauthorizednuclearweap onstransfer.pdf?sfvrsn=49ae1ef8_4.

10. Helene Cooper, "Air Force Fires 9 Officers in Scandal over Cheating on Proficiency Tests," *New York Times*, March 27, 2014, https://www.nytimes .com/2014/03/28/us/air-force-fires-9-officers-accused-in-cheating-scan dal.html.

11. Julian E. Barnes, "Air Force Fires General in Charge of Nuclear Missiles," *Wall Street Journal*, October 11, 2013, https://www.wsj.com/articles /air-force-fires-general-in-charge-of-nuclear-missiles-1381507728.

12. There are many sources that attempt to demystify the highly secret command and control procedures in the United States and other countries. A brief primer from the Union of Concerned Scientists can be found in "Whose Finger Is on the Button?," https://www.ucsusa.org/sites /default/files/attach/2017/11/Launch-Authority.pdf; an even briefer but useful blog post is Lt. Col. Gary Jacobsen," Command and Control of Nuclear Forces," US Naval Institute, March 15, 2019, https://blog .usni.org/posts/2019/03/15/command-and-control-of-nuclear-forces. An older treatment is Daniel Ford, *The Button* (New York: Simon and Schuster, 1985).

13. See Steven M. Bellovin, *Permissive Action Links, Nuclear Weapons, and the History of Public Key Cryptography*, Columbia University Department of Computer Science, lecture slides, October 21, 2005, https://web.stanford.edu/class/ee380/Abstracts/060315-slides-bellovin.pdf.

14. Ministry of National Defense, *2016 Defense White Paper* (Seoul, 2016), p. 8, http://www.mnd.go.kr/user/mndEN/upload/pblictn/PBLICTNE BOOK_201705180357180050.pdf.

15. Petrov was the subject of the documentary-drama, *The Man Who Saved the World* (2014); for an obituary, see Sewell Chan, "Stanislav Petrov, Soviet Officer Who Helped Avert Nuclear War, Is Dead at 77," *New York Times*, September 18, 2017, https://www.nytimes.com/2017/09/18/world/europe/stanislav-petrov-nuclear-war-dead.html.

16. For a discussion, see *Report of the Commission to Assess the Threat to the United States from Electromagnetic (EMP) Attack (2004)*, http://www.empcommission.org/docs/empc_exec_rpt.pdf.

17. A brief recap of the 1995 Norwegian rocket incident is "Nuclear Close Calls: The Norwegian Rocket Incident," Atomic Heritage Foundation, June 15, 2018, https://www.atomicheritage.org/history/nuclear-close-calls-norwegian-rocket-incident.

4

INDIA'S MISSING WOMEN

"I'd like to be a sales manager one day," muses the young lady with whom I'm having coffee in one of Chennai's upscale hotels. "But my parents have arranged a marriage for me, and it will be finalized next year." Her disappointment is palpable, yet muted by the odd formality with which she describes her upcoming nuptials, a mood matching the sober-if-stylish sari she is wearing. Like many of India's young urban women, Sita is educated and holds a professional position, yet her skills and dreams come second to respecting her parents' wishes. As India continues its torrid growth and its middle class expands, the evidence is mixed at best that traditional social bonds will loosen for many, perhaps most, Indian women. That may help maintain social stability in times of rapid development, but it may also limit the ultimate degree to which this country of 1.2 billion people will change. It also means that as India modernizes, it will miss out on the energies and talents of millions of its citizens, potentially hampering the broader role it can play in the world.

This essay is adapted from "India's Missing Women," *The American*, January 10, 2013. The names of some of the women interviewed for this article have been changed.

Sita may be resigned to her future, but she also seems to accept it readily. She has already had her life upended several times. She was born in India's poor northeast, then moved as a young child with her family south to Chennai, then up to India's capital, New Delhi, and finally back to Chennai. The moves, while disruptive, were actually done in no small measure for her well-being. Her parents prefer India's south for their daughter's sake, she tells me, believing it to be safer for young women. To an outsider, Sita's parents' concern for their daughter seems hard to square with their insistence on picking her husband. What is clear, though, is that her parents refused to ignore the dangers facing women in India.

Allowing women to participate fully in Indian society begins with making it safer for them. Violence against women is endemic but supposedly more prevalent in the north. Such violence was brushed under the rug for decades, but the country was galvanized by the horrific December 2012 gang rape and murder of a twenty-three-year-old student on a bus in New Delhi.[1] Yet despite the public outcry, violence against women continues to occur far too often in India, and for reasons that are not simply criminal. Culture and religion play their role in the dangers that Indian women face, too, as in the 2010 murders of two young Muslim women who had eloped with Hindu men, what was determined to be an honor killing by their mothers in Uttar Pradesh, the northern state bordering Delhi.[2]

No one knows for sure the amount of violence perpetrated against women, or specific numbers regarding rape, much of which goes unreported. Yet even when charges are brought, only 26 percent of rape cases result in convictions in court.[3] In part in response to such numbers, India's first women's court opened in West Bengal in 2013. The court is headed by two female judges, and all the staff and government lawyers are women.[4] More broadly, Indian laws have begun to try to change society, if slowly. A 2013 bill prohibiting sexual harassment in the workplace was touted as a way to protect Indian women in the labor force, but according to the Federation of Indian Chambers of

Commerce and Industry in 2015, fully a third of Indian companies, and 25 percent of multinational corporations in India, were not compliant with the Sexual Harassment Act.[5] And while not nearly as widespread as the #MeToo movement that swept the United States, India's own version of public sexual shaming took off in 2018, with well-known public figures trading charges of sexual assault, harassment, and improprieties.

While crimes of violence and of a sexual nature are increasingly in the public eye, other types of social pressure and discrimination against Indian women remain pervasive. As for Sita, my coffeehouse companion, she tells me she would like to move from Chennai, but perhaps only to Bangalore, several hundred miles to the west, which is the space industry and IT capital of India and a magnet for young, educated Indians. She hopes that there her talent will be respected and that she might be freer to pursue her interests.

Sita's career path has been as indirect as her migration through India. At university, she majored in biology, finishing her degree through correspondence courses after her family's move south. But she never had an interest in working in the sciences and instead has a good service-sector job connected with Chennai's booming tourist and business population. She was hoping to become a duty manager at the hotel where she works, but even if she is promoted, she has decided to leave within a year to try and move into a sales position. But then, she admits, that probably won't happen either, since her parents are adamant about that marriage.

I ask Sita about her engagement. Her somberness comes not just from having her life partner picked out for her, but because she is in love with someone else. She has a boyfriend who is also a professional, but "it won't work out," she says. Because of her arranged engagement? No, because she doesn't know if he loves her. He works in Bangalore, one reason she wants to move there, but he is not ready to commit. Not that it would matter, she adds, since her parents don't like him. Our whole conversation is like this, with her starting a topic by talking about her desires and the choices she would like to make, and then invariably admitting that none of it will happen since the choices have been made for her.

What her parents have decided to do is to marry her off to someone from the same caste, in fact with the same surname, living in the area where she was born. Her family is Hindu and Brahmin, and it is inconceivable to her parents that she would marry outside the caste. In India, democratic freedom rubs up regularly against traditional social models, such as the caste system and arranged marriages, which continue to play a significant role in shaping relationships and even economic ties.[6] I ask Sita whether she will go back to the north, to the poverty-riven state of Bihar where her husband-to-be lives. Yes, she answers, for the marriage. And what will she do there? She doesn't know. A job? She shrugs. But, she hastens to add, arranged marriages remain extremely popular in India, and they are the best way to ensure that marriages succeed. In the West, she believes, too many people divorce and never commit to making married life work. She makes marriage sound like a duty, and when I tell her that, she doesn't disagree.

I ask if she thinks she will come to love her husband. She answers that she doesn't know, since she doesn't know him. She has only met him once, when her family traveled to a city near his hometown to meet him and his parents. The two of them never talked directly, but only in a large crowd of relatives, as is common in the negotiating stage of arranged marriages. "How can I love someone I've never talked to?" she asks. Perhaps he feels the same way, I add, but she just shakes her head. He is thirty-three, she tells me, ten years older than she is, and eager to get married.

The pressure on Sita to get married is not only due to traditional Indian mores. The past decades have seen the birth of far more males than females in India, not only in poor areas but in richer regions as well. Traditionally, boys were more valued for their labor potential in this overwhelmingly agrarian country, as in China, leading to sex-based abortion and infanticide. India's most recent census, which revealed an astonishing net gain of 180 million persons from 2000 to

2010, also saw a widening of that sex imbalance, despite growth of the middle class. This should not be happening. In most development models, as a country becomes richer, its sex ratio evens out. In India, though, that gap has not narrowed, even though the rate at which it is widening did indeed slow over the past decade. Today's sex ratio of 914 females to every 1,000 males under age six ranks among the worst in the world.[7] Yet at the same time, decades of such a skewed sex imbalance make eligible young women an increasingly prized asset for males like Sita's fiancé.

The whole situation is her fault, she says, since her parents badgered her for years, ever since she was a teenager, to begin looking at an arranged marriage. She put them off numerous times and finally agreed, if only to end their exasperation. Her husband-to-be was the first one they looked at, and he said yes immediately. Sita doubts she'll bridge the age gap between them, and she's not even interested in trying. "I'm a quiet person," she says. "I don't talk to my parents much, since all they do is criticize me. So, I probably will talk to my husband when he talks to me." And yet, I muse, she is comfortable talking to a stranger about some of the most personal issues in her life. Perhaps the fact that I have no connection to anyone she knows makes it easier for her to talk this way, though it does nothing to solve her problems.

India's colleges and universities are full of young women with professional goals like Sita. My first day in India, I visit the University of Madras (the venerable city name for Chennai), one of India's three oldest institutions of higher learning, established in 1857 by the British and modeled on the University of London. There, amid its red-brick colonial grandeur, I learn that over half of its four thousand undergraduates are female, and regularly some of its top performers. From one perspective, India has made rapid gains in higher education, with 46 percent of women enrolling in some type of college or university in 2016.[8] By comparison, Japan has had a century and a half of higher education for women, yet in 2018 just over 50 percent of women went to college.[9]

When I reach Calcutta a week later, I stop at the elite Presidency University, founded by the British in 1817. I meet Professor Amita

Chatterjee, formerly the vice chancellor of the university. Chatterjee doesn't volunteer the information, but once I ask, she tells me that 60 percent of her three thousand undergraduates are women, many of whom do better than the men at their studies. This echoes what the vice chancellor at Madras told me. In fact, in recent years, women have excelled in India's national civil service examinations. From 2010 through 2012, and from 2014 through 2016, the top scorers among five hundred thousand applicants in the exam were women, sometimes taking the top four slots, as in 2014. In 2013, women made up half of the top twenty-five scorers, while in 2017, eight of the top twenty-five were women.[10]

Walking around several university campuses, I see far more young women than men studying in corridors or talking in classrooms. This female educational excellence also spills down to secondary education, where 87 percent of graduating high school girls passed their Class 12 (senior year) exams in 2012, compared to just 78 percent of boys.[11] As in the United States, women are increasingly the top grade earners on college campuses and in high schools. One would expect that they would thus be a national force in business, professional education, government, and the like. Yet such statistics are misleading, for in the country as a whole fewer than half of India's women are literate, leaving hundreds of millions far worse off than Sita and her college-educated friends.

If Sita is any guide, the talents of many of the twelve million women enrolled in undergraduate programs may not be put to full use once they've graduated, which is a condition facing most women throughout the Indo-Pacific region. Generalization is a fool's errand in India, with its billion diverse people, but during my discussion with Sita, she gave no indication that her situation was markedly different from her friends or workmates. When I ask a professor at the University of Calcutta what his female graduate students will do after their studies, he shrugs his shoulders. Some will get research and administrative jobs, he indicates, but marriage will end the careers and aspirations of many of India's young women. I wonder if the relative lack of young marriage-age women doesn't give those lucky enough to get a college education an advantage in picking a desirable mate, perhaps someone who will let them pursue a career. But then I'm reminded of how Sita's future is already picked out for her.

Sita's disappointment comes not from the thought of being married but from having no say in the marriage or what comes after. When I press her on this, she talks a bit about her mother, who has followed her father around India and now lives in an area where she doesn't speak the language. Westerners may think that Hindi is the national language, but it is spoken primarily in the north. Tamil is the language of hundreds of millions in the south, and Sita's mother can't understand it. Then with whom does her mother talk? Only her family and old friends back home, on the telephone, replies Sita. I see a shadow of fear on her face, maybe as she imagines being as isolated as her mother.

It will be particularly hard for Sita to move back north. Although she speaks Hindi as a native tongue, and therefore won't be as cut off from society around her as her mother, social conditions in the north may make life difficult. It is poorer than the south and its cities are comparatively worse. Driving around Calcutta a week later, I see thousands of Biharis who fled their state into Calcutta's West Bengal, and are now living in filthy, crumbling lean-tos and shanties on the city's streets. For someone like Sita, who has dreamed of living in Bangalore, the north offers little enticement.

The north of India is also more socioeconomically volatile than other areas of the country. During 2010, farmers rampaged against police near Delhi over land repossession, killing several officers, and Maoist guerillas from a decades-old insurgency ambushed eleven policemen in the northeast.[12] It is also relatively less educated. Tamil Nadu, the southern state in which Chennai is located, has hundreds of colleges and universities, from the flagship University of Madras to tiny private schools that can be hardly better than vocational centers. Regardless, the opportunities for education beyond secondary school are nonetheless readily available in the southern Deccan region. And as a glance at any of the moderately established higher education schools shows, females constitute a large proportion of those getting educated in the south.

No doubt such educational levels help explain why the Deccan is a key part of India's economic engine, as well as its gateway to the rest of Asia's vast trading network, with links throughout Southeast Asia and tie-ups to foreign corporations like Ford and Hyundai. Yet Sita will be part of that vibrancy for only a short while longer. If she wished, she could undoubtedly get that sales job and rise to become a manager, given the growth of business in places like Chennai and Bangalore. But that would mean turning her back on her parents. And from our conversation, it doesn't sound like she'd find a wide support group of friends who would either understand her choice or have taken the same road themselves.

The situation is not markedly different in cosmopolitan centers like New Delhi. While in the capital, I meet Aaliyah, a young, modern Muslim who is a reporter and anchor for one of India's large television stations. Like Sita, Aaliyah tells me that she's given in to her parents and agreed to an arranged marriage. She is far more negative about it than Sita, although her situation seems somewhat more palatable. Among Aaliyah's circle of female friends, some from work and some from university, many are not only married but also keeping their jobs. She is the same age as her prospective husband, who works in business. However, she has no interest in marrying him, especially after the usual one-and-only meeting of the families. What angers her most is that he is currently living overseas, so she will have to give up her job, though if he were in Delhi, she almost certainly would keep it. It may be only for a few years, she adds, but if she leaves India, she wants to do it for her own reasons, like getting a graduate degree in the United States.

Yet Aaliyah ultimately feels a responsibility to abide by her parents' wishes. Her parents are as traditional as Sita's and cannot conceive of her marrying a non-Muslim. I ask, probably impolitely, if he is an observant Muslim. "He's more traditional than I am," she remarks. "He prays twice a day, whereas I pray only once. Of course, we're both supposed to do it five times a day." Risking further offense, I ask if he wants her to wear the hijab. She shakes her head no. They are both modern Indian Muslims, far from the world of male dominance in places like Saudi Arabia or Afghanistan, or more fundamentalist forms of Islam. Yet the sting of feeling that she has no choice in the most important decision of her life makes her, like Sita, feel helpless. Can she love him, I ask? "I will make myself love him" is her response. I subsequently hear that she has had her first child, though I can't discover if she kept working in media.

It doesn't seem like that should be the case for an urban, educated female, given the prominence of many women today. Today's India is filled with images of powerful women, from politicians to movie stars. There seems to be little overt prejudice against female politicians in a country that was ruled by Indira Gandhi for nearly twenty years. The Congress Party, political home of India's first prime minister, Jawaharlal Nehru, and base for the Gandhi dynasty, was long dominated by Sonia Gandhi, the Italian-born widow of Indira's son, former prime minister Rajiv Gandhi, after his assassination in 1991. Sonia, despite her checkered political success, was the party president, controlling nearly every aspect of party management, and remains its parliamentary chairperson.

Not all of India's female leaders were born in the purple, however. Three of the country's most important states, including Chennai's Tamil Nadu, are now or recently have been run by elected female chief ministers from among the commoners. India's most populous state, Uttar Pradesh, with a population of nearly 180 million, was run four times by Kumari Mayawati, who built a minicult of personality around herself during her terms starting in 1995 and ending most recently in 2012. A trip through Lucknow, Uttar Pradesh's capital, during Mayawati's last chief ministership revealed massive billboards at every intersection with her image and a list of her accomplishments in office, while huge, pharaonic-like structures built on her orders dot the city. The fact that she is a Dalit, from the caste once known as "untouchable," and the first elected female Dalit chief minister, only adds to her mystique. Whether she is loved or hated, Mayawati has been one of the most powerful chief ministers of the past two decades.[13]

Perhaps even more interestingly, in West Bengal, a poor state in India's northeast where cosmopolitan Calcutta is located, a modest folk leader named Mamata Banerjee succeeded in May 2011 in ousting the Communist Party, which had held power for thirty-four years. Mamata, as everyone calls her, lives a frugal life with her mother and is clearly a populist icon in West Bengal. Her previous stint as national railways minister was not particularly successful, and many question whether she has a real agenda for reviving Bengal's economy despite nearly a decade in office. Regardless, she is a symbol of fearlessness to many Indians, men as well as women, for having survived imprisonment and physical abuse at the hands of the former ruling Communist Party.

Indian women are slowly breaking the political glass ceiling in other ways. For five years, from 2014 to 2019, Sushma Swaraj served as India's minister of external affairs, and in September 2017, Nirmala Sitharaman became the country's first independently appointed female minister of defense, then succeeding to the crucial post of Minister of Finance in 2019.[14] Two of India's ambassadors to the United States were women, serving consecutively from 2009 to 2013. Yet the Gandhis, Mamatas, and Mayawatis are the exception, no matter how prominent they are. Out of 790 seats in the national parliament, only 63 were held by female parliamentarians in 2017, while in 2014, women held just under 12 percent.[15] This means India ranks behind Afghanistan, Bangladesh, Pakistan, and Nepal in female parliamentarians, despite having elected a female head of state, Indira Gandhi, in 1966, the second country in the world to do so.

Beyond female politicians, Indian women increasingly appear in the spotlight. India's Bollywood leading ladies are everywhere, and many seem more popular than their male costars. Indian TV annually reports from Cannes, for example, where superstar Aishwarya Rai, among others, regularly takes the red carpet. As in any country, the life of an international celebrity like Rai is a poor yardstick by which to measure the lives of ordinary women, or men, for that matter. Yet even

Aishwarya Rai has taken her husband's surname and peppers her interviews with references to her role as a wife (though she is an admittedly equal partner in her dual superstar marriage). Perhaps the weight of tradition and social mores sits on the shoulders of all women to varying degrees. And perhaps only those like Mayawati or Rai are confident or ambitious enough to try and challenge convention.

Back in the real world, though, women are seen mostly with children or doing domestic chores. Most offices, shops, restaurants, and bookstores that I visit in different cities in India are staffed by men, who also act as drivers, waiters, hotel cleaners, street stall operators, and the like. Many women find jobs as teachers in public schools, or are librarians and research scholars like the ones I met while in Calcutta, but figures from the last decade show that women represented just 19 percent of the total workforce and made far less than their male counterparts; indeed, rural Indian women make less than two dollars per day. The female labor force participation rate in India was only 28.5 percent in 2017, versus 82 percent for males.[16] So far, no Indian government has come up with a program like Japanese prime minister Shinzo Abe's "womenomics," which has aimed at increasing female representation across the board in Japan's economy. In 2018, 67 percent of Japanese women of working age were in the labor force.[17] By contrast, in 2013, India ranked 98 out of 128 countries in *The Economist*'s measure of women's economic opportunity.[18]

Yet some Indian women who are fortunate enough to get an education, who come from an established family, or who find supportive partners, have far more chances at a successful career and personal happiness than others without such advantages. At a major hotel in Delhi, I talk with Gunvanti, a twenty-six-year-old professional. Gunvanti was married only a few months ago, to a man she met and fell in love with while working at the same office. They are both Hindu but from different castes. Her widowed mother, from an elite Brahmin subcaste who served as priests for the maharaja of Jaipur, was opposed to her marrying her beau, even though he was from an aristocratic Rajput caste. Gunvanti enlisted her uncle and other male family members to win over her mother, who herself encouraged her daughter to keep working.

Would she have gone ahead with the marriage had her mother continued to oppose it? No, she would have dropped it, Gunvanti tells me. She is as unwilling as the other women I've met to ignore her family's wishes. Yet Gunvanti is far more optimistic than Sita or Aaliyah. She, too, has moved around India, but in her case because she followed jobs that she wanted after graduating from university with a degree in classical singing. In fact, she turned down a more lucrative offer in order to come to Delhi to work at the same place as her then fiancé.

She and her husband continue to work together, and she says he will leave it entirely up to her to decide whether or not to hold a job. She clearly is very much in love, and her eyes sparkle when I suggest she is luckier than many of the other women that I've met. Many of her friends were also married in love matches, she tells me, though she recognizes they are still a minority. Like Aaliyah, she focuses on personal relations and doesn't raise national issues of violence against women or broader discrimination.

So given her fortunate situation, I ask, what does she think would do the most to help women in India? Education, she replies immediately, and having a job. "If you bring your own status to a marriage, then the man will respect you more," she asserts, even though she knows that many, if not most, women continue to face restrictions placed on them by family or husbands. "But [the prevalence of such restrictions is] starting to change."

India is indeed changing, though unevenly. Nearly everyone I talk with, male or female, stresses that India must build up its national strength, meaning its economy, in order to play a larger role in the world, especially in the Indo-Pacific region. All the young women I meet are part of that strength, yet many will undoubtedly drop out of the workforce. Government or business doesn't seem to be the hindrance so much as entrenched social mindsets and the powerful pull of the family unit. Qualified women appear more likely to be restrained at home than openly discriminated against at the employment office. For hundreds of millions of poorer women, moreover, change in India is coming all too slowly, if at all. As it looks ahead to becoming a great power, how to ensure that all women have more of a say in shaping their lives will be one of India's greatest challenges. Perhaps education will be the key, or the voices of prominent female leaders like Sonia Gandhi may change engrained attitudes. When women such as Sita are able to choose their future, Indians will find that both the family and society are strengthened, leading to a more powerful and confident India on the world stage.

Notes

1. Heather Timmons and Sruthi Gottipati, "Woman Dies after a Gang Rape That Galvanized India," *New York Times*, December 28, 2012, https://www.nytimes.com/2012/12/29/world/asia/condition-worsens -for-victim-of-gang-rape-in-india.html.

2. "India Mothers Accused in Honour Killing of Two Brides," *The Telegraph*, May 15, 2011, https://www.telegraph.co.uk/news/worldnews/asia /india/8515426/India-mothers-accused-in-honour-killing-of-two -brides.html.

3. Saptarishi Dutta and Aditi Malhotra, "Statistics: Rape Conviction Rates across India," *Wall Street Journal*, January 4, 2013, https://blogs.wsj.com /indiarealtime/2013/01/04/statistics-conviction-rates-for-rape-across -india.

4. Amitabha Bhattasali, "India First Women's Court Opens in West Bengal," *BBC News*, Calcutta, January 24, 2013, https://www.bbc.com/news/world -asia-india-21175738.

5. Arpinder Singh and A. Didar Singh. *Fostering Safe Workplaces: Sexual Harassment of Woman at Workplace (Prevention, Prohibition and Redressal) Act, 2013* (New Delhi: Ernst & Young, 2015), http://ficci.in/spdocu ment/20672/Fostering-safe.pdf.

6. Kaivan Munshi, "Caste in the Indian Economy," *Journal of Economic Literature*, June 2017, http://www.histecon.magd.cam.ac.uk/km/Munshi _JEL2.pdf.

7. Office of the Registrar General and Census Commissioner, India, *2011 Census Data Report: Chapter 5, Gender Composition*, 105, http://census

india.gov.in/2011-prov-results/data_files/mp/06Gender%20Composi
tion.pdf.

8. "More Indian Women Are Going to College, but Fewer Are Working,"
    Scroll.in, July 28, 2016, https://scroll.in/article/812591/more-indian
    -women-are-going-to-college-but-fewer-are-working.

9. Figure for Japan from "Gender Bias in Japanese Society Adds Up to Fewer
    Women in College," *Asahi Shimbun*, October 23, 2018, http://www.asahi
    .com/ajw/articles/AJ201810230001.html.

10. Annual reports detailing UPSC demographics can be found on the
    Union Public Service Commission's Annual Reports page, https://upsc
    .gov.in/annual-reports.

11. Senior School Certificate Examination Results, *Central Board of Second-
    ary Education Annual Report 2011–2012*, p. 21, http://cbse.nic.in/publica
    tions/ar/CBSE%20Annual%20Report%202011-12A.pdf.

12. "From Dantewada 2010 to Sukma 2017: How the Naxal Attack Narrative
    Has Not Changed in 7 Years," *India Today*, April 2017, https://www
    .indiatoday.in/india/story/from-dantewada-to-sukma-naxal-attack
    -narrative-has-not-changed-in-seven-years-973481-2017-04-25.

13. For more on Mayawati's political career, see Jason Burke, "Mayawati—
    The Untouchable Idol of India's Most Populous State," *The Guardian*,
    February 7, 2012, https://www.theguardian.com/world/2012/feb/07/ma
    yawati-profile-uttar-pradesh-chief-minister.

14. Indira Gandhi appointed herself defense minister in 1975 and 1980,
    while prime minister.

15. See UN Women and Inter-Parliamentary Union (IPU), *Women in Poli-
    tics 2017 Map*, https://www.ipu.org/resources/publications/infographics
    /2017-03/women-in-politics-2017.

16. *The Global Gender Gap Report 2017* (Geneva: World Economic Forum,
    2017), http://www3.weforum.org/docs/WEF_GGGR_2017.pdf.

17. See Abe's speech to World Economic Forum, January 2019, https://www
    .weforum.org/agenda/2019/01/abe-speech-transcript.

18. "Where to Be Female: Women's Economic Opportunity Index," *The
    Economist*, March 8, 2012, https://www.economist.com/graphic-detail
    /2012/03/08/where-to-be-female.

5

JAPAN'S EIGHTFOLD FENCE

Foreign Policy, National Identity,
and the Struggle for Internationalism

> Eight clouds arise. The eightfold fence of Idzumo makes an eight-
> fold fence for the spouses to retire [within]. Oh! that eightfold fence.
>
> —*Kojiki* (Records of ancient matters, 712 CE)

When the first Europeans landed on Japan's shores in the sixteenth century, the island nation appeared a land set apart from the rest of the
world. Shrouded in clouds, its peaks glowing verdantly, Japan seemed
to harbor endless mysteries just beyond the shoreline. Upon landing,
Portuguese missionaries and Dutch traders found a civilization almost
entirely different from any they had encountered before. By the standards of the day it was advanced, though without the technological
prowess of Europe. Divided into warring feudal domains, sixteenth-
century Japan was locked in the midst of a century-long civil war to
determine which samurai clan would rule the rest. Armies of tens of
thousands of armored warriors met in narrow plains, under the shadow

---

This essay originally appeared in *American Affairs* 1, no. 3 (Summer 2017).
Parts were adapted from articles originally published by *Politico Magazine* and
Standpoint Magazine.

of massive castles, wielding some of the deadliest weapons known to man, including the musket.

When the cinders from the last battle cooled in 1600, the Tokugawa family emerged supreme. Yet far from attempting to destroy all opposition, it instead instituted a quasi-centralized feudal regime, allowing 250 other semiautonomous domains to carve up the country. Then, roughly forty years after taking power, they promulgated a series of edicts designed to tightly control foreign relations, making supervision of overseas contacts a prerogative of the *shogunate*, the Tokugawa military bureaucracy, which served as a de facto government of the nation. These maritime exclusion edicts, restricting trade with Chinese and Dutch merchants primarily to the city of Nagasaki on the far southwestern home island of Kyushu, later gave rise to the legend of the era of isolation, the so-called *sakoku* or "closed country." Only when Commodore Matthew Perry arrived with his "Black Ships" in 1853 was Japan forced to "open" itself to the world, at least in the popular Western imagination.

Nearly four hundred years after the exclusion edicts were enacted, Japan retains the mystique of being a land apart, a country of the world but perhaps not fully in it. Some of this impression is sheer exoticization, a form of the "Orientalism" made famous (and abused) by the late Edward Said. Some of it has been used skillfully by the Japanese themselves, to deflect foreign pressure or criticism. And some of it is real, the fruit of a historical experience unique in its own ways. One of Japan's first recorded poems, in the imperial anthology *Kojiki*, from the early eighth century, celebrated an "eightfold fence" separating Japan from other lands and peoples, a realm where the gods dwelled.

Japan, of course, has never been isolated from the world around it. The emergence of Japan's first proto-state, in roughly the fourth century, was marked by the importation of metal goods from the continent, while Buddhism was introduced in 550, according to records. When Nara's Great Buddha statue was consecrated in 754, monks from as far away as India came to the ceremony, and glass from seventh-century Persia can be found today in Nara's Imperial Treasury. Most controversially, speculation has long abounded that around the third century Japan suffered an invasion of horse-riding Koreans, who went on to found the first great clans, including perhaps the imperial family itself.

Since Japan's modern period began with the 1868 Meiji Restoration, the country has been inextricably, and at times tragically, linked with the rest of the world. In many ways, Japan remains the test case of non-Western modernization, even one hundred and fifty years after the political event that drove it to radically break with its past. Yet in the century and a half since midlevel samurai overthrew the feudal hierarchy, the country has painstakingly navigated between embracing the outer world and retaining core elements of its culture and society. As much as Japan is celebrated for becoming the first non-Western, non-Christian country to develop a modern political and economic system, it is often criticized for keeping itself closed off from other nations and cultures.

These plaudits and criticisms have taken on particular relevance since current prime minister Shinzo Abe took office in late 2012. A conservative often labeled a nationalist, Abe has moved boldly to increase Japan's role abroad, increase its influence throughout Asia, and loosen restrictions on security cooperation that have been in place for decades. While some see Abe's moves as designed to erase Japan's seventy years of diplomatic and military impotence after 1945, others see him as a danger to continued peace and stability in Asia.

In reality, Abe's attempts to normalize Japan's foreign and security policies are limited by how much internal change he and other Japanese are willing to accept. Attempts by Japan to take a leadership role in Asia, largely in response to the rapid rise of China in the past quarter century, are constrained by an equally powerful desire not to get too involved in the outer world. In other words, Japan's role in the world remains tethered to its conceptions of "Japanese-ness" and a desire to maintain its national identity in a world of flux.

Japan's recent history forces us to consider how open borders need to be and to judge the trade-offs societies are willing to accept between growth and opportunity, and between a focus on domestic issues and engagement abroad. Can a country be globalized and modern yet not open? Japan offers an example of a society that is willing to be less engaged with the world and to maintain certain socioeconomic barriers, thereby trading some growth for physical security and economic and social stability at home. How, then, can Japan play a larger role in the world, as Prime Minister Abe wants?

Borders against the "Dangers from Without"

Naiyū gaikan (内憂外患; troubles within, dangers without)

—Mid-nineteenth-century phrase describing the weakening of Tokugawa *bakufu* and Western imperial encroachment

For Westerners now sympathetically acculturated to accepting radical multiculturalism, Japan offers an almost shocking vision of an alternate reality. As engaged as Japanese are with the world through trade, diplomacy, study, and the like, they also live in a society that celebrates both its uniqueness and its segregation from the rest of the world. Perhaps some of that is natural to an island nation, but this feeling of detachment exists in a society whose wealth, of course, has come primarily from economic exchange outside its borders, and the surface of whose national life is largely indistinguishable from the modern West.

When, in the mid-nineteenth century, the centuries of Tokugawa-imposed maritime restrictions were crumbling before the advance of the European imperial powers and the young United States, Japanese thinkers captured the sense of vulnerability to a world suddenly no longer safely kept outside the country's borders. The phrase *naiyū gaikan* (内憂外患) circulated among those who wondered how long it would be before the barbarians would force their way onto Japan's shores, and who saw that such a shock might even risk the survival of the Tokugawa shogunate, which was already struggling to maintain control of a society that had dramatically changed since the early seventeenth century. Translated roughly as "troubles within, dangers without," the saying recognized the intimate relation between domestic and foreign policy.

As a cardinal virtue of national strategy, it was accepted that a country that could not control what happened at its borders also could not control what happened within them. Even if Japan had to accommodate and drop the more restrictive maritime exclusion edicts, maintaining a distance from the world remained both a strategy and a national goal. In ways perhaps not fully appreciated, that tension between openness and insularity continued to influence Japanese history and government policy throughout the modern period, up to the present.

In some respects, Japan appears to have enshrined a form of "exclusionary nationalism." As used by scholars with respect to the European state-building experience, exclusionary nationalism was the means of forming modern, unified nation-states by the suppression of domestic minorities, particularly religious minorities.[1] Exclusionary nationalism has come to be used to explain not only ethnic conflict but also the racist nature of some modern European rightist parties such as France's National Front.[2] Even more recently, the concept of "national conservatism" has been championed by some on the American right who seek to privilege the concept of the nation and its particularistic culture over internationalism (even of the conservative variety) and cosmopolitanism.[3]

Yet Japan is exclusionarily nationalistic essentially due to its particular history, not simply by a conscious or overtly political choice. An island nation, its continental and Pacific island lineage groups long ago merged into one unified ethnicity, with long-term resident foreigners making up a negligible part of its population. The largest group of "foreigners" in Japan remains ethnic Koreans, many descended from those forcibly brought to Japan during the decades of colonization that ended in 1945. Being thus in their second or third generation of residence in Japan, these ethnic Koreans are usually indistinguishable from Japanese, and most consider themselves to be full members of the society. Nonetheless, Korean immigrants and their descendants have been singled out for legal discrimination as well as made scapegoats during crises; such ethnic riots as Japan has seen were perpetuated against resident Koreans, most notably after the 1923 Great Kantō Earthquake, when they were accused of poisoning water supplies.[4]

Given the miniscule number of foreigners in Japan in the nineteenth century, the modern Japanese state was not unified in the 1870s by the repression of foreign nationalities or ethnicities; nevertheless, the sense of "Japanese-ness" that accompanied modernization was driven by the exclusion of others from an already homogeneous society. Unlike in modern Europe—where ethnic groups compete not only for geographic but also political space—in Japan, a powerful sense of universal group identity serves to unify politics and society, particularly after World War II. Resistance to the state has been mainly driven by the importation of Western socialist ideology, expressed largely through workers' unions and leftist parties during the first half of the 1900s, along with a brief spasm of student-led rebellion in the 1960s, but little after that. Instead, most Japanese appear to welcome the physical security brought about by Japan's exclusionary nationalism, even as they choose how and when to integrate with the surrounding world.

Modernization in a Mirror

The triumphal post–Cold War West has lost, if it ever had, the understanding that societal openness and globalization are only a means and not an end. Victory over two existential geopolitical foes in one century may have engendered a hubristic sense that no enemy foreign or domestic could really threaten the West's survival. Ironically, this sense of security allowed for the internal spread of a cultural and moral relativism that proposed a radically altered conception of the nation and threatened to undermine the very tenets of traditional Western civilization. This relativism surreptitiously took over the commanding heights of society, starting in the 1960s, spreading from the universities to the mainstream media and popular culture. It demanded a nonexclusionary multiculturalism that dramatically changed the demographic composition of most Western nations in just a few decades. The question of national identity, state borders, and multiculturalism became, by the late 2010s, the most contentious, and occasionally violent, issue in Western domestic politics, fueling the election of Donald Trump as US president in 2016 and the revitalization of a host of nationalist parties in Europe.[5]

Japan has almost entirely escaped a similar cultural war over national identity. Its different approach to both openness and globalization goes back to its profoundly different view of modernity. In the West, ever since the American and French revolutions, modernity has been identified with the beginning of a new world, the radical reformation of reality, and the discarding of tradition. Since then, Western modernity increasingly became identified with the concept of openness to the world, moving from the realm of ideas and political philosophy to the field of economic competition, and more slowly to the opening up of the country to large-scale immigration. In reality, of course, all these strands intertwined and reinforced each other. As the belief in openness sank deep roots, it defined both national identity and government policy, particularly in America, evolving into the idea that greater diversity, achieved through ever-increasing openness, results in greater national strength.

Driven in part by the horrors of World War II, the concept of openness formed the core of the post-1945 European reintegration, initially among the western European nations and then, after 1989, the continent as a whole. Encouraged by Washington's Cold War global strategy, the idea eventually transcended national boundaries and evolved from a concern solely with the internal workings of a society to the idea of an integrated and united globe. Whether known as cosmopolitanism, one-worldism, or the more anodyne globalism, the idea soon became entrenched that the future lay in the effacing of national characteristics and the triumph of a managerial elite whose loyalties lay both with dispassionate science and transnational values.

In Japan, by contrast, modernity and the concept of openness have always been restrained by a tradition of social stability and hierarchy that goes back to the seven centuries of a feudal system headed by shoguns and emperors. Generations of a social caste system left an impression after the abolishment of the last formal vestiges of feudalism in the mid-1870s, even as the Japanese took full advantage of the freedom to choose their livelihoods, marriage partners, and places of residence. In complex ways, the social residue of those centuries persists in contemporary Japan, symbolized at its apex by the emperor. Such is one explanation both for the perplexing endurance of the imperial system and the concomitant attention paid to the Heisei emperor's unprecedented wish to abdicate the throne in favor of his son, in 2019.

The Japanese imperial clan traces its lineage back to the seventh century, making it the world's oldest dynasty, if not monarchy. Pruned dramatically after the Second World War by the American occupying forces headed by General Douglas MacArthur, the institution remains at the spiritual core of Japan. Yet despite continued controversy over 1940s-era war guilt and the occasional divinity question, the decades of peaceful postwar history have dulled any serious opposition to its continued existence. There is no republican movement in Japan, nor calls to reduce the expenditures of the imperial family. With only three emperors in the last century, the clan quietly continues along, avoiding scandal and entering the spotlight only in the most controlled of environments. As patrons and scholars in their own right, Japan's royals have been model constitutional monarchs, with the extended family dutifully performing their functions, much like the vast majority of their subjects.

After a reign of three decades, the Heisei emperor (known during his reign as Emperor Akihito) became the first Japanese sovereign to abdicate in over two centuries when he stepped down in April 2019. In an August 2016 television address, Akihito, then in the twenty-eighth year of his reign, made clear his desire to abdicate in favor of his son, Crown Prince Naruhito, because of his advanced age (eighty-two) and his poor health (he had undergone heart surgery and recovered from prostate cancer). With no abdication provision in place, the cabinet approved legislation permitting the move, sending it to the National Diet for passage. The emperor's announcement was carefully telegraphed beforehand, and while shocking to many, it nonetheless raised no questions or doubts about the future of the imperial system. As anachronistic as the system is, it is also an indelible part of contemporary Japan. Indeed the whole object of the 1868 Meiji Restoration, at least symbolically, was to rescue the imperial family from centuries of virtual imprisonment and elevate it to be the benign ruler of a modernizing nation that had overthrown seven hundred years of feudal control. It is this straddling of past and present, of manufactured tradition and political impotence, of unique roles and dutiful service, that explains the perseverance of the imperial family and its near-universal acceptance by the Japanese people.

The ambiguous role of the imperial family perhaps explains, or even mirrors, the continued tension in Japan between tradition and modernity. Unlike British monarchs, who touch ancient tradition only when crowned, Japanese emperors are surfeited on a near-daily basis with ceremonies that purport to reach back to the beginnings of the Japanese nation. Far more than other noble families, the imperial family continues in a private yet well-acknowledged capacity to intercede between their people and the gods, though like their foreign counterparts they too cut ribbons and attend exhibitions. Such juxtapositions, extending to religious and philosophical syncretism of widely divergent systems, has long fascinated and perplexed Western observers of Japan.

If aspects of premodern Japan linger in its culture, or are hidden in small villages and city side streets alike, then perhaps there is some connection with the continued existence of the imperial system. As a reminder of a premodern era—one that Japanese often mythologize as "purer" or simpler—the imperial family plays a cultural and moral role, in a way as the conscience of a nation forever reinventing itself, at least on the surface. The self-identity of the imperial family itself is hard to pin down. Is it the ancient and sacral representative of the Japanese people or a unique representative arm of the central government? The answer seems to be yes on both counts.

Yet the restoration of the emperor as a symbol of the state was not used as an excuse to try and seal Japan off from the world of the nineteenth century. When low- and middle-ranking samurai spearheaded the overthrow of the 265-year-old Tokugawa shogunate in 1868, they unleashed a fierce generational battle over the path forward for Japan. The debate centered on the idea of modernity and was encapsulated in geographic terms, with proponents of reform urging, "Out of Asia, into Europe" (*datsu-A nyu-O*). This was the era of Japanese "enlightenment," featuring the rapid translation of Western novels and works on politics, economics, and philosophy. Corresponding to the last half of the Victorian era, Japanese modernizers eagerly saw themselves as the vanguard of a new Asia that felt more at home in London than in Beijing. Unsurprisingly, they were opposed, and sometimes cut down in the streets, by those fighting against westernization and the loss of traditional identities.

Through those fraught decades, the Japanese government crafted images and messages that transferred supposedly ancient cultural practices and ways of living into a modern medium. The face that Japan presented both to itself and to the world deliberately merged the traditional and the avant-garde. Thus, kimono-clad maidens were pictured riding on steamships, while the Japan Tourist Bureau assured foreign visitors that they could encounter the unchanging charm of feudal Japan from the comfort of first-class railway carriages.

Japanese participation in various world's fairs during the late nineteenth and early twentieth centuries sent the same message, an Asian twist on Henry Adams's "The Dynamo and the Virgin" at the 1893 Chicago World's Exposition, as traditional Japanese craftsmen sat side by side with the newest mechanical equipment produced by the fledgling imperial power. Meanwhile domestically, older forms of social hierarchy, religious practice, and cultural expression remained alongside the new, all under the somewhat stern gaze of imperial portraits hung in every schoolroom, office, and house. More so than the turning of Gallic peasants into Frenchmen during the nineteenth century, the national project of creating modern Japanese struggled with the cultural default of syncretization—in other words, attempting to make traditional and modern coexist.

If there was a moment when the imperial system was most at risk, it was in the wake of the catastrophe of World War II, known in Japan as the Pacific War. The tension between modernity and tradition that had resulted in the unprecedented emergence of Japan as a world power, a tension intensified by continued European colonialism in Asia and the ravages of the Great Depression, destroyed oligarchic control of the government, allowing ultranationalist militarists to plunge the Pacific into conflict in the 1930s.

The death of at least four million Japanese in the war (against still untold tens of millions in Asia more broadly), and the destruction of most of the country's cities and industrial capacity, culminated in the atomic horror of Hiroshima and Nagasaki. After a war in which Japanese often died with the emperor's name on their lips, it would have been tempting to tear up root and branch the inspiration for such devastation.

Yet when General MacArthur landed in Japan just days after the surrender ceremony in Tokyo Bay, it was the words of Emperor Hirohito, played to the nation on a recorded disc, that ensured the Japanese laid down their arms and accepted the occupiers. Quickly discerning in the emperor a tool to ensure compliance with American wishes, MacArthur neither forced him to abdicate nor abolished the imperial system wholesale. The resulting stain on Hirohito personally and on the position of the emperor shadowed the succeeding decades of his reign, providing fodder for other Asians and left-wing Japanese to label him a war criminal and call for the dissolution of the imperial system.

Whatever moment for radical transformation of Japan's self-identity may have existed in the summer of 1945, it was lost during the US occupation. No longer is the imperial family or the emperor a serious object of attack for Japan's past actions. The quiet, steady reigns of

Hirohito and his son Akihito instead served as an accompanying symbolic note to Japan's reconstruction and emergence as an economic superpower. Postwar pacifism, the fruit of an alliance between the Left and the Right, was firmly embedded in the country, but Japan's essentially conservative social and cultural structures also remained intact, except for large-scale landowning, a victim of the occupation. Against all odds, the imperial family became identified as a fundamental element of stability anchoring a country once again rapidly modernizing.

Judging Modern Japan

As the persistence of the imperial system and the invented tradition surrounding it shows, the Japanese have always viewed modernity warily. They have forged their own path, one that has brought as much criticism as praise. After more than two decades of being dismissed, perhaps it is time to reconsider the long-tainted "Japan model."

At least in Western eyes, Japan has spent the past three decades under a cloud. After the Japanese asset price bubble popped in the late 1980s, the once-and-future Pacific superpower no longer interested investors, pundits, or the media. So-called Japanese models such as lifetime employment, so recently lauded, were quickly reinterpreted as rigidity, risk averseness, and a general inability to deal with a new era of innovation that valued the individual over the group. In particular, it became an article of faith in the West to decry Japan's insularity, whether economic or sociocultural. Japanese society, ethnically monolithic and anti-immigration, was derided as fatally parochial in the new, modern, borderless world.

Japan has found a separate existence—a separate peace if you will—from the globalization paradigm that has dominated the West since World War II. The country's experience over the past quarter century, since the popping of the asset and real estate bubble in 1989, raises a challenge to the fundamental question of Western modernity: How open does a modern nation need to be in order to be "successful"? The Japanese experience should prompt us to ask, in turn, whether the West has too confidently asserted the benefits of openness and globalization, and underestimated the virtues of social cohesion and stability. As one commentator recently claimed, "Closed societies are meaner, poorer, and more repressive."[6] Is that really the case? Can such a claim plausibly be made about Japan? If so, what qualifies as "closed" and what as "open"?

It is an almost heretical thought, but maybe Japan has made better national choices since the 1990s than the rest of the world has given it credit for. It has succeeded in providing a stable and secure life for its people, despite significant economic challenges and statistical stagnation. It has done so in part by maintaining cohesion at home and certain barriers against the world. By comparison, America and Europe appear increasingly confounded by their failures to ensure sociocultural integration, keep their economies growing equally for all, and provide security in the heart of their great cities. When historians look back on global history from the 1990s into the first decades of the twenty-first century, how will they judge which nations were successful and which failed to provide a good life for their people?

The metric employed by Americans in particular—how much personal freedom and economic growth one can calculate and accumulate—is not necessarily the measure favored by the Japanese. It is fair to say that in Japan, it is not the lack of individual restraint that counts, but the overall level of stability in society. Similarly, the West's adherence to neoclassical economics has been adapted in Japan to something that may be less efficient but also less disruptive to society.

The Japanese seem to have internalized the value of maintaining barriers against internal and external disruption. The assumption that openness is a prerequisite for modernity and economic success has led Western observers to dismiss—or has prevented them from understanding—the logic of an approach designed to maintain social cohesion and insulate a country from foreign economic and security disturbances. The anthropologist Edward T. Hall was one of the few Western scholars to consider the benefits of a different approach in his 1976 book, *Beyond Culture*, when he compared "low context," or diverse, cultures like the United States, with "high context," or more uniform, cultures like Japan. Low-context cultures, which merge many disparate traditions, encourage creativity but become increasingly unwieldy the larger they grow. High-context cultures, by comparison, often impose rigidity in thinking and certainly in social interaction but offer far greater cohesion, due largely to their monolithic ethnicity.

Forty years later, the trade-offs that Hall discussed are at the center of political conflicts throughout the West. Even America, whose national identity was built on immigration, finds itself at odds over the benefits of open borders and amnesty, forming odd alliances across socioeconomic lines. For many in the United States, openness has become an end in itself, with no reference to larger social questions. The fear of unassimilated immigrants is greatest in Europe, which is now forced to contemplate the effects of decades of largely unrestrained, largely Muslim, immigration, which is rapidly changing the continent's demographics while burdening its security and social services. All this has driven the rise of nationalist sentiments and new political movements, such as that which propelled Donald Trump into the presidency.

Reassessing Japan's recent history in the light of Western failures does not mean whitewashing its current weaknesses and challenges. A third of a century of anemic economic growth, averaging 2 percent from 1981 to 2015, is a signal that the mature Japanese economy will likely never again see double-digit growth. Unbalanced investment has left Japan's rural regions in parlous economic shape, and temporary workers now account for nearly 40 percent of the workforce. The country's regulatory environment is too stifling, corruption nests inside corporate and political cultures, the service sector is startlingly inefficient, and the nuclear industry is a mess. The government was widely criticized for its inept handling of the March 2011 nuclear crisis after the devastating Tohoku earthquake.

Socially, Japanese youth are widely reported to be dissatisfied with their future prospects, and the scope for individualism in the workplace remains tightly constricted. Foreigners are tolerated but not particularly welcomed, and Japanese of Korean descent still face discrimination. Immigration is all but absent. Moreover, Japan has faced its own homegrown terrorists, like the millennial Aum Shinrikyo cult, which set off a deadly toxin attack on Tokyo subways in 1995. Above all, the country faces a debilitating demographic collapse, one no modern democracy has ever encountered and which poses the single greatest threat to Japan's future.

Yet compared with the problems that both the West and many of its neighbors face, Japan's relative strength and stability should at the least cause us to rethink our assumptions about social and economic policy. The *Wall Street Journal*'s Jacob Schlesinger argued that, for two decades after the popping of the bubble, Japan's leadership consciously chose a deflationary course for the economy, seeking stability and a minimization of the social risk that would accompany radical economic restructuring.[7] Only the return of Shinzo Abe to the premiership in 2012 reversed this long trend, as he actively sought to modestly inflate the economy, privileging economic expansion over stability. The difference might be thought of as "value" policy versus "growth" policy, similar to stocks or mutual funds. The careful, moderate reforms of what is called "Abenomics" indicate that even the current government is seeking a mix of value and growth, again prioritizing social stability.

Despite decades of officially slow or stagnant macro growth, the real economic picture of Japan is better than many Westerners think. Writing in the *Financial Times*, Matthew C. Klein showed that, in the decade from 2005 to 2014, real GDP per person grew more in Japan than in the United States, Great Britain, and the Eurozone.[8] In the almost quarter century from 1990 to 2013, nearly the entire postbubble era, real household consumption in Japan also grew more than in the Eurozone, lagging behind only Great Britain, the United States, and Sweden.

As China's economy began to unravel openly during 2015 and the US equity markets precipitously declined in early 2016, Japan is a country neither sprinting ahead nor rocked by economic instability. The uncertainty that clouds so many of the world's economies exacts psychic and material costs, but Japan, where GDP growth has been sluggish for decades, seems less threatened by the roller coaster that is prevalent in the West, in part because its system remains more resistant to radical restructuring and the diktats of unrestrained market forces. In fact, things simply aren't all that bad.

Japan remains a high-income country by Organization for Economic Cooperation and Development (OECD) standards. Its GDP per capita at purchasing-power parity rates increased from $35,779 in 2011 to $42,823 in 2018, while the cost of living in Tokyo and other major cities declined, due in part to moderate deflationary trends.[9] Japan's Gini coefficient, which measures income inequality, stood at .32 in 2008 (the latest year available), according to the World Bank. Though higher than many European nations, it likely remains lower than America's 2013 measure of .41, indicating a more equal society.

Economic data tell only part of the national story. Other measures show a picture of social strength. To give just a few examples, Americans are fifteen times as likely to be murdered as their Japanese counterparts, according to the United Nations.[10] Japan, with approximately 40 percent of the population of the United States, recorded just 442 cases of intentional homicide in 2011, a rate of 0.3 per 100,000 inhabitants. Meanwhile in America, 14,661 persons were murdered intentionally, a rate of 4.7 per 100,000. While gun control advocates point out that Japan has far more stringent gun laws than the United States, crimes of all kinds, especially violent crimes, occur far less frequently in Japan than in America. Japan is a more peaceful society because of factors other than regulation of guns. There is less overall poverty, fewer impoverished inner city areas, and different segments of society rarely seem to see each other as threats or have contentious relations.

Japan remains a male-dominated society, and sexism is a pervasive problem, yet Japanese women also are among the most highly educated in the world, and they traditionally have controlled household budgets and many family decisions. Moreover, as the *Financial Times*'s Klein notes, more than half the growth in Japanese workers since 2003 has come from women entering the labor force, even as the overall population has shrunk. Prime Minister Abe's "womenomics" policy seeks to increase this number even more, as well as to break the glass ceiling in executive suites. Though no one would claim that Japan is yet close to real gender equality, society is slowly changing.

In education, Japanese students once again scored near the top of the OECD's global math, reading, and science rankings in 2015, ranking second after Singapore, surrendering the top spot they had held for years.[11] Americans, by contrast, scored significantly lower, thirty-sixth in math and twenty-fourth in reading, despite spending close to 30 percent more per student than Japan.[12] Meanwhile, Japan's unemployment rate is below 3.5 percent, which partly represents demographic decline but also the strong work ethic and expectation that able-bodied citizens will be in the labor force. Sixty-six percent of Japanese age fifteen to seventy-four were employed, according to the Federal Reserve Bank of St. Louis, while 63 percent of Americans age sixteen or older held a job, according to the US Department of Labor, a number that has been dropping steadily since 2007.[13]

Japan's public health picture is also brighter than America's and Europe's. While there are numerous factors that could be measured, a few stand out. Japan ranks as the least obese developed country according to the OECD, while America is number one.[14] Moreover, whereas Denmark, France, Austria, Belgium, Norway, and America have the six highest cancer rates in the world, according to the World Cancer Research Fund, Japan ranks forty-eighth for cancer.[15] The country had a negligible number of AIDS cases, only 7,658 by 2014, compared to the United States, which recorded 1,216,917 cases since the 1980s.[16] While amphetamines have been a problem in some of Japan's major cities, the country has nothing like the opioid epidemic sweeping the United States. Even areas where Japan was among the worst in the developed world, as in suicides, it is making progress. The number of suicides in Japan has fallen annually since 2009, and is down by a third from its peak in 2003, even though the country ranks second among industrialized nations in suicides.[17]

Again, such statistics of social strength tell only part of a far more complex story. Yet they can be adduced to support an argument that Japan has more successfully dealt with its myriad problems over the past quarter century than most observers have recognized. Whether Japan can continue to maintain its stability, social cohesion, and basic economic strength without opening up its borders, overturning some traditional social structures, and introducing an element of disruptiveness into its culture will be the great question of Japanese history over the next two generations. Yet even to ask such questions is to again presume a Western frame of reference.

Japan in the World, but Not of It?

A country as wealthy and socially stable as Japan might be expected to embrace an energetic, if not assertive, global role. On the other hand, its exclusionary nationalism may serve to dampen a wholehearted embrace of foreign adventurism. The tension between these two attitudes defines Japan's approach to the world. Above all, it is the benign regional environment in which Japan has existed, even thrived, since 1945 that has allowed it the leisure to debate such choices and not feel forced into one position or the other. Yet Japanese understand well the foreign challenges they face and their potential impact on Japan's security, and hence way of life.

Not that the Japanese aren't constantly questioning the level of their involvement in the world. "Do you think we should take in more Syrian refugees?" the head of one of Japan's leading cultural exchange organizations asked me in November 2015 in Tokyo. "It looks like we're not doing our part." I demurred, noting that Europe has yet to deal with problems the refugee flood may cause. Twenty-four hours later, the

Paris massacre burst onto Japan's television screens, a reminder of the type of danger that Japan does not face.

Unlike the West, consumed by the threat of terrorism for half a generation, Japan is a modernized and liberal society not directly at risk from the Islamic State, al-Qaeda, and homegrown Islamist radicals. Like any nation, it offers a plethora of soft targets, but the reality is that Japan is in comparatively little danger. Its people live in a reality entirely different from that of the West, spared from a seemingly endless fight against an implacable enemy who now lives among them. This is due in part to the fact that Japan prioritizes order over openness and stability over opportunity. It is also undoubtedly due to the fact that, until now, its regional environment has been largely benign and because of the security guarantees offered it since 1952 by the United States.

That benign environment has been growing more threatening since the mid-1990s, however, thanks to China's rapid military modernization program and assertive behavior, as well as North Korea's continuing nuclear and ballistic missile program. That these threats emerged right at the beginning of Japan's economic malaise added another level of worry for the public and policy makers. Despite a deepening of the alliance with the United States, including two revisions to the guidelines of the alliance that increased levels of cooperation between Tokyo and Washington, doubts continue to persist in Japan over the ultimate credibility of American guarantees for their security, given the scope of the challenges and the focus of US policy makers on the Middle East and other parts of the globe.

Polls show that Japanese have become increasingly concerned over the threats posed by North Korea and China in recent years. A Pew poll of September 2016 found that 86 percent of Japanese held unfavorable views of China, with 71 percent believing the Chinese were violent, a 21 percent increase from 2006.[18] Interestingly, fully 74 percent of Chinese interviewed in the same poll believed Japanese were violent, despite 70 years of a pacifist society and constitution and essentially no Japanese military presence abroad, underscoring the trust deficit in

Northeast Asia.[19] Worries over Chinese encroachment in the East China Sea, not to mention North Korea's nuclear program, are now a regular part of the national discourse, and an increasingly assertive posture toward the North Korean threat in particular has been adopted by successive Japanese governments. Over the past decade in particular, Tokyo has invested in antimissile defenses, placed orders for advanced fighter aircraft, and slowly added capabilities to project power in Asia, including through refueling tankers for fighters and building two new, large helicopter carriers, and the country has recently announced plans for its first aircraft carrier since World War II.[20]

Yet even with a greater awareness of foreign threats, Japan's position in the world remains a contested issue in domestic politics, as does the larger question of Japanese nationalism and patriotism. A 2015 international Gallup poll, for example, showed that only 11 percent of Japanese would be willing to fight for their country.[21] Granting that most Japanese share an instinctive desire to retain some boundaries against the rest of the world, the debate then is over the degree to which Japan should engage so as not to put at risk its natural separateness. It is here that Prime Minister Shinzo Abe's foreign policies are so controversial.

Abe returned to office in late 2012, determined to pick up from where he ignominiously left off in 2007. He quickly dusted off plans to increase the military budget, form a National Security Secretariat, end the restrictions on arms exports and defense industry cooperation, and pursue enhanced relations with a number of strategic countries, including India and Australia. Most notably, he submitted to the Diet a bill to allow for the exercise of collective self-defense, so as to deepen security cooperation with the United States and other potential partners. At nearly the same time, Abe was negotiating with the Obama administration on a set of revised guidelines for the US-Japan Alliance, designed to enhance security cooperation and embrace new areas, such as cyber and space.

From the beginning, both the security bill and the revised guidelines drew heavy criticism from the opposition party and domestic groups.

Consistent majorities opposed Abe's plans to allow Japan to more easily dispatch forces abroad. For example, in July 2015, just as the Lower House of the Diet was poised to pass the bill, 57 percent of those polled by the *Asahi Shimbun* opposed Abe's security bills allowing Japan to participate in collective self-defense activities.[22] These numbers held steady throughout the period of the legislation's debate and passage, ultimately ending in September 2015, when the Upper House assented to the bills. As the votes were set to begin, tens of thousands of protesters filled the streets near the Diet building, with gray-haired veterans of Japan's pacifist movements joined by students in their twenties, who had no experience of Japan's wartime past.[23] As always, a large proportion of left-wing teachers' groups joined the protests.

Similar controversy plagued the revised alliance commitments. In April 2015, as Japan and the United States unveiled new guidelines for the alliance, a poll by *Kyodo* found that 48 percent were opposed to the new measures, even though fully 70 percent of those polled backed US-Japan cooperation in defending far-flung islands claimed by Tokyo in the East China Sea.[24] In the same month, another *Kyodo* poll found that twice as many Americans, 47 percent compared to 23 percent of Japanese, believed that Japan should play a larger security role in Asia.[25]

In response, scholars such as Keio University's Yoshihide Soeya have argued that Japan must pursue a "middle power" strategy that acknowledges its gross power limitations.[26] Specifically, Soeya believes, Tokyo must embrace a "middle power internationalism" that seeks to maximize Japan's diplomacy and participation in multilateral forums and embed itself in a community of similar middle powers balancing off the demands of the United States and China. Suggestions such as these seek to counter a perceived trend toward "regressive nationalism," in Soeya's words. The belief that the cork needs to remain in the bottle of Japanese militarism more than seventy years after the end of World War II highlights just how strongly Japan's past continues to shape current views.

However, Japanese policy makers cannot shirk their responsibility to prepare to meet the threats they perceive to national security. Public opinion polls and scholarly arguments such as those mentioned point to the gulf between Japan's elected leaders and its population. As Soeya acknowledges, leaders from both major Japanese political parties, the Liberal Democrats and the Democratic Party (DPJ), have supported an expansionist role for Japan's diplomacy and security policies over the past decade. It was DPJ premier Yoshihiko Noda, for example, who publicly embraced revising the restrictions on collective self-defense, keeping alive a policy preference from the first Abe administration in 2006–7. Moreover, Noda made the decision to purchase the F-35 Joint Strike Fighter and to reorient Japan's security strategy to focus explicitly on defending the Senkakus and other southwestern islands. Though his policies have gone farther and are more controversial, Abe is no outlier among Japanese policy makers. Rather, he is pushing to a logical conclusion the modernization in Japan's security and foreign policies that began in earnest in 1998 with the first North Korean Taepodong ballistic missile launch over Japanese territory.

Perhaps the ultimate endpoint of Abe's attempts to broaden Japan's role in the world is the most symbolic: revision of the country's postwar constitution. Written over a matter of weeks by the American occupying force in 1946, the constitution was promulgated the following year, including its famous Article 9, forever renouncing "war as a sovereign right of the nation and the threat or use of force as means of settling international disputes." Despite the corollary abjuration of maintaining "land, sea, and air forces, as well as other war potential," the Japanese Self-Defense Forces have nonetheless developed into one of the world's most capable militaries, underscoring the incompatibility between the nation's fundamental political document and the reality required for self-defense.

Article 9 is perhaps the single most controversial political issue in postwar Japan, decried by conservatives, who question the double standard that seeks to limit Japan's sovereign right to maintain a military and act in its self-interest, and celebrated by liberals, who see it as the apotheosis of modern Japan's penance for the aggression and atrocities of the Pacific War era. While the article has done little to prevent Japan from maintaining a modern, effective military, it has left the issue of the legitimacy of Japan's military and security policies in limbo. The fact that the American alliance guarantee helped avoid addressing the inconsistency head-on only led to a hardening of opinion on both sides of the domestic debate, with neither having to consider the real-world effect of either maintaining or abandoning Article 9.

Now Abe has forced the issue, at least partway, by proposing that the constitution be amended by 2020 to explicitly acknowledge the status of the Self-Defense Forces. Shying away from dropping the renunciation of war as a means of state policy, Abe wants to normalize the idea of the military as a fundamental sovereign right. That such a move would be largely symbolic does not detract from its importance in making Japan a "normal" country in conservative eyes. Even so, Abe well understands how controversial, not to mention politically fraught, any change would be, and has urged the country to "hold fast to the idea of pacifism."[27] Polls taken in the days after his May 2017 announcement showed that a slim plurality of voters wanted to keep Article 9 unchanged, while even more expressed pride in the country's pacifist tradition, and others showed a minority approving of Abe's plans to acknowledge the SDF in the constitution.[28]

Even if Abe is successful in revising the constitution, both Japanese political culture and public opinion will continue to place limits on Tokyo's global engagement and security policies. Adventurism of the kind that marks Chinese expansion in the South China Sea, Russia's annexation of the Crimea, or America's various battles around the globe is almost inconceivable for the foreseeable future. Moreover, absent a true crisis of confidence in the US-Japan alliance, it is highly unlikely to impossible that Tokyo would pursue an indigenous nuclear weapons capability in the near term. The country is even unlikely to develop offensive strike capabilities such as ballistic missiles, despite the fact that its air and naval forces are increasingly able to project limited amounts of power outside the home islands. Nor is there any real prospect of the remaining restrictions on the deployment of Japanese forces abroad being lifted, especially for combat roles.

Japan instead is far more likely to take a middle path, improving its high-end defensive capabilities and modernizing its forces while maintaining political limits on what those forces can do. It is poised to export modest amounts of defense materials and engage in limited codevelopment and coproduction of armaments and assembly of major systems, such as the F-35 fighter. As for its security relationships, the alliance with the United States will remain at the center of Japan's security planning for the foreseeable future, with both Japanese policy makers and the public assuming that US forces will be the ultimate guarantor of the country's security in the case of a major conflict with China or North Korea.

Beyond that, future leaders who share Abe's vision likely will try to enhance relationships with key nations, including Australia and India, perhaps by joining in larger military drills and training. Meanwhile they will also ensure that smaller nations in Southeast Asia view Japan as a supplier of armaments. Doing so will indeed make Japan one of the more active regional actors in an Asia dominated by smaller and less developed nations. But Tokyo is unlikely to desire or sign any more mutual defense treaties, or to commit its forces in combat abroad. Even providing more public goods, such as conducting freedom of navigation operations in the South China Sea, will be difficult for a risk-averse government, as well as for a society that strongly distinguishes itself from the rest of the world.

A still-strong sense of being a country apart, a desire to maintain domestic social and political stability, and a wariness of draining national wealth on overseas interventions will continue to demarcate the limits of Japan's engagement with the world. As it has from time immemorial, the eightfold fence continues to ring, and to protect, the islands of Japan.

Notes

1. See, for example, Anthony W. Marx, *Faith in Nation: Exclusionary Origins of Nationalism* (New York: Oxford University Press, 2003).

2. Paul Collier, "How to Save Capitalism from Itself," *Times Literary Supplement*, January 25, 2017, http://www.the-tls.co.uk/articles/public/how -to-save-capitalism.

3. Israeli scholar Yoram Hazony, founder of the Edmund Burke Institute, is the driving force behind the national conservative movement, which held its first conference in Washington, DC, in July 2019.

4. See Joshua Hammer, "The Great Earthquake of 1923," *Smithsonian Magazine*, May 2011, https://www.smithsonianmag.com/history/the -great-japan-earthquake-of-1923-1764539.

5. The literature on contemporary multiculturalism and nationalism is immense and growing. See, among others, John Judis, *The Nationalist Revival: Trade, Immigration, and the Revolt against Globalization* (New York: Columbia Global Reports, 2018); Yoram Hazony, *The Virtue of Nationalism* (New York: Basic Books, 2018); Patrick Deneen, *Why Liberalism Failed* (New Haven, CT: Yale University Press, 2018); and Heather MacDonald, *The Diversity Delusion: How Race and Gender Pandering Corrupt the University and Undermine Our Culture* (New York: St. Martin's Press, 2018).

6. Philip Stephens, "Peace and Prosperity: It Is Worth Saving the Liberal Order," *Financial Times*, February 9, 2017, https://www.ft.com/content /b2db707e-ed61-11e6-ba01-119a44939bb6.

7. Jacob M. Schlesinger, "Japan's Economic Dilemma: Comfortable Decline or Painful Revival?," *Wall Street Journal*, December 3, 2014, https://www.wsj.com/articles/japans-economic-dilemma-comfortable -decline-or-painful-revival-1417640405?cb=logged0.351878400426358.

8. Matthew C. Klein, "Did Japan Actually Lose Any Decades?," *Financial Times*, December 4, 2014, https://ftalphaville.ft.com/2014/12/04/2059 371/did-japan-actually-lose-any-decades.

9. Organization for Economic Cooperation and Development, https:// data.oecd.org/japan.htm; World Bank, *World Development Indicators*, June 2017, http://data.worldbank.org/data-catalog/world-development -indicator.

10. United Nations Office on Drugs and Crime (UNODC), *Global Study on Homicide 2013* (Geneva: United Nations, 2013), https://www.unodc.org /documents/gsh/pdfs/2014_GLOBAL_HOMICIDE_BOOK_web.pdf.

11. Organization for Economic Cooperation and Development (OECD), *Pisa 2015 Results*, vol. 1, *Excellence and Equity in Education* (Paris:

OECD, 2016). The previous results, with Japan scoring at the top, can be found at OECD, *Japan-Country Note-Results from PISA 2012* (Paris: OECD, 2012).

12. OECD, *Education at a Glance 2016: OECD Indicators* (Paris: OECD, 2016).

13. "Employment Rate: Aged 15–74: All Persons for Japan," *Federal Reserve Bank of St. Louis*, February 2017, https://fred.stlouisfed.org/series/LRE M74TTJPM156S; "Labor Force Statistics from the Current Population Survey," *Bureau of Labor Statistics*, April 20, 2017, https://data.bls.gov /timeseries/LNS11300000.

14. "Obesity Update," *OECD Directorate for Employment, Labour and Social Affairs*, 2017, http://www.oecd.org/health/health-systems/Obesity-Up date-2017.pdf.

15. "Global Cancer Data by Country," World Cancer Research Fund, 2012 rankings, http://www.wcrf.org/int/cancer-facts-figures/data-cancer-fre quency-country.

16. Japan statistics from the UN: "Report to UNAIDS—HIV/AIDS Trends in Japan," http://www.unaids.org/sites/default/files/country/documents /JPN_narrative_report_2016.pdf; US statistics from the CDC: "HIV in the United States and Dependent Areas," Centers for Disease Control and Prevention, https://www.cdc.gov/hiv/statistics/overview/ataglance .html.

17. "Suicides Down, but Japan Still Second Highest among Major Industri-alized Nations, Report Says," *Japan Times*, May 30, 2017, http://www .japantimes.co.jp/news/2017/05/30/national/social-issues/preventive -efforts-seen-helping-2016-saw-another-decline-suicides-japan-21897 /#.WU7SABPytE4.

18. The poll did not differentiate between the Chinese government and the Chinese people in that question, but the implied meaning was Chinese as individuals or a nation. The same goes for the question in China about Japanese.

19. "Hostile Neighbors: China vs. Japan," *Pew Research Center*, September 13, 2016, http://www.pewglobal.org/2016/09/13/hostile-neighbors-china-vs -japan.

20. Brad Lendon and Yoko Wakatuki, "Japan to Have First Aircraft Carriers since World War II," *CNN*, December 18, 2018, https://www.cnn.com /2018/12/18/asia/japan-aircraft-carriers-intl/index.html.

21. "Only 11% of Japanese People Willing to Fight for Their Country: Gallup Survey," *Japan Today*, November 23, 2015, https://japantoday.com/category/national/only-11-of-japanese-people-willing-to-fight-for-their-country-gallup-survey.

22. "Asahi Shimbun Public Opinion Poll," Maureen and Mike Mansfield Foundation website, July 19, 2015, http://mansfieldfdn.org/program/research-education-and-communication/asian-opinion-poll-database/asahi-shimbun-public-opinion-poll.

23. Linda Sieg, "Japan Protesters Rally as Contentious Security Bills near Passage," *Reuters*, September 16, 2015, http://www.reuters.com/article/us-japan-security-idUSKCN0RG0DZ20150916.

24. "Nearly Half of Japanese Oppose New Joint Defense Guidelines with US: Poll," *Japan Times*, April 30, 2015, http://www.japantimes.co.jp/news/2015/04/30/national/politics-diplomacy/nearly-half-of-japanese-oppose-new-joint-defense-guidelines-with-u-s-poll/#.WPjtu_nythF.

25. "Poll Finds Trans-Pacific Gap on Role Japan Should Play in Region," *Japan Times*, April 8, 2015, http://www.japantimes.co.jp/news/2015/04/08/national/big-japan-u-s-opinion-gap-over-a-bombings-poll/#.WPjupPnythF.

26. Yoshihide Soeya, "Japanese Middle-Power Diplomacy," *East Asia Forum*, November 22, 2012, http://www.eastasiaforum.org/2012/11/22/japanese-middle-power-diplomacy.

27. Motoko Rich, "Shinzo Abe Announces Plan to Revise Japan's Pacifist Constitution," *New York Times*, May 3, 2017, https://www.nytimes.com/2017/05/03/world/asia/japan-constitution-shinzo-abe-military.html.

28. See "Kaiken 'jiki kodawarazu' 52% Asahi Shimbun 5-gatsu yoron chosa," *Asahi Shimbun*, May 16, 2017, http://www.asahi.com/articles/ASK5H4PPDK5HUZPS002.html; see also "Kenpo 9-jo ni Jieitai meiki 'sansei' 51% honsha yoron chosa shinkenpo no 2020-nen shikou mokuhou, 'sansei' 43% 'hantai' 39%", *Nihon Keizai Shimbun*, May 28, 2017, http://www.nikkei.com/article/DGXLASFS28H2N_Y7A520C1MM8000.

6

CHINA VERSUS JAPAN
Asia's Other Great Game

We confer upon you, therefore, the title Queen of Wa Friendly to Wei. . . . We expect you, O Queen, to rule your people in peace and to endeavor to be devoted and obedient.

—Letter of Emperor Cao Rui to Japanese empress Himiko in 238 CE, *Wei zhi* (History of the Kingdom of Wei, c. 297 CE)

From the emperor of the country where the sun rises to the emperor of the country where the sun sets.

—Letter from Empress Suiko to Emperor Yang of the Sui Dynasty in 607 CE, *Nihon shoki* (Chronicles of Japan, 720 CE)

I.

The specter of the world's two strongest nations competing for power and influence has created a convenient narrative for pundits and observers to claim that Asia's future, perhaps even the world's, will be

---

This essay is adapted from "China vs. Japan: Asia's Other Great Game," *National Interest*, no. 152 (November/December 2017).

shaped by the United States and China. From economics to political influence and security issues, American and Chinese policies are seen as inherently conflictual, creating an uneasy relationship, even a new Cold War, between Washington and Beijing that affects other nations inside Asia and out.

The focus on the Sino-US competition for global power ignores an intra-Asian competition, one that perhaps may have as much influence in the Indo-Pacific region as that between America and China. For millennia, China and Japan have been locked in a relationship even more mutually dependent, competitive, and influential than the much more recent one between Washington and Beijing. Each has sought to dominate, or at least be the most influential state in, Asia, and the relations of each with its neighbors have at various points been directly shaped by their rivalry.

There is little question that the current Sino-American competition has the greatest direct impact on Asia today, particularly in the security sphere. America's long-standing alliances, including with Japan, and provision of public security goods, such as freedom of navigation, remain the primary alternative security strategies to Beijing's policies. In any imagined major-power clash in Asia, the two antagonists are naturally assumed to be China and the United States. Yet it would be a mistake to dismiss the Sino-Japanese rivalry as a simple sideshow. The two Asian nations will undoubtedly compete long after US foreign policy has evolved, and will do so regardless of whether Washington withdraws from Asia, grudgingly accepts Chinese hegemony, or increases its security and political presence. Moreover, Asian nations themselves understand that the Sino-Japanese relationship is Asia's other great game and is in many ways an eternal competition.

II.

Centuries before the writing of Japan's first historical records, let alone the formation of its first centralized state, envoys from its leading clan appeared at the court of the Han Dynasty and its successors. Representatives of the land of Wa were recorded as first arriving in Eastern Han in the year 57 CE, though some accounts place the first encounters between Chinese and Japanese communities as far back as the late second century BCE. Not surprisingly, these earliest references to Sino-Japanese relations are in the context of China's intervention on the Korean Peninsula, with which ancient Japan had long-standing exchanges. Nor would an observer at the time be shocked by the letter from the Wei court quoted in the epigraph at the beginning of this chapter. Wei's expectation of deference is natural, as it was one of the three major post-Han states of the Three Kingdoms period in China (220–280 CE), successor to a great empire. Perhaps slightly more surprising is the letter from "empress" Suiko to the Sui Court. Supposedly written by the legendary Prince Shotoku, it reflects an upstart island nation just beginning to unify itself in the seventh century, asserting not merely equality but superiority over Asia's most powerful country.

The broad contours of Sino-Japanese relations thus became clear early on: a competition for influence, an assertion by both of their respective superiority, and an entanglement with Asia's geopolitical balance. Despite the passing of two millennia, the base of this relationship has changed little. Today, however, a new wrinkle has been added to the equation. Whereas over the previous centuries only one of the two nations generally was powerful, influential, or internationally engaged in any given era, today both China and Japan are strong, united, global players, well aware of the other's strengths and their own weaknesses.

Most American and even Asian observers presume that it is the Sino-American relationship that will determine Asia's future, if not the globe's, for the foreseeable future. Yet the competition between China and Japan has been of far longer duration, and its importance should not be underestimated. As the United States debates its global role after its wars in Iraq and Afghanistan, as it continues to struggle to maintain its widespread global commitments, and as the full scope of Donald Trump's desired readjustment of US foreign policy continues to take shape, the eternal competition between Tokyo and Beijing is poised to enter an even more intense period. This dynamic is as likely in its own way to shape Asia in the coming decades as that between Washington and Beijing.

III.

To make a claim that Asia's future will be decided between China and Japan may sound fanciful, especially after two decades of extraordinary economic growth has vaulted China into becoming the world's largest economy (at least according to purchasing power parity calculations)[1] and Japan has seen a concomitant quarter century of apparent economic stagnation. Yet the same claim would have sounded just as unrealistic back in 1980, except in reverse, when Japan had racked up years of double-digit and high single-digit economic returns while China had barely emerged from the generational disaster of Mao Zedong's Great Leap Forward and the Cultural Revolution. Just a few decades ago, Japan was predicted to be the global financial power par excellence, countered only by the United States.

For most of history, however, it would have seemed delusional to compare Japan with China. Island powers can rarely compete with cohesive continental states. Once China's unified empires emerged, starting with the Qin in 221 BCE, Japan was dwarfed by its continental neighbor. Even during its periods of disunity, many of China's fragmented and competing states were nearly as large as, or larger than, all of Japan. Thus, during the half century of the Three Kingdoms, when Japan's queen of Wa paid tribute to Cao Wei, each of the three domains, Wei, Shu, and Wu, controlled more territory than Japan's nascent imperial house. China's natural sense of superiority was reflected in the very word used for Japan, *Wa* (倭), which is usually accepted to mean "dwarf people" or possibly "submissive people," thus fitting Chinese ideology regarding other ethnicities in ancient times. Similarly, Japan's geographical isolation from the continent meant that the dangerous crossing over the Sea of Japan to Korea was attempted only rarely, usually only by the most intrepid Buddhist monks and traders. The early Chinese chronicles repeatedly introduced Japan as being a land "in the middle of the ocean," emphasizing its isolation and difference from the continent. Long periods of Japanese diplomatic isolation, such as during the Heian (794–1185) or Edo (1603–1868) eras also meant that Japan was largely outside the mainstream, such as it was, of Asian historical development for centuries at a time.

The dawn of the modern world turned upside down the traditional disparity between Japan and China. Indeed, what the Chinese continue to call their "century of humiliation," from the Opium War of 1839 to 1842 to the victory of the Chinese Communist Party in 1949, was largely contemporaneous with Japan's emergence as the world's first major non-Western power. As the centuries-old Qing dynasty and China's millennia-old imperial system fell apart, Japan overthrew its seven centuries of samurai rule and "restored" the emperor to a position ostensibly leading the government. In reality, lower-level ex-samurai deposed their feudal lords and took power, centralizing the state and forging Japan into a modern nation-state that within a generation would inflict military defeats on two of the greatest empires of the day, China itself in 1895 and czarist Russia a decade later. The sidelining of civilian government control during the 1930s allowed ultranationalist military officers to invade Manchuria and fight both the United States and other European powers, resulting in devastation throughout China and Asia. During these decades, Chinese reformers overthrew the Qing dynasty, yet the new republic soon descended into decades of warlordism following the 1911 Revolution. This was followed by decades of civil war between Chiang Kai-shek's Nationalists and Mao Zedong's Communists, and then the excesses of Mao's era, even as Japan emerged from the devastation of 1945 to become the world's second-largest economy. At the end of the Cold War, few observers would have judged China to be on the cusp of an unprecedented era of growth, or have suspected that Japan would soon stumble from its lofty perch, seemingly never to return.

Since 1990, however, the tide has reversed, and China has come to occupy an even more dominant global position than Tokyo could have imagined at the height of its postwar prominence. If international power can crudely be conceived of as a three-legged stool, comprising political influence, economic dynamism, and military strength, then Japan fully developed only its economic potential after World War II, and even then lost its position after a few decades. Beijing, meanwhile, has come to dominate international political forums while building the world's second most powerful military and becoming the largest trading partner of over one hundred nations around the globe.

Yet while one is "ranked" above the other, in comparative terms, both China and Japan today are wealthy, powerful nations. China has the world's largest economy by purchasing power parity measures, while Japan's per capita GDP is nearly four times the size of China's, at US$39,000.[2] Each is also guided by the strongest leader in at least a generation, both coming to power in 2012. Xi Jinping has become the most powerful Chinese ruler since Deng Xiaoping and possibly Mao himself, reorienting Chinese Communist Party (CCP) ideology to focus on himself as the "core" or "party center," and enshrining "Xi Jinping Thought" in the Chinese constitution. Meanwhile, Shinzo Abe will become Japan's longest-serving prime minister since World War II, and has pushed through a wholesale reorientation of Japan's security and foreign policies while overseeing significant economic reform. Indeed, though China has been the focus of global headlines for its modernization, despite nearly a generation of economic doldrums, Japan remains the world's third-largest economy. It also spends roughly $50 billion per year on its military, boasting one of the world's most advanced and best-trained defense forces. On the continent, with its audacious Belt and Road Initiative, free-trade proposals, and growing military reach, China is widely considered the world's second most powerful nation after the United States. This rough parity is new in Japan-China relations and has been perhaps the single greatest, if often unacknowledged, factor in their contemporary relationship. It is also the spur for the intense competition the two are waging in Asia.

IV.

Competition between countries does not inherently lead to aggression, or even particularly contentious relations. Indeed, looking at Sino-Japanese relations from the vantage point of the start of the 2020s may overemphasize just how vexed their ties traditionally have been. For long periods of its history, Japan looked to China as a beacon in a sea of darkness—as the most advanced civilization in Asia and as a model for political, economic, and sociocultural forms. While at times that admiration was perverted into an attempt to assert equality, if not superiority—as during China's Tang era (seventh to tenth century) or a millennium later in Japan, during the rule of the Tokugawa shoguns (seventeenth to nineteenth century)—it would be a mistake to assume there was no positive element to the interaction between the two. Similarly, Chinese reformers understood that Japan had achieved success in modernizing its feudal system in the late nineteenth century to a degree that made it, for a while, a model. It was not an accident that the father of the 1911 Chinese Revolution, Sun Yat-sen, spent time in Japan during his exile from China in the first years of the twentieth century. Even after Japan's brutal invasion and occupation of China during the Pacific War, the 1960s and 1970s saw Japanese politicians such as Prime Minister Tanaka Kakuei reach out to China, restore relations, and even contemplate a new era of Sino-Japanese relations that would shape Cold War Asia.

Such fragile hopes, not to mention mutual respect, now seem all but inconceivable. For over a decade, Japan and China have been locked into a seemingly intractable downward spiral in relations, marked by suspicion and increasingly tense maneuvering on security, political, and economic fronts. Except for the actual Japanese invasions of China in 1894–95 and 1937–45, the history of Japanese-Chinese competition was often as much a rhetorical or intellectual exercise as it was real. The current competition is more direct, even while taking place in an environment of Sino-Japanese economic integration and globalization.

The current atmosphere of Japanese-Chinese dislike and mistrust is marked. A series of public-opinion polls carried out by Genron NPO, a Japanese nonprofit think tank, in 2015–16 revealed the parlous state of relations.[3] Fully 78 percent of Chinese and 71 percent of Japanese polled in 2016 believed relations between their two countries were either bad or relatively bad. Both publics also saw significant increases from 2015 to 2016 in expectations that future Japan-China relations would worsen, from 13.6 percent to 20.5 percent in China and from 6.6 percent to 10.1 percent in Japan. When asked if Sino-Japanese relations posed a potential source of conflict in Asia, 46.3 percent of Japanese responded affirmatively while 71.6 percent of Chinese agreed. Such findings track with other polls, such as a 2016 survey by the Pew Research Center, which found that 86 percent of Japanese and 81 percent of Chinese held unfavorable views of each other.

The reasons for this public distrust reflect, in large part, the outstanding policy disputes between Beijing and Tokyo. The Genron NPO poll found that over 60 percent of Chinese, for example, cited both Japan's lack of apology or remorse over World War II and its September 2012 nationalization of the Senkaku Islands, claimed by Beijing as the Diaoyu Islands, for their unfavorable impression of Japan.

Indeed, the history question continues to dog Sino-Japanese relations. China's leaders have astutely used it as a moral cudgel with which to bash Tokyo. Pew's polling thus found an overwhelming 77 percent of Chinese claiming that Japan had not yet sufficiently apologized for the war, yet over 50 percent of Japanese believing their country had apologized enough.[4] Controversial visits to Yasukuni Shrine, where eighteen class A war criminals are enshrined, by current prime minister Shinzo Abe in December 2013 continued a spate of provocations in Chinese eyes that seemed to downplay Japan's remorse for the war at the very time Abe was pursuing a modest military buildup and challenging China's claims in the East China Sea. Chinese president Xi Jinping established two new national holidays early in his term, one to commemorate the "Rape of Nanking," and another to celebrate the defeat of

Japan in World War II, both events occurring over seven decades previously. A visitor to China in these years saw little abatement of anti-
Japanese portrayals on Chinese television; on any given night, at least a
third if not more of prime-time dramas on stations from all of China's
major provinces were about Japan's invasion of China, given verisimil-
itude thanks to actors speaking fluent Japanese.[5]

If the Chinese are focused on the past, the Japanese are most concerned about the present and future. In the same polls cited earlier,
nearly 65 percent of Japanese claimed that the ongoing Senkaku
Islands dispute accounted for their negative view of China, while over
50 percent cited the "seemingly hegemonic actions of the Chinese" for
leaving an unfavorable impression. Overall, 80 percent of Japanese
polled by Pew responded that they were either very or somewhat concerned that territorial disputes with China could lead to military conflict, versus 59 percent of Chinese.[6]

These negative impressions and fears of war come despite nearly
unprecedented levels of economic interaction between the two countries. Even with China's recent economic slowdown, according to the
CIA *World Factbook*, Japan was China's third-largest trade partner,
accounting for 6 percent of its exports and nearly 9 percent of its
imports; China was Japan's largest trade partner, taking 17.5 percent of
its exports and providing a full quarter of its imports.[7] Though exact
numbers are difficult to ascertain, it has been claimed that Japanese
firms directly or indirectly employ as many as ten million Chinese,
most of them on the mainland.[8] The neoliberal assumption that greater
economic ties raise the threshold for security conflicts is being tested
in the Sino-Japanese case, with both proponents and critics of the concept able to claim that so far, their interpretation is correct. Since the
downturn in relations during the administration of Junichiro Koizumi
(2001–6), Japanese academics such as Masaya Inoue have described
the relationship as *seirei keinetsu*: politically cool, economically hot.
That relationship is reflected in another way by the surging number of
Chinese tourists to Japan, who totaled nearly 6.4 million in 2016,[9]
whereas the China National Tourism Administration claims that nearly

2.5 million Japanese visited China, ranking second after South Korean tourists.

Yet the growing Sino-Japanese economic relationship has not been left unaffected by geopolitical tensions. Chinese protests against Japan over the Senkaku dispute led to steep declines in Japanese foreign direct investment in China during 2013 and 2014, with year-on-year investment dropping by 18 and 42 percent, respectively.[10] These declines were accompanied by a corresponding increase in Japanese investment in Southeast Asia, including Indonesia, Thailand, Malaysia, and Singapore.

Negative attitudes toward China on the part of Japanese business have been mirrored in the political and intellectual spheres. Japanese analysts have been concerned about the long-term implications of China's growth for years, but such concerns turned into open worry particularly after China's economy overtook Japan's in 2011. Since the crisis in political relations caused by repeated incidents in the Senkaku Islands starting in 2010, policy makers in Tokyo interpreted Beijing's actions as flexing newfound national muscle, and they grew frustrated with the United States for its seemingly cavalier attitude toward Chinese assertiveness in the East China Sea. At one international conference in 2016, a senior Japanese diplomat harshly criticized Washington and other Asian capitals for countering China's expansion in Asian waters with nothing but rhetoric and warned that it might soon be too late to blunt Beijing's attempts to gain military dominance. "You don't get it," he repeated in unusually blunt language, decrying what he (and perhaps his superiors) saw as undue complacency about China's encroachment throughout Asia. It is not difficult to get the sense that China is seen by some leading thinkers and officials as a near-existential threat to Japan's freedom of action.

As for Chinese officials, they are all but dismissive of Japan and its future prospects. One leading academic claimed in private conversation that China already has more wealthy citizens than the entire population of Japan, so that there could be no competition between the two; Japan simply can't keep up, he asserted, so its influence (and ability to oppose China) is doomed to evaporate. Similarly, a visit to one of China's most influential think tanks revealed an almost mono-lithically negative view of Japan. Numerous analysts expressed their skepticism about Japan's intentions in the South China Sea, perhaps revealing a concern for increased Japanese activity in the region. "Japan wants to get out from under the [postwar] US system and end the alli-ance," one analyst asserted in the closed-door session. Another criti-cized Tokyo for "playing a disruptive role" in Asia, and for creating a loose alliance against China. Underlying many of these feelings among Chinese elite is a refusal to accept Japan's legitimacy as a major Asian state, tinged with more than a little fear that Japan may be the only Asian nation, along perhaps with India, that can prevent China from reaching certain goals, such as maritime dominance in Asia's inner seas.

The sense of distrust between China and Japan reveals not only long-standing tensions but also a window into the insecurities felt by both countries as they contemplate their respective positions in Asia. These insecurities and tensions combine to create the competition that each is waging against the other, even as they maintain extensive economic relations.

V.

Increasingly, Chinese and Japanese foreign policies in Asia appear to be aimed at countering the influence—or blocking the goals—of each other. This competitive approach is taking place in the context of the deep economic interactions noted above, as well as the surface cor-diality of regular diplomatic exchanges. In fact, one of the more direct clashes is taking place over regional trade and investment.

With its head start on economic modernization and postwar polit-ical alliance with the United States, Japan helped shape Asia's nascent economic institutions and agreements. The Manila-based Asian Development Bank (ADB), founded in 1966, has always been led by a Japanese president working closely with the American-dominated

World Bank. The two institutions set most of the standards for lending to sovereign states, including expectations for political reform and broad national development. In addition to the ADB, Japan also expended hundreds of billions of dollars of official development assistance (ODA), starting in 1954. By 2003, Tokyo had disbursed $221 billion worth of aid globally, and in 2016, it still disbursed approximately $13.45 billion of ODA globally; $7 billion of this amount was spent in East and South Asia, mostly in Southeast Asia, and particularly in Myanmar.[11] The political scientists Barbara Stallings and Eun Mee Kim have observed that overall, more than 60 percent of Japan's overseas aid goes to East, South, and Central Asia.[12] Japanese assistance has traditionally been targeted for infrastructure development, water supply and sanitation, public health, and human-resources development.

In contrast, China's institutional initiatives and aid assistance traditionally lagged far behind Japan's, even though it too began providing overseas aid in the 1950s. Scholars note that it has been difficult to evaluate China's development assistance in part because of the overlap with commercial transactions with foreign countries. Moreover, over half of China's aid goes to sub-Saharan Africa, with only 30 percent going to East, South, and Central Asia.[13]

In recent years, Beijing has begun to increase its activity in both spheres, as part of a comprehensive regional foreign policy. Perhaps most notable has been China's recent attempt to diversify Asia's regional financial architecture by establishing the Asia Infrastructure Investment Bank (AIIB). Proposed in 2013, the AIIB formally opened in January 2016 and soon attracted participation from nearly every state, except Japan and the United States. The AIIB explicitly sought to "democratize" the regional lending process, as Beijing had long complained about the rigidity of the ADB's rules and governance, which gave China under 7 percent of the total voting share, compared to over 15 percent for both Japan and the United States. Ensuring China's dominant position, Beijing holds 31 percent of AIIB's shares with 26.65 percent of the voting power; the next-largest shareholder is India, with just 8.68 percent of shares and

7.65 percent of the voting power.[14] Compared to the ADB's asset base of approximately $160 billion and $30 billion in loans, however, the AIIB has a long way to go in reaching a size commensurate with its ambitions. Initially capitalized at $100 billion, by the end of 2016, $89 billion was subscribed and $19.6 billion of the $20 billion in authorized capital was committed to projects. Yet only $1.7 billion in loans was disbursed its first year, with $2 billion slated for 2017, and $7.5 billion in 2018.[15] By comparison, the Japan-dominated ADB made $35.8 billion in loans in 2018, far outstripping the AIIB. Moreover, the yen remains the third-most popular currency for international transactions, after the dollar and euro, well ahead of the Chinese renminbi.[16]

For many in Asia the apparent aid and finance rivalry between China and Japan is welcome. Officials from countries that desperately need infrastructure, such as Indonesia, hope that there will be a virtuous cycle in the ADB-AIIB competition, with Japan's high social and environmental standards helping to improve the quality of China's loans, and China's lower cost structure making projects more affordable. With an estimated need for $26 trillion in infrastructure development by 2030, according to the ADB, the more sources of financing and aid the better, even if Tokyo and Beijing view both financial institutions as tools for larger strategic and political goals.

Chinese president Xi Jinping has pegged the AIIB to his ambitious— some would say grandiose—One Belt One Road (OBOR) initiative, essentially turning the new bank into an infrastructure-lending facility along with the older China Development Bank and the newer Silk Road Fund. In comparison to Japan, China has focused most of its overseas aid on infrastructure, and the OBOR serves as the latest and largest incarnation of that priority. It is the OBOR, once known as the "new Silk Road," that represents one of the key challenges to Japan's economic presence in Asia. At the inaugural Belt and Road Forum, held in Beijing in May 2017, Xi pledged $1 trillion of infrastructure investment spanning Eurasia and beyond, essentially attempting to link land- and sea-based trading routes in a new global economic architecture. Copying a page from the ADB, Xi also promised that the

OBOR would seek to reduce poverty around Asia and the world. Since then, OBOR's envisioned reach has spread to Africa and Latin America, along with projected Maritime and Ice Silk Roads.

Despite widespread suspicion that the amounts ultimately invested in the OBOR would be significantly less than promised, Xi's scheme nonetheless sparked initial eagerness in countries like Pakistan and Malaysia, but backlash in other parts of Asia and beyond as previous and potential recipient nations balked at getting ensnared in what some called "debt-trap diplomacy." When Sri Lanka was forced in 2017 to hand over a strategic port to Chinese control due to its inability to repay debts, tighter economic integration with Beijing suddenly appeared as much a risk as a boon for cash-starved nations. Malaysia successfully reduced by one-third the loan amount for a rail line due to fears of strategic indebtedness to Beijing, while the Maldives, Sri Lanka, and even Pakistan were among the countries exploring stepping back from commitments to receive Chinese aid.[17] As a linchpin in Beijing's strategy, the hesitance of Islamabad to continue with some high-profile infrastructure projects was a particularly noteworthy shift in regional opinion.[18]

Functioning as a quasi-trade agreement, the OBOR also highlights the free-trade competition between Tokyo and Beijing. Despite what many consider a timid and sluggish Japanese trade policy, Japanese economist Kiyoshi Kojima had proposed a Free Trade Area of the Asia-Pacific as far back as 1966, although the idea was not taken seriously until the first decade of the 2000s, by the Asia-Pacific Economic Cooperation (APEC) forum. In 2003, Japan and the ten-member Association of Southeast Asian Nations (ASEAN) began negotiating a free-trade agreement, which came into effect in 2008.

Japan's major free-trade push came with the Trans-Pacific Partnership (TPP), which it formally joined in 2013. Linking Japan with the United States and ten other Pacific nations, the TPP would have accounted for nearly 40 percent of global output and fully a quarter of global trade. After the United States withdrew from the TPP in January

2017, Prime Minister Abe pushed ahead with the TPP 11, renamed the Comprehensive and Progressive Agreement for Trans-Pacific Partnership, with the remaining eleven nations. Coming into effect at the end of 2018, the reborn pact links Japan initially with Australia, New Zealand, Singapore, and Vietnam in the Asia-Pacific (along with Mexico and Canada), though other nations in Asia, including South Korea, Indonesia, Taiwan, and Thailand, have expressed interest in exploring negotiations to join the group.[19] For Tokyo, the TPP still remains the germ of a larger community of interests based on enhanced trade and investment, as well as adoption of common regulatory schemes, all designed to blunt China's dominant trade position in the region.

China has sought over the last decade to catch up with Japan on the trade front, signing its own FTA with ASEAN in 2010 and updating it in 2015, with the goal of reaching two-way trade totaling $1 trillion and investment of $150 billion by 2020. More significantly, China has adopted a 2011 ASEAN initiative, the Regional Comprehensive Economic Partnership (RCEP), which would link the ten ASEAN nations with their six dialogue partners: China, Japan, South Korea, India, Australia, and New Zealand. Accounting for nearly 40 percent of global output and linking close to 3.5 billion people, the RCEP increasingly has come to be seen as China's alternative to TPP. While Japan and Australia in particular have sought to slow final agreement over RCEP, Beijing has been given a huge boost by the Trump administration's withdrawal from the TPP and the widespread impression that China is now the global economic leader. Tokyo is finding little success in combating such opinion yet continues to try to offer alternatives to China-dominated economic initiatives. One such approach is to remain engaged in RCEP negotiations, and another is to have the ADB cofund certain projects with the AIIB. This type of cooperative competition between Japan and China may become the norm in regional economic relations, even as each seeks to maximize its influence both in institutions and with Asian states.

VI.

What long appeared to be a static security environment in Asia has dramatically changed over the past two decades. In the decades after World War II, Asia's leading nations focused on rebuilding from the devastation of the war, privileging economics over military policy. Tokyo subordinated much of its security within the framework of the US alliance, while China reeled from the domestic catastrophe of Mao's rule. A largely pacifist Japan and internally focused China did not conduct major military operations outside their borders, with China's 1962 war with India and its 1979 war with Vietnam being exceptions.

Since the end of the Cold War, however, the two began significant modernization of their militaries, in part in reaction to other regional trends, such as North Korea's nuclear and missile programs or the perception of US disengagement from the region. Today, on security matters, there is a far more direct struggle for influence and power in Asia between Beijing and Tokyo. This may sound odd when applied to Japan, which is well known for its pacifist society and the various constitutional restrictions on its military, but the past decade has seen both China and Japan seek to break out of traditional security patterns. In particular, Beijing is focused on the United States, which it sees as a major threat to its freedom of action in the Asia-Pacific region. But observers should not dismiss the degree to which Chinese policy makers and analysts worry about Japan, in some cases considering it an even bigger threat than America; this has led to a reaction in Japan fueling force modernization in light of China's dramatic military buildup.

Neither Japan nor China has any real allies in Asia, a fact often overlooked when discussing their regional foreign policies. They dominate, or have the potential to dominate, their smaller neighbors, making it difficult to create bonds of trust. Moreover, memories of each as an imperial power are ever present in Asia, adding another layer of often unspoken wariness.

For Japan, this distrust has been abetted by its fraught attempts to deal with the legacy of the Second World War and the sense on the part of most Asian nations that it has not sufficiently apologized for its wartime aggression and atrocities. Yet Japan's long-standing pacifist constitution and limited military presence in Asia after 1945 helped tamp down suspicions of its intentions. Since the 1970s, Tokyo has prioritized building ties with Southeast Asia, though until recently those were primarily focused on trade.

Since returning to power in 2012, Prime Minister Abe has moved to increase Japan's defense spending and expand its security partnerships around the region. After a decade of decline, each of Abe's defense budgets since 2013 has modestly increased spending, now totaling roughly $50 billion per year. Next, in reforming postwar legal restrictions, such as the ban on arms exports or the ban on collective self-defense, Abe has attempted to offer Japan's support as a way to blunt some of China's growing military presence in Asia. Sales of maritime patrol vessels and airplanes to countries including Malaysia, Vietnam, and the Philippines are designed to help build up the capabilities of these nations in their territorial disputes with China over the Spratly and Paracel Islands. Similarly, Tokyo hoped to sell Australia its next generation of submarines, as well as provide India with amphibious search and rescue aircraft, though both of these plans ultimately fell through or were put on hold.[20]

Despite such setbacks, Japan has increased its security cooperation with a variety of nations in Asia, including in the South China Sea area. It has formally joined the Indo-US Malabar naval exercises and sent its largest helicopter carrier to the July 2017 exercise after three months of port visits in Southeast Asia. The Japanese coast guard remains actively engaged throughout the region and plans to set up a joint maritime safety organization with Southeast Asian coast guards to help them not only deal with piracy and natural disasters but also improve their ability to monitor and defend disputed territory in the South China Sea. Most recently, then Foreign Minister Taro Kono announced a $500 million maritime security initiative for Southeast Asia, designed to help build capacity among nations in the world's most congested waterways. Abe has in particular formed a close relationship with Prime Minister Narendra Modi of India, discussing a strategic partnership between Asia's most powerful democracies that could be seen as a gambit to counter Chinese hegemony in the region.

If Tokyo has attempted to build bridges to Asian nations in a cooperative gamble, Beijing has staked out a more hegemonic position in trying to change the balance of power in the region. China has built an overwhelming military force, consisting of the world's largest navy, advanced fighter jets, ballistic missiles, and space and cyber capabilities. In the South China Sea, it has constructed and militarized artificial islands in an attempt to be the dominant power in the world's most vital waters.

China faces a more complicated security equation in Asia than Japan does, given its assertive claims in the East and South China Seas, and its territorial disputes with many of its neighbors, including large nations such as India. The dramatic growth of China's military over the past two decades has resulted not merely in a more capable navy and air force but in policies designed to defend and even extend its claims. The high-profile land reclamation and construction of bases in the Spratly Island chain exemplify Beijing's decision to assert its various claims and back them up with a military presence that dwarfs those of other contestant nations in the South China Sea. Similarly, the increase in Chinese maritime exercises in areas far from its claimed territory, such as the James Shoal, near Malaysia, or in the Indian Ocean, has worried nations that see Beijing's increasing capabilities as a potential threat.

China has, of course, attempted to assuage these concerns through maritime diplomacy, such as engaging in an ongoing set of negotiations with ASEAN nations over a code of conduct in the South China Sea, or conducting joint exercises with Malaysia. Yet repeated acts of intimidation and direct warnings to Asian nations have blunted any goodwill, forcing smaller states to consider how far to acquiesce in China's expansionist activities. Small nations in the region well remember China's then foreign minister reminding Southeast Asian nations at a regional meeting in 2010 that "China is a big country and you are small countries."[21] Adding to the region's unease was Beijing's flat rejection in July 2016 of The Hague's Permanent Court of Arbitration's ruling against China's South China Sea claims, stripping away the fiction that international law would moderate Beijing's behavior when strategic interests were at stake. Unlike Japan, moreover, China has not sought to win friends by providing defensive equipment; the bulk of China's military sales in Asia goes to North Korea, Bangladesh, and Burma, forging, along with Pakistan (the largest recipient of Chinese arms transfers), a loose grouping that is isolated from those nations cooperating with both Japan and the United States.

Yet for all its bluster and intimidation, China's approach, a combination of realpolitik and limited *machtpolitik*, is more likely to secure its goals, at least in the short run, if not longer. Smaller nations are under no illusion that they can successfully resist China's encroachments; they hope for either a natural moderation of Beijing's behavior or an overreach that will allow communal pressure to influence Chinese decision making. In this calculation, Japan appears primarily as a spoiler. While Tokyo is able to protect its own territories in the East China Sea, it knows that its power in the region is limited. This mandates not only a continuing, if enhanced, alliance relationship with the United States but also an approach that helps complicate Beijing's decision making, such as by providing defensive equipment to Southeast Asian nations. Tokyo understands that it can potentially help disrupt, but not deter, Chinese expansion in Asia. Put differently, Asia is faced with competing security strategies from its two most powerful nations: Japan seeks to be loved; China, feared.

VII.

A deeper manifestation of Sino-Japanese rivalry is the model for national development that each implicitly offers for Asia. It is not the case that Beijing simply expects governments around the Pacific to adopt "socialism with Chinese characteristics" or that Tokyo looks to help install parliamentary democracy. Rather, it is a more fundamental question of how each state is viewed by its neighbors and how much influence each state may have in the region thanks to perceptions of its national strength, governmental effectiveness, social dynamism, and opportunities provided by its system. From this perspective, the two are competing for regional authority, each pitting its political leadership against the other in making what Chinese scholar Yan Xuetong calls "strategic credibility" the litmus test for their influence.[22] This competition has been particularly active since 2012, when both Xi Jinping and Shinzo Abe came to power, each the most powerful national leader in decades.

It should be acknowledged that attempting to identify models of national development is an extremely subjective approach, and the evidence for determining which of the two countries is more influential will likely be more anecdotal, inferential, and indirect than explicitly discoverable. Nor is this question of serving as a model for other nations the same as the ubiquitous concept of soft power. Soft power is usually defined as an element of national power—specifically, the attractiveness of a particular system in creating the conditions through which that state can achieve policy goals. While both Beijing and Tokyo are undoubtedly interested in advancing their state interests, that is a question distinct from how each is viewed and what benefits each derives from the policies they pursue.[23]

The postwar period in Asian development divides neatly at roughly 1990, when Japan's economic "bubble" burst and China's reform policy was revitalized and its takeoff began.[24] For decades, Japan was the standard for development in Asia, but long gone are the days when a Mahathir Mohamad could declare Japan a role model for Malaysia and when even China considered Japan's modernization model a paradigm. Tokyo's hopes to leverage its economic ties with Southeast Asia, the so-called Flying Geese model, into broader political influence were derailed by China's rise in the 1990s.[25] Because Beijing is the largest trading partner for all Asian states, it occupies a central position. Yet Sino-Asian relations have remained largely transactional, due both to lingering concerns over Beijing's assertiveness and fears of being economically overwhelmed. From a short-term perspective, China may appear more influential thanks to its economic power, but that too has translated only fitfully into political gains. Nor has there been an increase in Asian nations attempting to mimic China's political model, as opposed to eagerly accepting its development assistance in most cases. Instead, both Tokyo and Beijing continue to jockey for position and influence. Each interacts with largely the same set of Asian actors, thus offering what Asians consider an almost market-based competition, in which smaller states are able to drive better deals than they would if dealing with either power alone.

Yet it is in this Sino-Japanese competition that the role of the United States becomes a driver of national strategy. Both China and Japan base their policies in part on their perceptions of US policy in Asia. Japan's alliance with the United States serves in essence to merge Tokyo and Washington into one bloc versus Beijing, while also creating an underlying uncertainty as to American intentions. Japanese concern over the credibility of American promises to remain engaged in the Indo-Pacific drives Tokyo's military modernization plans, in part to be a more effective partner and in part to avoid overdependence. At the same time, uncertainty over America's long-term policy enhances Japan's desire to deepen relations and cooperation with India, Vietnam, and other nations that share its worries about China's growing military strength. On the other hand, Beijing's response to the Obama administration's involvement in the South China Sea territorial disputes was a program of land reclamation and base building in the Spratly Islands. The same could be said for China's financial and free-trade initiatives, which are designed at least in part to blunt the TPP, which was championed though not started by Washington, or the continued influence of the ADB and World Bank in regional lending.

From a mere material perspective, Japan should come off worse in any direct competition for influence between the two nations. Its economic glory days are far behind it, and it never successfully translated its still comparatively powerful economy into political influence, let alone a military that could dominate the region. Perceptions of its sclerotic political system, despite the achievements of Abe since 2012, add to the sense that Japan will likely never again regain the dynamism it showed in the postwar decades.

Yet as a stable democracy with a largely content, highly educated, healthy (if aging) population, Japan is still regarded as the benchmark for many Asian nations. Having long ago tackled its pollution problem and boasting a low crime rate, Japan offers an attractive model for developing societies. Its benign international policies and minimal overseas military operations, combined with its generous foreign aid, make Japan the most admired country in Asia, according to a 2015 Pew Research Center poll—71 percent of respondents voiced a favorable view. China garnered only a 57 percent approval rating, with fully one-third of respondents having a negative view.[26]

But current perception and likability benefit Japan only so much. When Genron NPO, the Japanese polling company, asked in 2016 if Japan would increase its influence in Asia by 2026, only 11.6 percent of Chinese and 23 percent of South Koreans answered in the affirmative; perhaps surprisingly, only 28.5 percent of Japanese themselves thought so.[27] When Genron asked the same question about China in 2015, fully 82.5 percent of Chinese, 80 percent of South Koreans, and 60 percent of Japanese expected China's influence in Asia to increase by 2025.[28] Two decades of Chinese economic growth and Japanese economic stagnation undoubtedly are the causes of such findings, but China's recent political overtures under Xi Jinping likely play some role.

Despite scoring lower than Japan in regional opinion polls, China has ridden a wave of anticipation that its ultimate strength will make it the most dominant nation in the Indo-Pacific, if not the world. This has made it easier to attract cooperation or wary neutrality from Asian nations. The AIIB is just one example of Asian nations flocking to a Chinese proposal; One Belt One Road is another. Beijing has also used its influence in negative ways, for example by pressuring Southeast

Asian nations such as Cambodia or Laos to oppose stronger criticisms of China's territorial claims in joint ASEAN communiqués.

At times, China's very dominance has worked against it, and Japan has taken advantage of the region's unease at China's power. When ASEAN nations proposed what would become the East Asia Summit in the early 2000s, with the participation of China, Japan, and South Korea, Tokyo successfully lobbied with Singapore for Australia, India, and New Zealand to be included as full members. This inclusion of an additional three democratic nations was designed to blunt China's influence over what was expected to become the largest pan-Asian multilateral initiative and was decried by Chinese media for doing so.

For all their attempts, neither Japan nor China has succeeded in establishing a dominant position as the undisputed great power of Asia. Southeast Asian nations above all want to avoid being drawn into a Sino-Japanese—or, much the same thing, Sino-US-Japan—political and security dispute. The scholars Bhubhindar Singh, Sarah Teo, and Benjamin Ho have argued that, in recent years, ASEAN nations have focused more on the US-China relationship, since it is the United States that has formal Southeast Asian allies and has inserted itself into the South China Sea dispute.[29] Yet all also consider Sino-Japanese ties to be of critical importance for Asian stability in the short and long term. While this particular concern is largely centered on security issues and less on the larger questions of national models, when attention has turned to national development, the focus on China and Japan becomes even clearer. None dismiss the continuing importance of the United States to Asia's short- and medium-term future, but awareness of the long history of Sino-Japanese relations and competition is a primary element of the larger regional perception of power, leadership, and threat that will shape Asia in the coming decades.

It is a truism, though not unhelpful, to observe that neither Japan nor China can leave Asia. They are stuck with each other and with their neighbors, and each has an intense relationship with the United States. Japan and China's economic ties are likely to deepen in future years, even as both look for alternative opportunities as well as seek to structure Asian trade and economic relations in ways most beneficial to their own interests. There will undoubtedly be periods of greater political cooperation between Beijing and Tokyo, such as that trumpeted by Xi and Abe in the fall of 2018, along with the minimal quotidian diplomatic niceties.[30] There will continue to be grassroots exchange—at the very least, unorganized exchange through millions of tourists.

Their histories and civilizational achievements, however, all but ensure that they will remain the two most powerful Asian nations, and that implies an ongoing competition. Whether Japan remains allied to the United States or not, or whether China successfully forges a pan-Asian Belt and Road community, the two will continue to try to shape the Asian political, economic, and security environment. With a United States that continues to be challenged by its global commitments and interests, thereby leading to periods of relative lassitude in Asia, China and Japan will stay bound in a complex, often tense, and competitive relationship that is Asia's eternal great game.

Notes

1.   World Bank, International Comparison Program Database, "GDP, PPP (current international $), China," https://data.worldbank.org/indicator /NY.GDP.MKTP.PP.CD?locations=CN&year_high_desc=true (accessed July 26, 2019).
2.   See 2018 World Bank statistics at https://data.worldbank.org/indicator /NY.GDP.PCAP.CD?locations=JP-CN (accessed July 26, 2019).
3.   *The 12th Japan-China Joint Opinion Poll Analysis Report on the Comparative Data* (Tokyo: Genron NPO, 2016), 3, http://www.genron-npo.net /pdf/2016forum_en.pdf.
4.   Bruce Stokes, "Hostile Neighbors: China vs. Japan," Pew Research Center, September 13, 2016, http://www.pewglobal.org/2016/09/13/hostile -neighbors-china-vs-japan.
5.   Philip J. Cunningham, "China's TV War Machine," *New York Times*, September 11, 2014, https://www.nytimes.com/2014/09/12/opinion/chinas -tv-war-on-japan.html.

6. Stokes, "Hostile Neighbors."

7. "East Asia/Southeast Asia: China," in *The World Factbook* (Washington, DC: Central Intelligence Agency), https://www.cia.gov/library/publica tions/the-world-factbook/geos/ch.html (accessed July 26, 2019).

8. Martin Fackler and Ian Johnson, "Sleepy Islands and a Smoldering Dispute," *New York Times*, September 12, 2012, https://www.nytimes.com /2012/09/21/world/asia/japan-china-trade-ties-complicate-island-dis pute.html.

9. According to data from Japan National Tourism Organization (JNTO), which can be accessed at https://www.tourism.jp/en/tourism-database /stats/inbound/#country.

10. Reinhard Drifte, "The Japan-China Confrontation over the Senkaku/ Diaoyu Islands—Between "Shelving" and "Dispute Escalation," *Asia-Pacific Journal: Japan Focus* 12, issue 30, no. 3 (July 27, 2014), https://apjjf .org/-Reinhard-Drifte/4154/article.pdf.

11. See chart III-2, "White Paper on Development Cooperation," Ministry of Foreign Affairs, https://www.mofa.go.jp/policy/oda/page22e_000864 .html (accessed July 26, 2019).

12. Barbara Stallings and Eun Mee Kim, *Promoting Development: The Political Economy of East Asian Foreign Aid* (London: Palgrave, 2017).

13. Axel Dreher et al., AIDDATA Working Paper 46: *Aid, China, and Growth: Evidence from a New Global Development Finance Dataset* (Williamsburg, MD: William & Mary, 2017). http://docs.aiddata.org/ad4/pdfs /WPS46_Aid_China_and_Growth.pdf.

14. *Members and Prospective Members of the Bank*, Asian Infrastructure and Investment Bank, Beijing, China, https://www.aiib.org/en/about -aiib/governance/members-of-bank/index.html (accessed July 26, 2019).

15. *Annual Report*, Asian Infrastructure and Investment Bank, https:// www.aiib.org/en/news-events/annual-report/2018/_common/pdf/2018 -aiib-annual-report-and-financials.pdf (accessed July 28, 2019).

16. Mike Bird, "Japan's Silent Belt and Road Is Beating China's," *Wall Street Journal*, April 22, 2019, https://www.wsj.com/articles/japans-silent-belt -and-road-is-beating-chinas-11555923604.

17. Panos Mourdoukoutas, "Modi Should Not Bail Out China in Maldives," *Forbes*, November 28, 2018, https://www.forbes.com/sites/panosmourdou koutas/2018/11/28/modi-should-not-bail-out-china-in-maldives/#573af 52941d8.

18. Gerry Shih, "Pakistan Has Second Thoughts on Chinese Investment. It Probably Won't Be the Last Country to Get Cold Feet," *Washington Post*, September 11, 2018, https://www.washingtonpost.com/world/2018/09/11/pakistan-has-second-thoughts-chinese-investment-it-probably-wont-be-last-country-get-cold-feet/?noredirect=on&utm_term=.e718d3677b36.

19. Fumi Matsumoto, "TPP-11 to Take Effect on Dec. 30," *Nekkei Asian Review*, October 31, 2018, https://asia.nikkei.com/Politics/International-Relations/TPP-11-to-take-effect-on-Dec.-30.

20. Purnendra Jain, "Japan: The World's Next Big Arms Dealer?" *National Interest*, February 17, 2017, https://nationalinterest.org/blog/the-buzz/japan-the-worlds-next-big-arms-dealer-19477.

21. Joshua Kurlantzik, "The Belligerents," *New Republic*, January 27, 2011, https://newrepublic.com/article/82211/china-foreign-policy.

22. Yan Xueton, *Leadership and the Rise of Great Powers* (Princeton, NJ: Princeton University Press, 2019), esp. ch. 1. Yan would deny that Tokyo is able to compete with China's political, economic, and military capability, but in the sphere of the Indo-Pacific, his model of great power competition works well when applied to Japan and China.

23. Yan, *Leadership*, 13–14.

24. Specifically, 1989, with the collapse of Japan's asset price boom, and 1992, with Deng Xiaoping's famous "southern tour" to restart economic reform.

25. The "Flying Geese" paradigm, the process by which older technology and know-how is passed down the chain of developing economies, was popularized in the 1960s by Japanese economist Kaname Akamatsu. The theory initially spoke to technological development in Southeast Asia, drawing upon Japanese technological and industrial know-how.

26. Bruce Stokes, "How Asia-Pacific Publics See Each Other and Their National Leaders," Pew Global, September 2, 2015, http://www.pewglobal.org/2015/09/02/how-asia-pacific-publics-see-each-other-and-their-national-leaders.

27. *The Genron NP Poll 2016: The Future of Northeast Asia and Public Opinions* (Tokyo: Genron NPO, 2016), 10, http://www.genron-npo.net/pdf/genronnpo_poll2016.pdf.

28. Yasushi Kudo, *The Genron NPO Japan-U.S.-China-ROK Opinion Poll Report* (Tokyo: Genron NPO, 2015), 4, http://www.genron-npo.net/en /opinion_polls/archives/5321.html

29. Bhubhindar Singh, Sarah Teo, and Benjamin Ho, "Rising Sino-Japanese Competition: Perspectives from South-East Asian Elites," *Australian Journal of International Affairs* 71, no. 1 (2017): 105–20, DOI: 10.1080 /10357718.2016.1157849.

30. Shunsuke Shigeta, "Xi and Abe Pledge 'New Era' of Cooperation," *Nikkei Asian Review*, October 27, 2018, https://asia.nikkei.com/Politics /International-relations/Xi-and-Abe-pledge-new-era-of-cooperation.

7

THE QUESTION OF AMERICAN STRATEGY IN THE INDO-PACIFIC

From the beginning of the Republic, Americans have been drawn to the Pacific. Fur traders and wagon train pioneers were preceded in their western expansion across the continent by American ships heading into the great western sea. As American engagement with the vast Pacific world, whether public or private, waxed and waned for decades, individual initiative often seemed unconnected to a broader national strategy beyond desiring the region remain free and open to all states.[1]

Indeed, a self-conscious, coherent, and well-resourced American global strategy is a relatively new phenomenon, coming fullest into being during the early Cold War with the assumption of worldwide commitments. Even then, the Pacific Ocean region was just one part of a necessarily broad global picture. Perhaps only with China's rise after the Cold War, and with Asia becoming a vital part of the global economy, can one realistically talk about the concomitant emergence of a US global strategy at the center of which lies the Indo-Pacific. Yet,

---

This essay is adapted from "The Question of American Strategy in the Indo-Pacific," Hoover Institution Working Group on Islamism and the International Order, July 17, 2018, https://www.hoover.org/sites/default/files/research/docs/auslin_webreadypdf.pdf.

ironically, just at the moment when Asia has become central to US grand strategy, Washington's influence and power in the region is now significantly challenged, perhaps for the first time since 1945. US policy makers are being tested to formulate a truly effective, comprehensive strategy toward the Indo-Pacific that preserves stability and protects US and allied interests, all in the context of a growing strategic competition between Washington and Beijing, the threat of a nuclear-capable North Korea, and the overall deterioration in international order.

Traditionally, Americans have referred to this region as Asia or the Asia-Pacific, and often have focused on even narrower subregions, such as Northeast Asia or South Asia. Not only have American academic programs in universities similarly divided their studies, but many US government departments split up responsibility for Asia among multiple geographically narrow bureaus. The result has been to limit the ability to conceptualize the area in its totality, including the various linkages that cross ethnic, cultural, and linguistic lines, not to mention the challenges that the region faces. Only recently has it become more prevalent to speak of the Indo-Pacific. This is a relatively new term, intended to provide an integrated sense of the region and its manifold interests. It corresponds largely to the military "area of responsibility" allocated to the US Indo-Pacific Command (see figure 2).[2]

The Indo-Pacific, on this definition, is perhaps the most diverse region on earth. It comprises thirty-six countries that are continental, peninsular, and archipelagic, including tens of thousands of inhabited islands, and covers much of the Pacific and Indian Oceans, as well as the inner seas of Asia. With over three billion people, it contains more than half of the global population, including the world's two most populous nations, India and China, and is where over three thousand languages are spoken. It has the world's largest democracy, India, and two of the world's three largest Muslim nations, India and Indonesia. The Indo-Pacific is home to more than 40 percent of global economic output, including the leading economies of China, Japan, and South Korea. It also contains some of the world's largest and most developed military

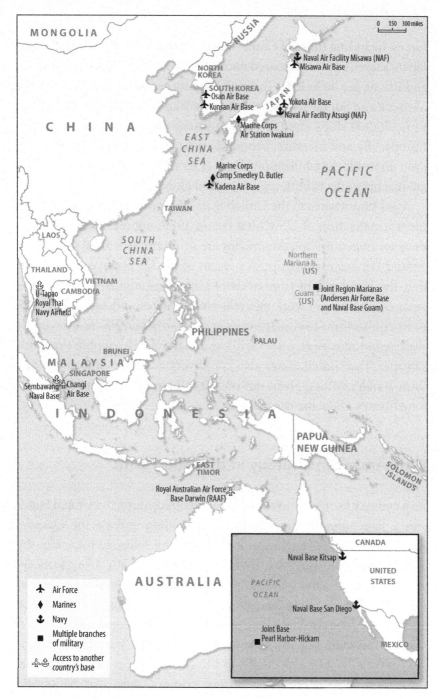

Figure 2. US Military Bases in the Indo-Pacific

forces, including those of China, North Korea, South Korea, India, and Japan; as well as three declared nuclear powers (five, if the United States and Russia are included). Through its strategic waterways, such as the Malacca and Sunda Straits, transit some 70 percent of global trade and some 75,000 ships annually, linking Asia with the Middle East and Europe.[3] By any measure, economic disruption, regional conflict, or even domestic destabilization of any of Asia's major nations could have far-reaching effects both regionally and globally.

Asia's importance to the United States has grown dramatically since the normalization of US-China ties in 1979, not least because more than seventeen million Americans are immigrants from Asia or have Asian heritage, making up 5.8 percent of the US population.[4] Add to that the hundreds of thousands of Chinese, Indians, Koreans, and Japanese studying or working in the United States, and America's grass-roots connections to Asia have never been stronger. US trade in goods with Asia totals nearly $1.5 trillion dollars, nearly double that with Europe.[5] The United States also could very easily be drawn into any intra-Asian conflict, given not only its alliance commitments but its long history of Pacific engagement.

Early American Strategy in the Indo-Pacific

As a country born only in the late eighteenth century, the United States was a latecomer to the waters of the Indian and Pacific Oceans. European nations, starting with Portugal and followed by Spain, the Netherlands, and England, traded for centuries with Asian princely states, kingdoms, and islands. Eschewing the costly, land-based routes of the Silk Road, European sailors rounded the Cape of Good Hope and followed the sea-lanes long opened by Arab traders into the Indian Ocean. This incursion from the western edge of the Eurasian landmass led inexorably, if unexpectedly, to the establishment of colonial outposts to protect the European traders, primarily spice merchants, and their small settlements. Starting on the western coast of the Indian subcontinent in the early sixteenth century, by the mid-nineteenth century, the Europeans had ensconced themselves throughout the Indo-Pacific, reaching into Chinese territory, yet hardly into the Pacific Ocean itself.[6]

When the Americans came in the late eighteenth century, they initially followed the familiar European route but soon shifted to the far more daunting Pacific route, approaching from the east across the vast ocean, thus opening up an entirely new set of sea routes.[7] American trading ships traversed thousands of miles of barely known maritime territory, stopping at small, widely separated island chains before suddenly arriving in Asia proper, congested with empires and kingdoms, and dotted with European colonial fortresses.

Yet as much as trade drove early Americans across the oceans, it was war that brought American power proper into the Indo-Pacific. For the new country, the Pacific was a region of geopolitical competition with its former colonial master, Great Britain, as well as other European nations who looked askance at the new merchant intruders. American military power, limited and inexperienced as it was, initially was deployed to uphold US neutrality rights in shipping that were threatened by other European maritime powers. The protection of American commerce in the Pacific thus catalyzed the emergence of an official US presence in the region, represented primarily by the US Navy, with only sporadic consular representation for the first third of the nineteenth century. Yet there was little in Washington's policy that initially could be considered a comprehensive or consistent strategy, let alone a truly grand strategy on the part of the young republic. Scattershot American attention overrode sometimes ambitious intentions, and it is not until the middle of the nineteenth century that even the beginnings of a true strategy toward the Indo-Pacific can be discerned. That should not, however, lead us to overlook the fact that the new nation sought to project what maritime power it could into the Pacific decades before a more comprehensive strategy emerged.

It is well known that the first American merchant ship to trade with Asia, the *Empress of China*, sailed for China across the Atlantic Ocean from New York Harbor in early 1784, just months after the signing of the Treaty of Paris that ended the American Revolution. It was not until May 1800, during the "Quasi War" with France, that the USS *Essex* became the first US Navy vessel to reach Asia, porting at Batavia (now Jakarta) in the Dutch East Indies. Having crossed the Atlantic and rounded the Cape of Good Hope into the Indian Ocean, taking the same route as the *Empress of China* previously, the *Essex* was to escort back to the United States a convoy of merchant ships and protect them from French privateers, which were equally potential prizes, should they be encountered.[8] For the young nation, then, "Asia" was initially reached via the Atlantic and Indian Oceans, and the "Indo" part of what we today call the Indo-Pacific was not considered inseparable from the rest but was actually the main theater of operations in these earliest years.

Yet America was destined to focus its Asian energies through and in the Pacific Ocean. Perhaps ironically, given the name of the ocean, it took another armed conflict, the War of 1812, to pull American power into the Pacific. In January 1813, the same USS *Essex* became the first US naval ship to round Cape Horn and transit into the Pacific, though without any specific orders to do so.[9] She was again in search of prizes, this time British. *Essex* nearly decimated British whaling ships in the rich hunting grounds in a few short months, forcing London to send the Royal Navy to hunt the American predator. Captain David Porter, commander of *Essex*, recklessly decided to confront the Royal Navy at Valparaiso, Chile, in March 1814, leading to the capture of his ship in one of the bloodiest battles in early US naval history.[10] Meanwhile, at the other end of the great ocean, near Batavia, the USS *Peacock* captured the British East India Company brig *Nautilus* in June 1815, after the war had ended but before word of the armistice reached across the globe. In the action, *Peacock* killed a number of the British crew, who were probably the last casualties of the war.[11]

Not until 1818 was a regular US Navy presence established in the eastern Pacific Ocean. In that year, the USS *Macedonian* was dispatched as the first ship of the United States Naval Forces on "Pacific Station," soon renamed the Pacific Squadron, cruising along the western coasts of North and South America. A year later, the USS *Congress* became the first American naval vessel to enter Chinese waters, followed only sporadically afterward for over a decade, until the formation in 1835 of the East India Squadron, based in Asia proper, which was later renamed the Asiatic Squadron.[12] These two squadrons, of varying sizes and effectiveness, but never more than a handful of ships, patrolled the Indo-Pacific region for the rest of the century, occasionally intervening on behalf of scattered merchants and missionaries.

If there was an overall American approach to the Pacific world in the first century of its engagement, it might be conceived of as consisting of different types of activity in three "zones." These zones were never explicitly articulated as such, nor were they consciously thought of as distinct spaces, but the differing ways Americans approached the Pacific during the nineteenth century reveal an understanding of the scope and limits of US power in the Pacific until the dawn of the twentieth century.

First, along the western coast of the American continent, a "zone of control" was eventually established, patrolled by the US Navy. This zone operated as part of the broader imperial competition between the United States, Great Britain, Spain, Mexico, and Russia over the new territories of western North America. In particular, this zone saw American moves to counter British attempts to carve out a permanent presence deep into what would become the Oregon Territory, protected by the Royal Navy.[13] The Treaty of Oregon, signed on June 15, 1846, set the forty-ninth parallel as the border between British Canada and the United States, thereby incorporating the future states of Washington and Oregon into American territory and blocking British expansion southward. At the same time, the wresting of California from Mexico during the Mexican-American War of 1846–48 ensured the control of some of the most fertile land on the entire continent and gave the United States a coastline reaching from the northern Pacific down to temperate waters off the Baja California peninsula. Within this zone of control, the United States exercised complete maritime and territorial power, and gradually extended its naval reach down along the South American coast, as well.

Next, from off the western American coast all the way across the trackless Pacific to the Philippine and Indonesian archipelagos, a liquid desert confronted American ships. Widely scattered oases, such as the Sandwich (Hawaiian) Islands or atolls and islands of Polynesia, offered stopping points on the months-long voyages. Here, the United States established a "zone of influence." Outside of the Sandwich Islands and occasional larger islands such as Guam, there was little territory to be taken or controlled, unlike in continental America or Asia proper. US naval ships instead sailed freely in and out of these waters, dispatched to convoy American trading ships or to punish violent or recalcitrant Pacific potentates for impeding trade or threatening missionaries. The two Sumatran expeditions during the 1830s were examples of how Americans operated in the zone of influence: exercising US power against smaller or less powerful adversaries but almost always leaving their territory alone throughout the first three-quarters of the nineteenth century.

Finally, when the US Navy reached Asia itself, it encountered a crowded, complex geopolitical region of ancient states, such as China, Japan, and Korea, along with European colonies, such as the Philippines, and dozens or hundreds of smaller principalities. Here, American power was extremely limited, and there was no possibility, let alone desire, to attempt to control territory directly or even have influence to the same degree it did over isolated islands in the middle of the Pacific. Instead, the United States participated in a "zone of cooperation," more often than not working in tandem with European powers to pressure regional states, enter into diplomatic agreements, and occasionally employ force, such as against the Chinese in 1859, during the Second Opium War, and the Japanese in the 1863 Shimonoseki Expedition.[14] Even when the Americans acted unilaterally, as against Formosa in 1867 or Korea in 1871, they were well aware of the limited nature of their military power, as well as the interests of other Western nations, which demanded comparatively restrained US objectives. The apotheosis of American activity in the zone of cooperation was reached with secretary of state John Hay's "Open Door" policy of 1899, seeking to mitigate the effect of European spheres of influence in China in limiting trading access, and with American participation in allied military operations in China in the summer of 1901 during the Boxer Rebellion.[15]

America's zones in the Pacific emerged due to geopolitical, economic, and cultural pressures. The growth of the country's whaling fleet in the Pacific Ocean in the middle of the nineteenth century led to general arguments for a stronger US military presence in the region, eventually becoming the main impetus for Commodore Matthew Perry's famous mission to "open" Japan in 1853–54. Yet for decades, US trade in Asia lagged other regions and grew only slowly, with imports from Asia far outpacing exports. In 1840, five years after the establishment of the East India Squadron, trade with Asia amounted to just over $12 million, 90 percent of which involved imports to the United States.[16] On the eve of the Spanish-American War in 1897, US exports to Asia were still under $40 million, while nearly $92 million worth of goods were imported. Yet politics and other interests were at least as important as actual profits. Trade treaties during the mid-1800s with China (1844 and 1858), Japan (1858), and Siam (now Thailand) (1837), combined with an expatriate community of American Christian missionaries throughout the Pacific, mandated at least a modest US force in the region. Such forces were needed to protect both merchant rights and the lives of American citizens and consular officials, as attacks on American shipping in waters around far-flung Sumatra and Japan and violence against American diplomatic residences in Japan in the early 1860s proved.

American strategy, however, lagged commerce and religion, and emerged only fitfully in relation to the Pacific. During the 1860s, William Henry Seward, Abraham Lincoln's secretary of state, held perhaps the most articulated concept of US strategy in the region. Seward, echoing former president and secretary of state John Quincy Adams, argued that domination of global commerce was America's destiny, and that the Pacific would serve as a great highway to the riches of Asian markets.

Seward oversaw the signing of a more expansive treaty with China in 1868, and advocated for the annexation of the Hawaiian kingdom and the building of the Panama Canal. In terms of actual territorial expansion, Seward was less successful, known for purchasing Alaska, but only the small atoll of Midway, claimed in 1867, marked any absorption of Pacific islands.[17] Seward was decades ahead of his time, however, for not until 1898 did the United States become the type of colonial power envisioned by the most passionate expansionists. Fueled by concepts of maritime supremacy popularized by Alfred Thayer Mahan and promoted by policy makers such as Theodore Roosevelt and Henry Cabot Lodge, US forces annexed Hawaii, invaded and captured the Philippines, and took over Guam and part of Samoa, all in 1898–99. In one fell swoop, America overturned nearly a century of tradition and became one of the leading colonial powers in the Pacific. The new imperial policy collapsed the long-standing "zone of influence" into the "zone of control," thereby unifying American action across the Pacific, from the western coast of the United States all the way to the Philippines. From 1898 on, despite its limited power, the United States envisioned the Pacific Ocean, up to Chinese and Japanese waters, as a zone of control through its naval presence and string of territories reaching nearly to the Asian littoral. Only after 1945 would Washington consider all of Asia proper to be within a zone of control designed to prevent the emergence of any other hegemonic military power in the region, and to keep the Pacific "free and open."

Yet even with this broader orientation, US strategy continued to lag expansion. Despite the growing shadow of Japanese power after its defeat of China in 1895 and Russia in 1905, Washington's thinking in the early twentieth century was limited to relatively modest, and insufficient, planning for defending America's far-flung possessions. Other than the US Navy's War Plan Orange, there was little, if any, discussion about how to maintain stability in the Indo-Pacific.[18] Inertia in strategic planning came from the complexity of dealing with the multiple spheres of influence of the region's colonial powers, as well as the presumption that the Washington and London naval arms limitation treaties of 1921 and 1931 would prevent an arms race that could result in great power conflict in Asia between the navies of Japan, the United States, and Great Britain, primarily.[19] The creeping Sino-Japanese military conflict, begun in Manchuria in September 1931, did not spur further US preparedness in case a wider war broke out, nor did it cause a coalition of Western colonial nations to consider collective defense of their territories in Asia from what was an increasingly belligerent Japanese policy.

The Japanese attacks throughout Asia on December 8 (December 7, in Hawaii), 1941, were a direct bid for hegemony in the western Pacific. Alone, they might not have spurred any truly strategic thought on the part of the United States, but coming in conjunction with the Nazi threat to Europe, they generated the first serious, sustained strategic planning for Asia in the context of US global interests. That America had no grand strategy prior to World War II, let alone a strategy for Asia, was recognized by contemporaries. The columnist and foreign policy analyst Walter Lippmann, for example, excoriated the very lack of US grand strategy prior to and during the war, reiterating what he called the "common principle" of genuine foreign policy—namely, that a nation must balance its commitments with its power. Without adequate resources, a state cannot uphold its commitments, and thus its foreign policy will remain out of balance. In particular, Lippmann argued, Washington left its frontiers unguarded, its armaments unprepared, and its alliances unfounded.[20] This "gap" was particularly noticeable in eastern Asia, where America's Philippine possessions were all but undefended.

As for the overarching US strategy required in a global environment, contemporary observers were equally clear. Lippmann argued that the continental limits of the United States did not equal the country's defensive frontiers.[21] This mirrored the wartime arguments of geopolitical scholar Nicholas Spykman, who stated that the goal of US foreign policy must be to preserve the balance of power in Europe and Asia as the first line of defense for the United States. Spykman argued that America's unique geographical advantage of being protected by two great oceans would be irrelevant if Europe and Asia were both dominated by aggressive empires, thus isolating the country from global trade and threatening its ultimate security. To Spykman, continental defense (what he called "quarter-sphere" defense) was unviable without full hemispheric defense, including South America; that, in turn, could not be ensured without a favorable balance of power in both Europe and Asia in the Eastern Hemisphere.[22] Thus, American forces had to be present in those far-flung regions, which became part of the argument for near-permanent forward basing of US troops in both Europe and Asia after 1945.

This shift in strategic thinking led to concrete planning for the postwar era, forming the basis for US policy in the Pacific throughout the Cold War and beyond. Beginning with the need to neutralize a potential future Japanese threat, the first two pillars of Washington's strategy were the permanent militarization of the US presence in Asia and the democratization of Japan. The US occupation of Japan from 1945 to 1952 ensured that both these approaches became the basis of US policy.[23] The outbreak of the Korean War, in June 1950, further spurred a military-first strategy for Asia, while reinforcing the containment of Soviet-sponsored communism as the third major pillar of US strategy, as already codified in the then top secret NSC-68 document of April 1950. The threat of communist subversion in newly decolonized Asia led to the fourth element of US strategy, which was to create a regionwide system of defensive alliances.[24] Between 1951 and 1960, Washington would sign a series of formal security treaties, attempting to create a network of multilateral agreements mirroring those in Europe, including the Australia–New Zealand–United States (ANZUS) Treaty in 1951 and the Southeast Asia Treaty Organization (SEATO) in 1954.

The US multilateral treaty system did not succeed in Asia, with SEATO and ANZUS breaking apart, ultimately leading instead to enduring bilateral alliances with Australia (1951), the Philippines (1951), South Korea (1953), Thailand (1954), and Japan (1960). American forces were anchored by major air and naval bases located in Japan in the northeast, and the Philippines in the southeast. These strategically located and extensive installations allowed US forces to project power, intervene when necessary, and provide a constant level of insurance and security for public goods such as freedom of navigation; they also served as the major bases for America's Vietnam War efforts. While concerned about communist subversion of Asian countries, Washington did not face a significant traditional great-power challenge in Asia's common seas or skies throughout these decades. The major American military priorities were to prevent another North Korean attack across the thirty-eighth parallel and to bottle up Soviet ballistic missile submarines in their littoral bastions in the Sea of Okhotsk and nearby waters; this latter was undertaken in conjunction particularly with Japanese naval and air forces.

As Asian economies took off in the 1960s and 1970s, beginning with Japan and then spreading to the "Four Tigers" of South Korea, Singapore, Hong Kong, and Taiwan, an economic element to Asia's strategic importance came to the fore. As America's economy became more tied to Asian manufacturers, concern with ensuring freedom of navigation and the high seas, and protecting crucial lanes of sea transport, concurrently rose in importance. Subsidiary to that was a growing US interest in ensuring overall stability in Asia, so that the economies of key allies such as Japan and South Korea were not threatened by external aggression or internal upheaval. The rise of Asia during the final decades of the Cold War occasioned the melding of geoeconomic interests with long-standing geopolitical and security interests, but the region was still treated in many ways as simply one part of a global anti-Soviet/anticommunist grand strategy.

American Strategy in the Indo-Pacific after the Cold War and the Rise of China

Contemporaneous with the collapse of the Soviet Union and the bursting of the Japanese economic bubble at the beginning of the 1990s, China began its unprecedented rise to global power. During the Cold

War, US policy toward China was a combination of geopolitical maneuvering against the Soviet Union and aspirations of unlocking its massive market for American businesses. When Richard Nixon traveled to meet Mao Zedong in 1972, few in the United States imagined that within a generation, China would be the second most powerful nation on earth and would become an unambiguous challenger to America's leading global role. Even after the 1989 Tiananmen Square massacre, US policy was focused on integrating China into the global economy and giving Beijing a place at the table of international politics. From normalization of US-China ties in 1979 through Beijing's accession to the World Trade Organization in 2001, in addition to high-level Sino-US government exchanges such as the Strategic and Economic Dialogue, Washington consistently worked to promote deeper economic and political bonds with Beijing. The US approach was perhaps best summed up by Robert Zoellick, then deputy secretary of state, who in 2005 called on China to become a "responsible stakeholder" in the global system, pointedly distinguishing between early twenty-first-century Sino-US relations and the Cold War competition between America and the Soviet Union.[25]

The early post–Cold War years saw attempts by both the Bill Clinton and George W. Bush administrations to come up with a new grand strategy for the United States. With Europe taking a backseat in US interests for the first time in two generations, Asia rapidly began to fill the vacuum. Both administrations acknowledged the unique unipolar moment following the collapse of the Soviet Union but did not yet argue that Asia would become the cockpit of international relations. However, by the time Clinton left office, tensions were already appearing in Sino-US relations that would lead to reconsiderations of American strategy in the region.

Reflecting the central role of military capability in maintaining America's presence in Asia, the Department of Defense in 1998 issued a US Security Strategy for the East Asia–Pacific Region, which remained until 2019 the only formally published US government strategy for the Indo-Pacific region. Coming as it did when the full extent of the

Japanese economic slowdown was not known, when China was just a few years into the relaunch of then paramount leader Deng Xiaoping's economic reforms, and before North Korea had progressed in its nuclear and ballistic missile programs, the strategy adopted a more optimistic, if not relaxed perspective on Asia than many subsequent statements of US interest. America's central goals in Asia, the strategy proclaimed, are "to enhance security by maintaining a strong defense capability and promoting cooperative security measures; to open foreign markets and spur global economic growth; and to promote democracy abroad." These goals would be achieved by focusing on strengthening long-standing alliance relationships and other partnerships, maintaining a robust forward-based US military presence in the region, and encouraging the "constructive integration" of China into the international community.[26]

While the overall goals and means in Asia espoused by the US government did not formally change over the succeeding decades, US strategy began to shift in Asia in the 2000s in response to China's rise and more assertive policies, the growing North Korean threat, and the gradual economic integration of the region. Early post–Cold War problems in Asia centered on Taiwan and its moves toward democracy, as early as the 1996 presidential election, which was the first direct election of Taiwan's leader. Beijing feared the potential independence leanings of then president Lee Teng-hui, of the Kuomintang Party, as well as the granting of a US visa to visit his alma mater, Cornell University, and, in an attempt to intimidate both him and Taiwanese voters, fired ballistic missiles into the waters off the island nation in July and August 1995 and March 1996. In response, the Clinton administration sent two US aircraft carrier battle groups to the Taiwan Strait as a show of force. Beijing's naval buildup over the next two decades was designed to counter US strength in waters it increasingly considered its sphere of influence.[27] This modernization centered on what became known as the "anti-access, area-denial" (A2/AD) strategy, whereby the Chinese People's Liberation Army (PLA) began developing a set of capabilities to target qualitatively superior US forces in Asia's inner seas and the western Pacific Ocean. The new weapons systems included antiship ballistic missiles, attack submarines, stealth fighters, swarming missile boats, and the like.[28] During the same period, in 1994, the first North Korean nuclear crisis occurred, raising the specter of US military strikes on the Korean Peninsula and spurring diplomatic negotiations between the Clinton administration and the Kim regime that led to the so-called Agreed Framework to halt Pyongyang's nuclear development program in exchange for two light-water nuclear reactors.

Though the 9/11 terror attacks consumed the attention and energies of the Bush administration during the first decade of the twenty-first century, China's undeniable growth, the discovery of North Korean cheating on the Agreed Framework, and a breakthrough in US-India relations pushed Washington to begin focusing more on the Indo-Pacific region.[29] Much effort was spent on attempting to balance America's long-standing alliance commitments with the rising influence of China, seeking ever closer cooperation with Beijing so as to turn it into a willing partner in maintaining stability. Central to this strategy was the establishment of the "Strategic and Economic Dialogue" between the top officials in Washington and Beijing, an attempt that some compared the forging of a G-2 condominium to settle major global issues.[30] As for North Korea, the Bush administration initiated the Six-Party Talks mechanism as a multilateral diplomatic approach for solving the peninsula's nuclear crisis.

The 2008 financial crisis threw a wrench into Washington's plans, convincing Chinese leaders that their communist system was superior to America's dangerously out-of-control capitalist model. This led to growing hubris on the part of top Chinese Communist Party (CCP) officials, like then Chinese president Hu Jintao, and a belief that China would soon displace American power in Asia. By the end of Bush's second term, little progress had come of the G-2, and Pyongyang had claimed its first nuclear detonation. These two poles, China and North Korea, increasingly shaped US strategy in the region, challenging prior assumptions about Asia's peaceful rise and questioning the commitment Washington would have to make to maintain stability and promote prosperity in the Indo-Pacific.

It was not until the Obama administration that a new, overarching concept came to be articulated, the so-called pivot or rebalance to Asia. First rolled out by then secretary of state Hillary Clinton in an article titled "America's Pacific Century," the argument behind the pivot was repeated by President Barack Obama and a host of administration officials; they asserted that the United States would pursue a multipronged approach of military buildup, diplomatic engagement, and free-trade negotiation to shore up its position in Asia.[31] The pivot envisioned a renewed push for Sino-US cooperation, symbolized by the 2013 Sunnylands summit between Obama and new Chinese leader Xi Jinping. Yet by enhancing America's military presence in Asia, the pivot was interpreted by many, not least in China, as an attempt to contain a rising power.[32] Further, by publicly asserting that the United States had a "national interest" in seeing China and its neighbors peacefully resolve South China Sea territorial disputes, the Obama administration threatened to intervene in areas that Beijing considered to be core interests.[33]

China's response was not only to continue its rapid military modernization but to begin a massive land reclamation program in the contested Spratly Islands, creating islands out of submerged reefs and militarizing them with three-thousand-meter runways, defensive weaponry, radars, and porting facilities. China further continued its predatory cyberattacks on US businesses and was charged in the theft of the confidential personal information of over 22 million American citizens from the US Office of Personnel Management. Its repeated watering down and undermining of UN sanctions against North Korea, as well as its support for authoritarian regimes around the world, further strained ties with the United States.

As for North Korea, the Obama administration's policy of "strategic patience" resulted in largely eight years of neglect of the issue, with only one, quickly broken agreement (the so-called 2012 Leap Day

Agreement) to show for diplomatic engagement. Pyongyang doubled down on its nuclear and missile program development during Obama's years, conducting nuclear tests in 2009, 2013, and twice in 2016, while launching ballistic missiles on at least a dozen occasions. By the end of Obama's term, Pyongyang was deemed to have a nuclear arsenal of several dozen warheads and had largely perfected intercontinental ballistic missile technology, a capability it demonstrated in the early months of the succeeding Trump administration.

Other elements of Obama's pivot added to complications in relations with Beijing, making an increasingly aggressive Chinese leadership believe that America was seeking to contain China the way it had the Soviet Union. Underscoring the continuing importance of allies, Washington deepened its bilateral security alliance with Tokyo through a revision of the "guidelines" for mutual cooperation. With the return of conservative prime minister Shinzo Abe to office in late 2012, the Obama Asia team found in Japan a willing partner to begin countering Chinese influence in Asia. Japan, with a $50 billion annual defense budget and a highly trained, modernized military, was regarded by Beijing as the Asian nation most capable of opposing Chinese power. Abe moved to dilute or change legal restrictions on Japan's ability to participate in collective self-defense, sell defensive arms equipment abroad, and engage in defense industrial cooperation. Tokyo also increased its commitment to support US forces engaged in military operations in Northeast Asia and continued modernizing its forces, including purchasing up to 140 F-35 stealth fighters, making Japan the largest foreign buyer of the new jet. Abe's cabinet further approved plans to modify its two new helicopter carriers, the largest surface ships in its fleet, to carry new F-35B vertical takeoff and landing jet aircraft. These ships would be the country's first fixed-wing aircraft carriers since World War II, displacing 27,000 tons and giving the Japan Maritime Self-Defense Forces the ability to better protect Japan's far-flung territorial possessions and the potential of working more closely with US naval expeditionary forces throughout the region.[34]

Japan was not the only Asian country with which America attempted to deepen security relations in the light of China's military development. Washington enhanced its security cooperation with Southeast Asian nations, many of which have ongoing territorial disputes with China in the South China Sea. The Obama administration pursued closer ties with Singapore and Malaysia, and negotiated a breakthrough pact with the Philippines to allow US military forces access to bases on the archipelago; this last accomplishment, however, was derailed by the breakdown in relations between Washington and Manila after the electoral victory of Rodrigo Duterte, a populist politician who moved closer to China after criticism by the Obama administration for his supposed support of vigilantes in cracking down on the Philippines' drug trade. And while ties with India during the Obama years did not achieve the warmth of the Bush years, any overtures by Washington to New Delhi were eyed suspiciously by Beijing.

A final element of the Obama administration's pivot to Asia was the negotiating of the Trans-Pacific Partnership, a twelve-nation free-trade pact. Begun in 2005 by Brunei, Chile, New Zealand, and Singapore, the TPP eventually attracted Obama's attention, as well as Japan and America's NAFTA partners, Canada and Mexico. However, the Obama administration did not succeed in getting the pact ratified by the US Senate before its term ended, and the new US president, Donald Trump, withdrew from the agreement after criticizing it during the 2016 campaign (as did his opponent, Hillary Clinton). Despite the lack of implementation, the TPP presented China with the potential of a new free-trade area developing among largely market economies, with high standards for labor and environmental issues that would leave Beijing on the outside. China's response to TPP was to propose a massive new trade network, the One Belt One Road initiative, underpinned by $1 trillion in infrastructure spending across Eurasia and tying together land- and sea-based trading routes with China at the center.

By 2017 and the inauguration of Donald Trump, American strategy in Asia was being questioned as to its coherence, effectiveness, and resources. Despite the promises of the Obama-era pivot and a number of achievements, world opinion believed America was in retreat from Asia while China was ascendant.[35] Obama's rebalance was increasingly seen as mainly rhetoric, while Beijing was not deterred from militarizing the South China Sea, threatening Taiwan, or continuing its military buildup. Not only did Washington seem outmaneuvered in the South China Sea, but China's new economic initiatives seemed to promise more opportunity than the TPP, especially given US domestic opposition to the pact from both Democrats and Republicans. And while American policy makers would repeatedly argue that the United States was more engaged in Asia than ever before, the impression was of a country overpromising and underdelivering. Washington seemed without a clear strategy for maintaining its influence and countering the rise of China.

The Trump Era: Fundamental Change in Strategy or More of the Same?

Donald Trump ran for office promising to challenge the consensus on US foreign policy, not least in Asia, as part of his "America First" approach. He regularly attacked China on the campaign trail, asserting not only that lopsided bilateral trade practices contributed to a $350 billion trade deficit with China, but also that the decades of opening up American markets to Chinese goods had resulted in the hollowing out of American industries and the loss of millions of jobs. Further, Trump lambasted previous administrations' Korea policy, stating that he would meet with dictator Kim Jong-un and promising that he would prevent North Korea from getting a nuclear weapon that could hit the United States. Overturning decades of practice, Trump explicitly linked security to economic ties with China, arguing that if Beijing did not help solve the North Korean crisis, he would "make trade very difficult."

Surprising many in Washington and Asia, candidate Trump openly questioned the value of the US alliances with Japan and South Korea.

He claimed that both countries should be paying more to offset the costs of basing US forces in their countries and intimated he might consider walking away from the alliances if Tokyo and Seoul did not contribute more funds. Even more shockingly, he suggested that he might encourage both countries to develop their own nuclear capabilities in response to North Korea. This threatened to undermine the long-standing US nuclear guarantee of so-called extended deterrence, by which Washington promised to defend both Japan and South Korea from nuclear attack in exchange for both countries forgoing an indigenous nuclear deterrent.[36] Trump's surprising electoral victory, then, portended a potentially significant revision of US strategy in Asia, in part by reducing US commitments and confronting China. His unprecedented phone conversation with Taiwan's president, Tsai Ing-wen, during the transition period, further reinforced beliefs that he would not play by the traditional rules of diplomacy.

Once in office, however, the Trump administration adopted a more recognizable approach of reaffirming alliance relationships and engaging with China. Confounding critics who assumed he would pay little attention to the Indo-Pacific, Trump in reality made Asia a centerpiece of his foreign policy, stating that America's goal was a "free and open" Indo-Pacific region (indeed, the Trump administration formally changed the government-employed nomenclature to "Indo-Pacific"). He emphasized his personal relationships in early meetings with Japanese prime minister Shinzo Abe and Chinese president Xi Jinping, but Trump's diplomacy for the most part hewed to traditional discussions over deeper engagement. In addition, Trump attended the major gatherings of international and Pacific leaders and made repeated visits to the area, including the longest presidential trip to the region in decades.

If the Trump administration adopted a specific strategy for US Asia policy, it was to use US pressure to resolve seemingly intractable security and economic problems, while quietly retiring the concept of the overhyped "pivot" to Asia. In two specific ways, Trump departed from the policy of his predecessors. First, following outgoing president Barack Obama's warning that his greatest foreign policy challenge would be North Korea, Trump dramatically ratcheted up rhetoric against the rogue regime, warning that Pyongyang would face "fire and fury" if it threatened the United States or its allies with nuclear weapons. Trump increased military shows of force near the peninsula and sponsored a series of stronger UN sanctions to financially squeeze the Kim regime. This activity was capped by threats from the administration that it would preemptively strike North Korea, raining down "fire and fury" to degrade its nuclear and ballistic missile capability. Pyongyang's response through 2017 was to conduct another nuclear test and launch ballistic missiles on at least sixteen different occasions, including launching two over Hokkaido, Japan's main island, and theoretically achieving the capability of striking the US homeland.[37]

At the same time, Trump and his senior officials, including then secretary of defense James Mattis and then secretary of state Rex Tillerson, held open the possibility of another round of negotiations with Pyongyang. In a flurry of diplomatic activity in the spring of 2018, South Korean president Moon Jae-in announced that he would meet with Kim Jong-un, and Trump accepted an unprecedented offer for a summit with the North Korean dictator in Singapore in June 2018. Trump and his team credited their threatening rhetoric with bringing Kim to the negotiating table and quickly returned to the long-standing US goal of "complete, verifiable, and irreversible denuclearization" of the Korean Peninsula. Yet with little follow-through after that summit and a second one in Hanoi in February 2019, and amid reports that North Korea had restarted work on missile launching pads and nuclear facilities, it was clear that denuclearization of North Korea was as far away as it had been under prior administrations.

Of even greater significance, Trump adopted an approach toward China of alternating cooperative gestures with confrontational moves. The administration's first National Security Strategy, under the direction of then national security adviser H. R. McMaster and released in December 2017, laid to rest the idea that China would any longer be considered a unique partner of the United States, as pursued initially by the Obama administration. Rather, the document singled out

China's challenge to American "power, influence, and interests," arguing that the United States was engaged in a "geopolitical competition" with Beijing, one between "free and repressive visions of world order."[38] The document signaled that while Trump would pursue cooperation where possible with China, his administration would put China's aggressive security and predatory economic policies at the top of the agenda. The National Security Strategy was followed in mid-2019 by the Department of Defense's *Indo-Pacific Strategy Report*, the first such US document since the Clinton administration more than two decades previously.[39] Explicitly claiming that the Indo-Pacific is the Pentagon's "priority theater," the strategy report sharpened the idea that the United States and China are engaged in a long-term struggle for influence and power in the Indo-Pacific.

Following up on his campaign promises, Trump announced in early 2018 a series of new tariffs on Chinese steel, and demanded that the bilateral trade deficit be reduced by at least $100 billion. Though darkly warning of a trade war and imposing a retaliatory 10 percent tariff on $60 billion worth of US goods, Beijing nonetheless responded with various proposals for evening out the unbalanced trade between the two countries. Throughout 2018 and 2019 the two sides failed to reach agreement on market access for US firms and the reduction of trade barriers. This led Trump to levy 25 percent tariffs on $250 billion worth of Chinese goods and to announce 10 percent tariffs on a further $300 million worth.[40] By the summer of 2019, relations between Beijing and Washington had cooled significantly, with Chinese media and diplomatic officials blaming America for everything from China's economic slowdown to anti-Chinese demonstrations rocking Hong Kong.

The Fundamentals of US Strategy in the Indo-Pacific Region

Acknowledging Asia's new realities during the late-Obama and Trump eras started a process of reshaping US policy to achieve national goals, including a return to the fundamentals of US interests and strategy that held since the nineteenth century. Old and outdated assumptions about the geopolitical direction of the Indo-Pacific were discarded, and Washington was forced to reformulate American strategy, even as its overarching goals remained the same. The objectives of US strategy in the Indo-Pacific in the twenty-first century remain constant—namely, maintaining peace and stability, promoting democracy, and developing trade relations. These ambitious goals are becoming more difficult to achieve given the many problems noted above, as well as others that afflict Asian nations, including democratic backtracking, demographic pressures, corruption, political paralysis, environmental devastation, and the like.[41]

In particular, China's determination to dominate the skies and waters of the Indo-Pacific raises the question of the shape of future US strategy in the Indo-Pacific. Rising tensions in Asia, whether over disputed borders, historical issues, or rogue nations like North Korea, also draw the United States closer to the region. America's five formal treaty alliances and close relations with other nations remain the bedrock of its presence in the Indo-Pacific. These relations have endured because Washington has been willing to promise to spend American lives and treasure on the defense of its allies and to provide public goods such as protection of vital waterways.

The US security presence in Asia begins with the US Indo-Pacific Command (USINDOPACOM), headquartered on Oahu in Hawaii and composed of nearly 330,000 service members and civilian employees. The US Pacific Fleet comprises roughly 130,000 sailors and civilians; 200 ships, including five carrier strike groups; and 1,100 aircraft. Pacific Air Forces fields over 420 aircraft, including advanced F-22 fighters; while US Army Pacific has 106,000 personnel; and US Marine Corps Forces, Pacific, deploys 86,000 Marines and 640 aircraft.[42] Forward based throughout the region, particularly in Japan, Guam, and South Korea, these forces maintain a constant presence to defend US interests, allies, and regional stability. Added to this is US diplomatic representation in over thirty countries in the Indo-Pacific, as well as the aforementioned trade ties.

Any strategy for the Indo-Pacific must be comprehensive in nature, given American interests and commitments in the region. Strategy begins with appropriate means for achieving political ends. This means ensuring the robust nature of America's multifaceted institutional presence, both civilian and military. Reducing the US diplomatic or security presence undercuts attempts to play an engaged role that helps shape regional conditions.

The very size of the Indo-Pacific, with more than half of the world's population, along with its complexity, political diversity, and numerous problems, means that no one power can dominate the region, as seems possible in a smaller, territorially contiguous realm like Europe. But if absolute control is impossible, hegemony too is difficult, even for great powers in Asia. The traditional Asian great power, indeed even hegemon in early modern times, was of course China, with India playing a dominant role in its subregion. Utilizing political and economic power, ideology, and military power when necessary, Chinese dynasties from the Han (second century BCE–second century CE) onward sought to and often succeeded in structuring political relations and trade routes, propped up client states, and either battled or bought off barbarian tribes that threatened its borders.[43] By the mid-nineteenth century, however, attempts at reform had failed, European imperialism had sapped Chinese strength, and Chinese power had collapsed. In response, from the end of the 1800s through 1945, a newly modernized Japan attempted to build a colonial empire that would make it the dominant state in the Indian Ocean region and the South Pacific.[44]

Given this complex history, America's post–World War II strategy was comparatively ambitious. Washington's goal for the Indo-Pacific was reconstruction of battle-scarred countries, political and socioeconomic reform of Japan, and prevention of the rise of another dominant, aggressive power in the region.[45] The core of US strategy since 1941, it may fairly be said, is to block the emergence of any hostile hegemon in

Asia. Over time, promotion of democracy and expansion of trade networks were added to the core set of US goals.

America's current forward-based posture and alliance network in the Indo-Pacific is a legacy of its success in achieving that postwar goal. Yet it is also true that Washington did not face a significant challenger for dominance in Asia during the Cold War. This is not to say, of course, that there were no challenges at all to American policy and goals during those decades. Although a secondary theater for the Soviet Union, Asia saw a great deal of Soviet activity and attempted subversion of regional governments, but Moscow was never able to bring major power to bear in a way that could have defeated US forces or taken over significant amounts of territory. Similarly, China during the Cold War was internally focused, veering from consolidation after the Chinese Communist Party victory in 1949 to Mao's domestically destructive policies like the Great Leap Forward and the Cultural Revolution. India, too, during these decades hewed to a Nehruvian nonalignment policy and put much of its energies into leading the global nonaligned bloc. Japan, the region's erstwhile great power, poured its energies into domestic production and settled into a subordinate role as Washington's key Asian ally. Despite fighting brutal and domestically divisive wars in Korea and Vietnam, the United States was never forced to defend its position in Asia the way it was in Europe.

In other words, it is not misleading to conclude that for half a century after World War II, strategy in Asia was relatively easy for Washington. Not so today. In the case of China particularly, Washington confronts the difficulty of dealing with a "near-peer" competitor whose goals are increasingly antithetical to its own.

The Chinese challenge does not obviate seven decades of US strategy, but it mandates that policy be tailored to protect core American interests. Washington can neither surrender its alliances and interests nor undertake a chimerical attempt to freeze the Indo-Pacific in place. Overreach is a natural temptation in a region as large as the Indo-Pacific, as is the converse, a fatalism that engenders a timidity preventing the adoption of clear goals, the formation of a realistic strategy, and the will to attempt to implement it. Undersourcing American commitments and failing to articulate a clear and credible strategy—re-creating the Lippmann Gap between ends and means—would be particularly dangerous in an environment where China is regularly testing US resolve. Instead, US interests will be best served by occupying a middle ground of being committed to maintaining the vast gains made in stability and prosperity while recognizing limitations on American power.

Since 1945, America's primary interest has been to maintain a balance of power in the Pacific and prevent the rise of an aggressive hegemon that would threaten its freedom and peace. This should remain Washington's top priority. China has every right to operate in international waters and protect its own national interests, but not at the expense of regional stability. The United States cannot intervene in every dispute between Beijing and its neighbors, but China equally cannot be allowed to unilaterally set maritime or aerospace rules of conduct or alter national boundaries, whether through intimidation or force. Rather than containing China at every turn, constraining its assertive and aggressive behavior when necessary should be America's goal.

A strategy to ensure this outcome rests on a continued forward-based US naval and air presence in the region, so as to make credible our promises to ensure freedom of navigation and defend our allies if need be. Washington should focus on countering and preventing any attempts to restrict freedom of navigation or to intimidate states from fully exercising their right to peaceful passage and transit on the high seas. American freedom of navigation operations should continue to be conducted regularly, as the Trump administration has begun doing—if possible, with regional partners. Attention should be paid above all to the East and South China Seas, the eastern Indian Ocean, and the vital waterways of the Malacca, Sunda, Taiwan, and Tsushima Straits. Washington should make further efforts to form maritime communities of interest that develop common operating procedures and cooperate more closely, particularly in crucial waterways. Greater joint training, military exercises, and sharing of sensitive information can help forge more capable and confident Asian defense forces and intraregional relationships. There should be no rush to war for any but the gravest reasons, but China's salami-slicing tactics need to be met with greater resolve on the part of the United States and regional nations alike. Beijing may choose to try and force its preferred solutions on its neighbors, but it must understand the political, economic, and potentially even military costs of doing so.

More broadly, the US approach of incentivizing disruptive Chinese behavior by ignoring provocations needs to end. Beijing must be made to recognize that it can no longer take advantage of trading partners or materially harm other nations with impunity. Going forward, US strategy must impose reciprocity in bilateral relations in order to hold the line on China's attempts to undercut US influence, alter norms of conduct, and contravene the spirit of international agreements. As Beijing moderates its behavior, US pressure can ease and tension can abate. The Trump administration has begun to do this, by levying tariffs on Chinese goods, targeting Chinese espionage agents, as well as by increasing US military operations in the South China Sea. There must be a consistent approach, however, across future US administrations of seeking to work with Beijing while immediately responding to cyber espionage, aggression against US forces in international waters and skies, and the intimidation of US partners.

A potentially significant step toward strengthening US policy in the Indo-Pacific was taken with the Asia Reassurance Initiative Act of 2018 (ARIA), signed into law on December 31, 2018. The act is the most comprehensive statement of US interests in Asia in at least a generation, and complements the 2019 Department of Defense *Indo-Pacific Strategy Report*. It was no accident that President Trump signed the ARIA just one day before the fortieth anniversary of the normalization of US-China relations. The act, sponsored by Sens. Cory Gardner (R-CO) and Edward Markey (D-MA), gives support to the administration's belief that China is the greatest global threat to US interests. It authorizes over $7.5 billion through 2023 to enhance US alliance relations, increase arms sales, promote grassroots programs, develop trade, and upgrade ties with India and Taiwan, among other goals.

Much of this is aimed squarely at China, which is identified in the act as the primary threat to the liberal order that has allowed for Asia's peaceful development since 1945. Such funding represents a material commitment to Trump's call for a "free and open Indo-Pacific" far beyond what supported Barack Obama's pivot. Yet without a comprehensive strategy to maintain the balance of power in Asia, the billions of dollars will be ineffective in responding to China's security, economic, and cyber challenges.[46]

As for North Korea, a quarter century of US diplomacy has failed in its primary goal of preventing Pyongyang from developing a nuclear arsenal and the ballistic missile force to deliver it. Short of war or the deposition of the Kim family regime, there is little likelihood of North Korea fully denuclearizing, even if the US offered a complete withdrawal of forces from the peninsula. While Trump's gambit of trying to obtain denuclearization through a combination of threats, sanctions, and negotiations should be given time to work, the bulk of US strategy toward Pyongyang should shift to considering how to deter and contain a nuclear North Korea, as well as take advantage of any opportunities to weaken the Kim regime. This will have to include articulating clear and credible red lines beyond which American retaliation will occur. Sustaining our allies to the fullest extent possible and making further efforts to force Japan and South Korea to work more closely together, despite worsening relations over trade and history issues, should also be a priority.

The role of America's allies is indispensable to helping maintain a favorable balance of power in the region. Japan remains Washington's most steadfast ally, and continuing to deepen alliance cooperation, as well as provide defense materials, should be a priority. While relations with South Korea are being tested by Seoul's current outreach to Pyongyang, Washington's credibility throughout the region rests in no small part on its willingness to reaffirm its commitment to South Korea's defense. Until Seoul determines that it desires a different relationship with Washington, US promises should be kept, and all possible assistance should be given to South Korea to maintain a robust defense posture vis-à-vis the north. Similarly, Washington's support for Taiwan should remain steadfast. Many nations in the region carefully watch the strength of American ties with Taiwan as an indicator of how far Washington will go to help Asian nations resist Chinese pressure. While Taiwan is admittedly a special case, nonetheless to abandon its thriving democracy not only would deliver a blow to stability in the region by encouraging China but would undermine US credibility as a political partner.

Working with Japan and Australia, the United States should continue to develop closer relations with India and with nations in Southeast Asia, particularly those with liberal political systems or those leaning toward liberalism. Though formal alliances with such nations are unnecessary, the more a viable community of interests is formed, the more likely it is that Washington will find political and even security support for its efforts to maintain a free and open Indo-Pacific. Countries such as India and Vietnam can be valuable partners in expanding regional maritime cooperation, which in turn can lead to closer political ties.

No small part of American strategy in Asia should be a fair free-trade area. Though the Trump administration withdrew from the Trans-Pacific Partnership, it or its successors should either consider rejoining the successor TPP 11 or come up with some viable alternative that begins linking largely free-market economies in a closer trading network. Some movement along these lines was indicated by new US trade talks with Japan during Trump's first term. Such agreements, even if smaller in scope than the TPP, will help offset the inroads that Beijing is making with its One Belt One Road initiative and the creation of the Asian Infrastructure Investment Bank.

In promoting these policy ends, America will be protecting its own interests. These are under direct attack from a confident China that too often ignores its own problems, from a North Korea that seeks the means to threaten all around it, and from governments that are at risk of turning toward more authoritarian and confrontational policies. While supporting democracies and liberal ideas is not inherently controversial, Washington has too often failed to articulate the reasons behind such goals—namely, that all nations benefit from an open system that respects national sovereignty, upholds international law, peacefully resolves disputes, and seeks cooperation rather than confrontation. American strategy should not be to try and get states to surrender their own interests, but rather to create mechanisms, relationships, and patterns of behavior that attempt to harmonize transnational goals. Yet it is also clear that avoiding all risk only leads to a deterioration in security. Acting when necessary to maintain stability is thus the best way to avoid greater danger later on. A strategy guided by clear principles and prudently taking advantage of American strengths and partner self-interest is the surest route to keeping the world's most dynamic region open and pacific.

Notes

1. This is the argument of Tyler Dennett, *Americans in Eastern Asia: A Critical Study of United States' Policy in the Far East in the Nineteenth Century* (New York: MacMillan, 1922), especially for much of the nineteenth century, but the argument can be carried forward to the mid-twentieth century without much alteration.
2. US Pacific Command, established in 1947, was renamed US Indo-Pacific Command in May 2018. For use of the term Indo-Pacific as an organizing principle, see Michael R. Auslin, *The End of the Asian Century: War, Stagnation, and the Risks to the World's Most Dynamic Region* (New Haven, CT: Yale University Press, 2017).
3. Marcus Hand, "Malacca and S'pore Straits Traffic Hits New High in 2016, VLCCs Fastest Growing Segment," *Seatrade Maritime News*, February 13, 2017, http://www.seatrade-maritime.com/news/asia/malacca-and-s-pore-strait-traffic-hits-new-high-in-2016-vlccs-fastest-growing-segment.html.
4. Demographic figures are from the US Census Bureau, https://www.census.gov/quickfacts/fact/table/US/PST045216.
5. Trade figures are from the US Census Bureau, https://www.census.gov/foreign-trade/balance/c0016.html.

6. For a still valuable analysis, see George Sansom, *The Western World and Japan: A Study in the Interaction of European and Asiatic Cultures* (New York: Knopf, 1949); on the spice trade, see Charles Corn, *The Scents of Eden: A History of the Spice Trade* (New York: Kodansha, 1998). For an older study of the Pacific, see J. C. Beaglehole, *The Exploration of the Pacific*, 3rd ed. (London: Adam and Charles Black, 1966).

7. For general treatments of the American Pacific experience, see Tyler Dennett, *Americans in Eastern Asia: A Critical Study of United States' Policy in the Far East in the Nineteenth Century* (New York: MacMillan, 1922); Foster Rhea Dulles, *America in the Pacific: A Century of Expansion* (Boston: Houghton Mifflin, 1932); and Jean Heffer, *The United States and the Pacific: History of a Frontier*, trans. W. Donald Wilson (Notre Dame, IN: University of Notre Dame Press, 2002).

8. A brief account can be found in Frances Diane Robotti and James Vescovi, *The U.S.S. Essex and the Birth of the American Navy* (Avon, MA: Adams Media, 1999), 53–64.

9. For an account, see Irving Werstein, *The Cruise of the Essex: An Incident from the War of 1812* (Philadelphia: Macrae Smith, 1969).

10. John S. Rieske, ed., *Hunting the Essex: A Journal of HMS Phoebe 1813–1814 by Midshipman Allen Gardiner* (Barnsley: Seaforth, 2013).

11. The casualties of the *Nautilus* are commemorated on a plaque in the American Bar of the East India Club in London.

12. The best account of the Pacific Squadron is by Robert Erwin Johnson, *Thence Round Cape Horn: The Story of United States Naval Forces on Pacific Station, 1818–1923* (Annapolis, MD: United States Naval Institute, 1963). For the East India and Asiatic Squadron, see Robert Erwin Johnson, *Far China Station: The U.S. Navy in Asian Waters, 1800–1898* (Annapolis, MD: Naval Institute Press, 1979). The Asiatic Squadron became the Asiatic Fleet in 1902. In 1907, it and the Pacific Squadron were combined into the Pacific Fleet. See also Curtis T. Henson, Jr., *Commissioners and Commodores: The East India Squadron and American Diplomacy in China* (University: University of Alabama Press, 1982).

13. For a broader discussion of the international competition for the American West, see William H. Goetzmann, *Exploration and Empire: The Explorer and the Scientist in the Winning of the American West* (New York: History Book Club, 2006), esp. ch. 1, 170–80, ch. 7.

14. For an early discussion of the zone of cooperation, see Tyler Dennett, "Seward's Far Eastern Policy," *The American Historical Review*, vol. 28, no. 1 (October 1922), 45-62.

15. Dennett, *Americans in Eastern Asia*, chs. 32–33; a more recent treatment is Diana Preston, *The Boxer Rebellion: The Dramatic Story of China's War on Foreigners That Shook the World in the Summer of 1900* (New York: Berkley, 2000).

16. *Historical Statistics of the United States, 1789–1945* (Washington, DC: US Government Publishing Office, 1949).

17. On Seward's diplomacy, see Ernest N. Paolino, *The Foundations of American Empire: William Henry Seward and U.S. Foreign Policy* (Ithaca, NY: Cornell University Press, 1973), esp. chs. 1, 5, 6, and 7.

18. Edward S. Miller, *War Plan Orange: The US Strategy to Defeat Japan, 1897–1945* (Annapolis, MD: Naval Institute Press, 1991).

19. On the naval treaties and great power competition in this period, see William G. Beasley, *Japanese Imperialism, 1894–1945* (Oxford: Oxford University Press, 1987); and Akira Iriye, *After Imperialism: The Search for a New Order in the Far East, 1921–1931* (Cambridge, MA: Harvard University Press, 1965).

20. Walter Lippmann, *U.S. Foreign Policy: Shield of the Republic* (Boston: Little, Brown, 1943), 5.

21. Lippmann, *U.S. Foreign Policy*, 62.

22. Nicholas John Spykman, *America's Strategy in World Politics: The United States and the Balance of Power* (New York: Harcourt, Brace, 1942). See, for example, 6, 447, 457.

23. On the planning for postwar Japan, see Christopher D. O'Sullivan, *Sumner Welles, Postwar Planning, and the Quest for a New World Order, 1937–1943* (New York: Columbia University Press, 2008); Dayna Leigh Barnes, "Armchair Occupation: American Wartime Planning for Postwar Japan, 1937–1945," PhD diss., London School of Economics, 2013; and older treatments such as Michael Schaller, *The American Occupation of Japan* (New York: Oxford University Press, 1985), esp. chs. 2–4.

24. Among others, see Hal M. Friedman, "Modified Mahanism: Pearl Harbor, the Pacific War, and Changes to U.S. National Security Strategy for the Pacific Basin, 1945–1947," in *Hawaiian Journal of History* 31 (1997): 179–201; and Ji-Young Lee, "Contested American Hegemony and Regional

Order in Postwar Asia: The Case of the Southeast Asia Treaty Organization," *International Relations of the Asia-Pacific* (2017): 1–31.

25. Zoellick's speech can be found at https://www.ncuscr.org/sites/default /files/migration/Zoellick_remarks_notes06_winter_spring.pdf, accessed April 21, 2018.

26. US Department of Defense, "U.S. Security Strategy for the East Asia-Pacific Region," February 1995.

27. See Andrew Scobell, "Show of Force: The PLA and the 1995–1996 Taiwan Strait Crisis," paper presented to the Shorenstein Asia-Pacific Research Center, Stanford University, http://aparc.fsi.stanford.edu/sites/default /files/Scobell.pdf, accessed May 3, 2018.

28. For an overview, see Andrew Krepinevich, Barry Watts, and Robert Work, *Meeting the Anti-Access and Area-Denial Challenge* (Washington, DC: Center for Strategic and Budgetary Assessment, 2003), https://csba online.org/uploads/documents/2003.05.20-Anti-Access-Area-Denial -A2-AD.pdf, accessed May 3, 2018.

29. Nina Silove, "The Pivot before the Pivot," *International Security* 40, no. 4 (Spring 2016): 45–88.

30. See, for example, Richard C. Bush, "The United States and China: A G-2 in the Making?," Brookings, October 11, 2011, https://www.brookings .edu/articles/the-united-states-and-china-a-g-2-in-the-making.

31. Hillary Clinton, "America's Pacific Century," *Foreign Policy*, October 11, 2011.

32. See, for example, Joseph S. Nye, Jr., "Work with China, Don't Contain It," *New York Times*, January 25, 2013.

33. See the statement by Hillary Clinton on July 22, 2011, https://2009-2017 .state.gov/secretary/20092013clinton/rm/2011/07/168989.htm.

34. The 2018 National Defense Program Guidelines can be accessed at http://www.mod.go.jp/j/approach/agenda/guideline/2019/pdf/2018 1218.pdf.

35. Full survey findings can be found at http://www.pewresearch.org/fact -tank/2018/10/19/5-charts-on-global-views-of-china.

36. A recap of Trump's campaign positions can be found at Council on Foreign Relations, "Transition 2017," https://www.cfr.org/interactives /campaign2016/donald-trump/on-north-korea, accessed May 4, 2018.

37. An overview and timeline can be found at Missile Threat: CSIS Missile Defense Project, https://missilethreat.csis.org/country/dprk; a simpler timeline for 2017 can be found in Joshua Berlinger, "North Korea's Missile Tests: What You Need to Know," *CNN*, December 3, 2017, https://www.cnn.com/2017/05/29/asia/north-korea-missile-tests/index.html.

38. The National Security Strategy can be found at https://www.whitehouse.gov/wp-content/uploads/2017/12/NSS-Final-12-18-2017-0905.pdf.

39. Department of Defense, *Indo-Pacific Strategy Report*, June 1, 2019, https://media.defense.gov/2019/Jul/01/2002152311/-1/-1/1/DEPARTMENT-OF-DEFENSE-INDO-PACIFIC-STRATEGY-REPORT-2019.PDF.

40. Alan Rappeport, "Trump Says US Will Hit China with More Tariffs," *New York Times*, August 1, 2019, https://www.nytimes.com/2019/08/01/us/politics/china-trade-trump.html.

41. For a discussion of problems in Asia, see Auslin, *The End of the Asian Century.*

42. "About USINDOPACOM," U.S. Indo-Pacific Command, https://www.pacom.mil/About-USINDOPACOM.

43. The literature on Chinese foreign policy is vast. For some recent works, see, for example, Feng Zhang, *Chinese Hegemony: Grand Strategy and International Institutions in East Asian History* (Stanford, CA: Stanford University Press, 2015); and Ji-Young Lee, *China's Hegemony: Four Hundred Years of East Asian Domination* (New York: Columbia University Press, 2016).

44. See William G. Beasley, *Japanese Imperialism, 1894–1945*, rev. ed. (Oxford: Clarendon Press, 1991).

45. See Michael Schaller, *The American Occupation of Japan: The Origins of the Cold War in Asia* (Oxford: Oxford University Press, 1987); Dayna Barnes, "Think Tanks and a New Order in Asia," *Journal of American-East Asian Relations* 22 (2015): 89–119.

46. The full text of the Asia Reassurance Initiative Act of 2018 can be found at https://www.congress.gov/115/bills/s2736/BILLS-115s2736enr.xml.

8

THE SINO-AMERICAN LITTORAL WAR OF 2025

A Future History

More than two decades after the fact, the reasons why the United States and the People's Republic of China (PRC) avoided total war, let alone a nuclear exchange, during their armed conflict in the autumn of 2025 remain a source of dispute. What is clearer is why the Sino-American Littoral War broke out in the first place and the course it took. The result—the establishment of three geopolitical blocs in East Asia—continues to this day. The United States retained a rump alliance system, but the losses of Taiwan and the US alliance with South Korea were seen as major strategic defeats for Washington, leading to a tacit US withdrawal from the western Pacific. On the other hand, though seemingly victorious in the war, China's subsequent domination over a resentful bloc of allies and its broader diplomatic isolation narrowed the range of foreign policy initiatives that Beijing's military superiority should have made possible. The resulting cold war between the United States and China became the defining feature of geopolitics in the Asia-Pacific in the middle of the twenty-first century.

This essay was originally written for David Berkey, ed., *Disruptive Strategies: The Military Campaigns of Ascendant Powers and Their Rivals* (Stanford, CA: Hoover Institution Press, 2020).

To understand what happened and why, any history must start with the political environment between Washington and Beijing in the years leading up to the war, as well as look at the military assets each possessed and assess the balance of power in the western Pacific at the outset of hostilities. Only then will analysts be able to interpret the political and military decisions taken by both sides.

I. The Political Background

The influence of existing political relations on subsequent policy decisions is often downplayed by historians attempting to assert that rational actors had clearly articulated reasons for choosing a path that led to armed conflict. Yet the decade before the outbreak of war between China and America witnessed a steady erosion in Sino-US relations that poisoned the various links built up between the two nations since the 1970s and made crisis management increasingly difficult. The Cold War paradigm established by Richard Nixon and Jimmy Carter, where the United States sought to play the PRC and Soviet Union off each other, had evolved during the Reagan administration into a more transactional approach that sought to develop Sino-US relations for their own sake while attempting to get Beijing's support for US policies that pressured Moscow, such as in Afghanistan and Cambodia.

With the end of the Cold War, American policy makers turned to constructing a new great-power relationship with China, despite growing strains between the two countries. Though the George H. W. Bush administration largely downplayed the regime's Tiananmen Square massacre of prodemocracy student demonstrators in June 1989, the Clinton administration sent two aircraft carriers to the Taiwan Strait in March 1996 after Beijing fired ballistic missiles off the island during Taiwan's first presidential campaign.[1] Yet under administrations of both political parties, Washington steadily attempted to integrate China into what liberal internationalists called the "rules-based international order." Thus, the Clinton and George W. Bush administrations midwifed the PRC's entrance into the World Trade Organization, and successive US leaders ignored growing evidence of China's industrial and cyber espionage of both US government and private American business secrets. The 1999 Cox Commission Report detailed how Chinese agents stole some of America's most sensitive nuclear and ballistic missile technology, and a later report by Mandiant Corporation, in February 2013, revealed years of cyber espionage against a variety of US targets.[2]

However, it was during the Barack Obama administration that the real seeds of the 2025 Littoral War were laid. Building off the Bush administration's elevation of high-level bilateral talks into the "Strategic and Economic Dialogue," the Obama administration energetically engaged the Chinese government. Ostensibly pushing back against Beijing's rampant cyber espionage, Obama and new Chinese leader Xi Jinping agreed at the 2013 Sunnylands Summit that China would rein in its official and quasi-official hackers.[3] Like his predecessors, Obama traveled to China, though his 2016 visit revealed strains in bilateral ties when he was subjected to protocol insults on his arrival at the airport and hotel.[4]

Petty jockeying aside, however, serious challenges to Asian regional stability emerged during Obama's two terms. Most egregious was Beijing's decision to build and fortify islands in disputed maritime territory in the South China Sea. Ownership of various coral reefs and shoals in the Spratly and Paracel island chains had long been contested between China and a host of Southeast Asian countries. Many had built modest defensive installations on some of their possessions, yet Beijing claimed that then secretary of state Hillary Clinton's comments at a regional security meeting in 2010 demonstrated US antagonism toward China's rightful claims.[5] Clinton had stated that the Obama administration considered the peaceful multilateral resolution of competing territorial claims to be in the United States' national interest. Clinton's statements were combined with articulation of a "rebalance" or "pivot" to Asia, an assertion by Obama officials that the Asia-Pacific was the key geopolitical focus for America. To buttress the pivot, in addition to a new multilateral free-trade agreement, the Trans-Pacific Partnership (TPP), the Pentagon announced increased troop deployments to the Asia-Pacific and the shifting of US Navy assets to the region to account for fully 60 percent of all US naval strength.[6]

In response, Beijing claimed the entire South China Sea as its territorial waters and a "core national interest."[7] Reports and eventually video trickled out of People's Liberation Army (PLA) Navy ships harassing US Navy ships operating in the South China Sea on various occasions, raising memories of the March 2001 collision between a US Navy surveillance plane and a Chinese fighter jet, caused by the reckless flying on the part of the Chinese pilot, who died in the incident.[8]

When Washington failed to support Manila during the Scarborough Shoal crisis of mid-2012, allowing China to take effective control of the shoal, Beijing felt assured that US commitments to support allies in the South China Sea were hollow. New Chinese leader Xi Jinping added more concrete action to rhetoric, staging seemingly uncoordinated encounters once he came to power in late 2012. Starting around 2013, despite the Obama administration's continuing high-level bilateral meetings, the PRC began a major land-reclamation campaign in the Spratlys and then proceeded to militarize its new possessions, as well as some older ones in the Paracels.[9] The Chinese military built three Pearl Harbor–size port facilities, laid runways capable of handling fighter jets and bombers, installed radar and antiship and antiaircraft weapons, and built barracks and storage facilities, among other actions. The emplacement of airfields and weaponry on its claimed possessions gave Beijing the ability to effectively control the heart of the South China Sea, through which as much as 70 percent of global trade passed, and to project power throughout the region. It also launched its first aircraft carrier and conducted military exercises hundreds of miles from its recognized territorial waters, near the strategic waterways of Southeast Asian nations. PLA Navy (PLAN) ships regularly transited into the Indian Ocean and through strategic straits near Japan into the western Pacific Ocean.

The Obama administration's response to these Chinese moves was muddled and hesitant. It initially downplayed the island-building campaign, then condemned it, belatedly demanding that Beijing cease its actions, in response to which Chinese officials darkly warned of war should the United States not stop its pressure campaign. Washington also failed to take advantage of international law in its response to Beijing, even after The Hague's Permanent Court of Arbitration ruled in July 2016 against Chinese claims in a case brought by the Philippines.[10] Declaring that Beijing could not assert ownership over low-elevation landforms, even if they had been built up, and that it had no standing for its historical claims in the South China Sea, The Hague's court should have been a deterrent to China's course. Beijing, however, simply ignored the court's ruling, and the Obama administration did nothing to rally regional pressure on China.

Most noticeably, Obama hesitated to conduct military operations in the contested area, which would have sent clear signals to Beijing that the United States would not meekly surrender the area to China. It took the administration months to decide on freedom of navigation operations (FONOPS) that would come within twelve nautical miles of China's new islands, the territorial limit for legitimate possessions. Only four FONOPS were conducted during Obama's last two years in office, and the US Navy muddied the waters by claiming that it was conducting "innocent passage," which is a different category of transit under international law.[11] Chinese ships and aircraft did not actively interfere with American forces during these operations but instead shadowed them, issuing repeated warnings to leave the area. The end result of Obama's approach was to make the United States appear irresolute and confused about how to blunt China's advances. It further raised doubts in the minds of Asian allies, especially the Philippines, about whether Washington would live up to its treaty commitments.

Donald Trump became president having taken perhaps the hardest line of any presidential candidate toward China. Rejecting prior presidential approaches, Trump explicitly linked trade and security issues, promising to end China's unfair trading practices and warning that he would challenge Beijing in the South China Sea. After his first few months in office, when it appeared that he would revert to a more traditional posture toward China, Trump levied major tariffs against Chinese goods, ultimately encompassing $550 billion, or nearly all of China's exports to the United States. At the same time, he increased military spending and authorized more FONOPS and aerial overflights in the South China Sea, ultimately increasing them to approximately one every three weeks by the beginning of 2025. Trump's approach was codified in the December 2017 National Security Strategy, which labeled China a "revisionist power" seeking to "displace the United States in the Indo-Pacific region . . . and reorder the region in its favor."[12] Openly acknowledging the strategic competition with China, the Trump administration targeted Chinese technology companies, mused about restricting the numbers of Chinese students in American universities, and sought a decoupling of the two countries' intertwined economies.

Through these years, tensions between Washington and Beijing rose dramatically, and multiple unsafe encounters occurred between the forces of the two nations, always instigated by PLAN ships or Air Force planes. Xi Jinping, who was chairman of the Central Military Commission in addition to being general secretary of the Chinese Communist Party (CCP) and president, had told his military as far back as 2018 to "prepare for war," and his exhortations against American interference in China's "rightful" sphere of interest increased over the succeeding years, leading to risk-taking actions on the part of Chinese sailors and pilots.[13] While high-level bilateral diplomatic meetings continued to take place, they resulted in no solutions to the festering problems, and both sides recognized that such gatherings were increasingly for show. Beijing attempted to use Chinese students studying in US universities to whip up pro-Chinese sentiment on campuses and in major US cities, but the efforts backfired after a few student ringleaders revealed the Chinese government's organizing role. While the vast majority of Chinese Americans supported Washington, some activists, likely plants from China, vocally urged concessions to Beijing, using social media to spread their message. Meanwhile, US allies in Asia sought to prevent an outright breach between the two giant nations, but at the same time saw advantages in having both Beijing and Washington attempt to curry favor with them, whether through lessening demands on them, offering trade blandishments, or elevating diplomatic exchanges.

All this took its inevitable toll on the publics of both nations. At the 20th National Party Congress of the Chinese Communist Party, in November 2022, Xi stayed on as paramount leader, which was widely expected, and inserted a plank seen as a preemptive declaration that China would seek hegemony over the South China Sea by 2049. Public opinion polls taken in 2024 showed that the number of respondents in China and the United States having a positive opinion of the other country had dropped to single digits and that each considered the other its number one potential adversary. In short, the political relationship between the United States and China had deteriorated to such a degree by 2025 that relations seemed nearly unsalvageable.

II. The Antebellum Military Balance

As relations worsened, military planners in both countries stepped up their contingency and operational planning. While few professional military officers believed they would face the other side in actual combat, their responsibility lay in ensuring that their political leaders had the most complete set of military options available and that their forces were trained and equipped for potential conflict.

The subsequent events of the war depended in large part on the military balance that held between the two at the outbreak of hostilities. For the United States, it was the first time it had conducted large-scale military operations in Asia in a half century, since the end of the Vietnam War. For the PRC, its last full-scale conflicts had been the 1962 Sino-Indian War and the shorter but intense 1979 border war with Vietnam. Yet despite rhetoric about becoming a global power, Beijing had focused its military development on being able to conduct regional operations and control both sea and sky space for extended periods of time, within the so-called first and second island chains, encompassing the Yellow, East China, and South China Seas.[14] This allowed a concentration of forces at strategic points in the regional theater, generated from continental bases and on Hainan Island in the South China Sea, and with access to Chinese bases in both the Spratly and Paracel island chains in the same sea.

Chinese doctrine had steadily moved toward a more prominent role for naval, air, rocket, and strategic forces. The PLAN had increased its number of surface and subsurface vessels and fielded two aircraft carriers (but only one fully outfitted for naval operations), twenty-six destroyers equipped with Aegis-like antiair systems or advanced radar arrays, and thirty smaller ships, along with fifty attack submarines, almost all conventionally powered.[15] The combined PLAN Air Force (PLANAF) and PLA Air Force (PLAAF) boasted over one hundred J-31 and J-20 advanced fighters with stealth features, in addition to six hundred fourth-generation fighters, primarily J-10, J-11, and J-15 carrier variants.[16] China's first, understrength squadron of H-20 long-range stealth bombers also entered service in 2025, putting at risk American bases in Guam and as far as Hawaii. Beijing also deployed over one thousand short-range ballistic missiles with ranges up to 1,000 kilometers, and two hundred fifty medium-range missiles that could reach targets 3,000 kilometers away. Central to its missile force was the DF-21D antiship ballistic missile, which boasted a range of 1,500 kilometers and included maneuverable reentry vehicle warheads that could autonomously track targets, and the intermediate-range DF-26, with a range of 3,000 to 5,400 kilometers.[17]

With the world's largest defense budget and decades of forward deployment throughout the world, the US military appeared to have the edge over any potential competitor. Though on paper it seemed to have no peer, its force was aging, and it had not yet recapitalized some of its major systems. As an expeditionary force, the US military appeared postured to respond quickly to any conflict, but as would be shown, it lacked the depth to maintain a long campaign. The US Pacific Fleet provided the main naval presence in the region, composed of the US Third and Seventh Fleets. With the USS *Gerald R. Ford*, the US Navy's newest aircraft carrier, homeported in Yokosuka, Japan, the US Seventh Fleet had twenty-two ships in Asian waters—including two cruisers, eight guided-missile destroyers (DDGs), four nuclear-powered attack submarines, and an amphibious assault ship—with another forty available based in Hawaii and the Pacific Coast of the United States.[18] Third Fleet forces, drawn from California, Washington, and Hawaii, provided the potential of another two active carriers, with one hundred forty airplanes and ten more submarines.[19] The continental-based US naval forces faced a two-week transit to Japan and three weeks to the Strait of Malacca, while those in Hawaii were a week away from US bases in Japan. Added to the naval forces were the airplanes of the Pacific Air Forces, based at Anderson Air Force Base in Guam and Kadena, Yokota, and Misawa air bases in Japan (the South Korea–based air force squadrons remained detailed for peninsular defense). These roughly three hundred aircraft included two squadrons of F-35s and F-22s, with the remainder being older F-15s and F-16s.[20]

III. The Gray Rhino: September 8–9, 2025

The Littoral War began with a series of accidental encounters in the skies and waters near Scarborough Shoal, in the South China Sea.[21] (See figure 3 for a map of the theater of operations.) Beijing had effectively taken control of the shoal, long a point of contention between China and the Philippines, in 2012.[22] After Philippines president Rodrigo Duterte, who had steadily moved Manila toward China during the late 2010s, was impeached and removed from office, the Philippines' new president moved to reassert Manila's claim to the shoal, including sending coastal patrol boats into waters near the contested territory during the summer of 2025. When armed People's Armed Forces Maritime Militia (PAFMM)

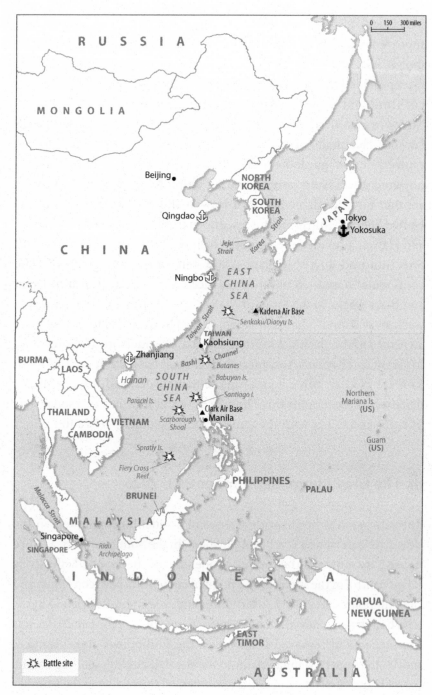

Figure 3. Theater of Operations, Sino-US Littoral War of 2025

vessels pushed out the Filipino forces in early July, Manila appealed to Washington under its security treaty for assistance.[23]

Prior Philippine requests for US help in dealing with China had been largely shunted aside by Washington, even during the Trump administration. However, new US president Gavin Newsom, who had been dogged during the 2024 campaign by allegations that Chinese cyber operations had benefited his candidacy, saw the Philippine request as an opportunity to show his willingness to take a hard line against Beijing. Newsom increased US Air Force flights over the contested territory, using air bases made available by Manila, and sent the *Gerald Ford*, along with escort vessels, on a short transit. On two occasions in late July, US and Chinese ships came close to running into each other due to aggressive PLAN maneuvering, and a US Navy FA-18 operating from the *Gerald Ford* was forced to take emergency evasive action to avoid colliding with a PLANAF J-15.[24] Despite the increasing tensions, the US Navy ships returned to Japan at the beginning of August, yet no diplomatic attempts were made to alter the trajectory of events. The fact that both sides knew some type of armed encounter was increasingly possible, if not probable, yet seemed to ignore the risk, led pundits to call the events surrounding the clash an example of a "gray rhino," unlike the complete surprise represented by a "black swan" occurrence. Ironically, Xi Jinping himself had warned about the dangers of "gray rhinos" back in 2018 and 2019.[25]

In response to the brief uptick in US Navy FONOPS near other Chinese-claimed territory in the Spratly and Paracel island chains, Beijing decided to fortify Scarborough Shoal, building airstrips and naval facilities as it had done in the Spratlys. As Scarborough lay only 140 miles from Manila, China's announcement set off alarm bells in the Philippines.[26] As Chinese naval construction ships approached Scarborough on September 4, dozens of small Philippine boats, many of them private, attempted to block them. On the second day of the maritime encounter, a Chinese frigate rammed a Philippine fishing boat, sinking it, with the loss of two seamen.[27] As news spread over the next several days, dozens more Philippine vessels, including the country's entire coast guard, confronted the Chinese. Though no further ship collisions occurred, worldwide broadcast of video of the maritime confrontation further inflamed tensions.

At this point, on Saturday, September 6, US Indo-Pacific Command, acting directly under orders from US secretary of defense Michele Flournoy, dispatched one guided missile destroyer, the USS *Curtis Wilbur*, and the *Independence*-class littoral combat ship the USS *Charleston* (LCS-18) to the waters off Scarborough, and ordered the USS *John C. Stennis* aircraft carrier to head from its home port in Bremerton, Washington, to Pearl Harbor.[28] In order not to inflame the high tensions, however, the White House and Pentagon decided not to send its Japan-based aircraft carrier, the USS *Gerald Ford*, to the area. Instead, another US guided-missile destroyer, USS *Stethem* (DDG 63), and a mine countermeasures ship, the USS *Patriot* (MCM 7), were ordered to transit the Taiwan Strait. The next day, Beijing announced an air defense identification zone over the entire South China Sea, demanding that all non-Chinese aircraft submit their flight plans to Chinese military authorities and receive clearance to proceed.[29] While the US Air Force and Navy immediately rejected China's authority over the South China Sea, PLAAF and PLANAF aerial patrols increased, and international civilian airliners complied with Beijing's demands.

On Monday, September 8, at approximately 18:30 local time (10:30 Greenwich time; 00:30 Hawaii time; 05:30 eastern time), a US Navy EP-3 surveillance flight out of Japan over the Spratlys was intercepted by a PLAAF J-20 taking off from Fiery Cross Reef, in the same chain. After warning off the EP-3, the J-20 attempted a barrel roll over the American plane. The Chinese pilot sheared off most of the EP-3's tail and left rear stabilizer; the Chinese plane lost a wing and went into an unrecoverable spin into the sea. The EP-3 also could not recover and plunged into the sea, killing all twenty-two Americans aboard.[30] Tragically, the EP-3 was not even supposed to be flying, as the US Navy had intended to replace the fleet with unmanned surveillance drones by 2020, but cost overruns and delays in the drone program led to occasional use of a limited number of aging manned aircraft in the region, especially when real-time interpretation of data was required.[31]

Roughly thirty minutes later, before word of the EP-3's downing had reached US Indo-Pacific Command in Hawaii, let alone Washington or Beijing, 13 nm northwest of Scarborough Shoal, the *Bertholf* (WMSL-750), a US Coast Guard cutter returning from a training mission along with the Japan Coast Guard *Kunigami*-class patrol vessel *Motobu*, out of Naha in Okinawa, was approached by a cutter-class armed Chinese Coast Guard (CCG) ship. After broadcasting warnings for the *Bertholf* and the *Motobu* to leave the area, the Chinese ship attempted to maneuver in front of the American ship, to turn its bow.[32] The CCG captain miscalculated and struck the *Bertholf* amidships, caving in the mess and one of its enlisted crew compartments. The *Bertholf* began taking on water and attempted to turn east toward the Philippines while emergency crews attempted to keep the ship afloat. The CCG ship immediately left the scene without rendering assistance. Six US sailors later were declared missing and presumed dead in the collision, while three Chinese CCG sailors were swept overboard and lost at sea.

Being the closest US naval vessel to the downed EP-3, the *Curtis Wilbur* raced toward the site of its crash, while the *Charleston* moved to assist the *Bertholf*. Nighttime darkness caused confusion for rescue and patrol operations on both sides. Two PLAN ships returned to the scene of the maritime collision to search for the lost Chinese seamen, coming in close quarters with the *Motobu*—which was helping in rescue operations to stabilize the American vessel—as well as with the littoral combat ship *Charleston*, which arrived several hours later. Mechanical trouble kept the *Bertholf* from making way under her own power, and she began to drift back toward PLAN vessels. In the darkness, US ships and the Japanese attempted to disengage with the Chinese vessels, while continually warning the other side to stand down so rescue operations could continue.

After several close encounters, one Type 052D Luyang III class PLAN destroyer, the *Taiyuan*, activated its fire-control radar and locked on the *Motobu*.[33] The captain of the thousand-ton Japanese patrol ship, knowing he could not survive a direct hit from the PLAN destroyer, radioed repeated demands that the radar be turned off. When no Chinese response was forthcoming, and with rescue operations ongoing, the *Motobu*'s commander fired one round from his Bushmaster II 30 mm chain gun across the bow of the *Taiyuan*. In response, a nearby Chinese frigate, thinking it was under attack from the Japanese Coast Guard ship, fired a torpedo in the direction of the *Motobu*. In the congested seas, however, the torpedo hit the *Charleston*, which was transiting between the Chinese and Japanese ships, ripping a hole below the waterline. The lightly armored littoral combat ship, with a complement of fifty officers and seamen, foundered in just twenty-five minutes, with an unknown loss of life, at 01:30 (17:30 Greenwich time; 07:30 Hawaii time; 10:30 eastern time) on Tuesday, September 9.[34] US surveillance drones flying over the melee recorded parts of the encounter and flashed images back to US commanders in the region.

IV. The Choice for War: September 9–23, 2025

When word of the aerial and maritime encounters began filtering in to the USS *Blue Ridge*, flagship of the US Navy's Seventh Fleet, and US Pacific Fleet headquarters in Hawaii, rescue operations were immediately ordered. As the late-night and early-morning melee developed, US commanders watched in near real time as the *Charleston* sank. Within ten minutes, the *Curtis Wilbur* was ordered to leave the site of the downed EP-3 and instead move to pick up all US survivors from the two lost ships. Within twenty minutes, the four-star admiral in command of US Indo-Pacific Command had directed the commander of the US Pacific Fleet to order the *Gerald Ford* to steam to the location, provide rescue operations, and protect all US and allied ships in the South China Sea area. Over the previous decade, as Chinese naval and missile capabilities increased, it became a working assumption that US carriers would be kept out of the "kill zone" of Chinese missiles and submarines in the case of any hostilities. However, with the loss of American lives, the White House ordered the Pentagon to send the *Gerald Ford* as a message to Beijing. This tactical decision would have strategic consequences in the coming weeks. It would take two days to get underway and seven days total for the *Gerald Ford* to reach the scene; in the meantime, only one US ship, the *Curtis Wilbur*, was in the waters of the accident, as the USS *Wasp*, an amphibious assault ship that carried ten US Marine Corps F-35s, was paying a port visit to Chennai, India, for a series of scheduled naval exercises with the Indian Navy.

US forces needed air protection, but with the *Gerald Ford* days away, the commander of US Indo-Pacific Command ordered US Pacific Air Forces to scramble four F-35As to the South China Sea from Kadena Air Force Base in Okinawa, a distance of approximately 920 nm (the F-22 Raptor's combat radius of 490 nm was deemed insufficient for the mission). The F-35s would then be deployed to Clark Air Base in the Philippines, to allow for longer-duration operations in the area. With a combat radius of 669 nm, the F-35 required refueling, and the mission was delayed until KC-46A tankers reached approximately half-way stationing points northwest of Luzon Island in the Philippines. After reaching the patrol station in the early afternoon of September 9, the F-35s encountered two PLAAF J-20 fighters launched from Fiery Cross Reef.[35] The Chinese radioed for backup, and two more J-20s soon arrived. After ten minutes of shadowing each other with repeated calls from each side for the other to withdraw, one of the Chinese jets attempted another close encounter head on, clipping the wing of one F-35. Both pilots were forced to eject, and almost simultaneously, a second J-20 launched an air-to-air missile at one of the remaining F-35s. At this point, the American pilots, who had received permission to defend themselves if fired upon, targeted and destroyed the three remaining J-20s, but not before one J-20 destroyed another F-35, with the loss of the American pilot. When the Chinese learned about the aerial encounter, the PLA chief of staff recommended missile attacks on US air bases in Okinawa; this, however, was vetoed by Xi Jinping, in his role as chairman of the Central Military Commission (CMC). While American war planners did not know of Xi's decision, they anticipated the horizontal escalation of hostilities to US bases in the region and were surprised at the lack of enemy action against them.[36] For many Chinese postconflict commentators, Xi's decision not to attack Japan in the earliest stages of the conflict was a strategic error that prevented complete victory.

At this point, as intelligence about the aerial dogfight streamed into the US Pacific Fleet's Maritime Operations Center, the PacFleet commander sent orders to the US Seventh Fleet commander for the *Curtis Wilbur* to defend the *Bertholf* and disable any Chinese ship that interfered with ongoing rescue and repair operations. Similar orders went out to Pacific Air Forces to maintain steady air cover and intercept any Chinese fighter jets from entering a twenty-mile radius of the accident site. At the same time, he issued orders for all mission-ready Seventh Fleet combat forces to steam from Yokosuka, Japan, at full speed toward the Spratlys. This consisted of one cruiser, the USS *Antietam*, and three *Arleigh Burke*–class destroyers, making roughly twenty knots; in addition, a nearby nuclear-powered attack submarine was diverted to lurk in the waters near Scarborough Shoal. However, given that the additional US forces would not reach the Spratlys for close to a week, while the *Wasp* began the trip back from India, US firepower was limited to the *Curtis Wilbur*, with the ship taking up a visible position near Scarborough Shoal and the site of the clashes. To intimidate the Chinese, B-52s based in Guam commenced regular overflights of Chinese bases in the Spratlys on Wednesday, September 10.[37]

The American response was designed to sanitize the immediate area of the clash, but not to widen the theater of operations or prevent Chinese ships and planes from transiting the South China Sea, except for the area where the Americans were concentrating on rescue operations. This "minimum deterrence" approach made political sense but ultimately created opportunities for Beijing to take military advantage of US hesitancy.[38] President Newsom had been informed within minutes of the sinking of the *Charleston* and, eager to dispel lingering rumors that he was beholden to China for his electoral victory, confirmed the operational plans of Indo-Pacific Command issued on September 9, while approving further deployments of a second aircraft carrier, the *John C. Stennis*, and three more destroyers from Hawaii to the South China Sea, along with three nuclear attack submarines (SSNs), including the USS *Illinois*, from Submarine Group 7 in Guam to positions off the Strait of Malacca, the Paracel Islands, and Hainan Island. After making this decision, President Newsom went on national television to brief the nation, promising that he would protect American interests and never back down from America's role in the Pacific.

The Failure of Diplomacy

An urgent phone call between President Newsom and Chairman Xi that evening did little to stabilize the situation, and on the evening of September 10, Beijing time, a doctored video of the ramming of the *Bertholf* was spread in China that made it look like the Americans were to blame for the accident. Chinese internet censors allowed the clip to become a viral sensation, and stage-managed crowds soon thronged the gates of the American and Japanese embassies, shouting slogans denouncing the United States and Japan, throwing stones and trash onto the grounds, and demanding compensation from Washington and Tokyo.[39] Xi took to the airwaves to chastise the Americans, but also to try to rise above the fray, announcing that China would not further deepen the crisis. This tactic backfired, and crowds began moving toward Tiananmen Square, demanding that China push America out of Asia, while the internet lit up with criticism of Xi that questioned his mental state. Chinese overseas students and provocateurs under guidance from the CCP's United Front Work Department propaganda unit began coordinated protests in Sydney, Seoul, London, Paris, Toronto, and Vancouver, while small groups of Chinese students at US universities, including Harvard, Columbia, UC Berkeley, and UCLA, staged demonstrations that garnered widespread media coverage.[40]

At an emergency meeting of the Chinese Communist Party's Standing Committee and then the Central Military Commission (CMC) on September 11, Xi reversed his previously cautious course. He ordered the PLAN to block all US ships from coming into China's "historic waters" of the South China Sea, and to either escort out or capture any US vessels remaining in the sea. He also ordered a no-fly zone over the Spratlys and Paracels. Moreover, he promised to target any Japanese naval ships that accompanied US vessels into the South China Sea. However, Xi continued to reject suggestions that US air bases in Japan, or Japanese air bases, immediately be targeted with ballistic missiles, a decision that caused deep resentment within the PLA.

China's Choice to Expand the War

Nonetheless, Xi's decision to confront US forces and essentially turn a skirmish into a war has been hotly debated by historians. Without access to the papers of the Standing Committee or CMC, and with diplomatic and academic ties between China and the United States severely curtailed after the war, it is largely guesswork as to why Xi chose the path he did. Some analysts point to the weakness of the Chinese economy, which had resulted in growing public dissatisfaction for several years, and surmise that the war was a way to divert public attention. Others argue that shrinking military budgets, which were used by China's political adversaries in Asia to claim that its days as the most powerful Asian military were drawing to a close, caused fear among China's top leadership that their military strength was a wasting asset. Many, however, argue that Beijing's grand strategy had been clear for years, underscoring Xi's belligerent rhetoric stretching back to the 2010s and his assertion that Taiwan would be absorbed into China, as evidence that he was waiting for an opportunity to give a black eye to an America he believed was unwilling to put up a major fight.[41]

Whatever the actual reason, it seems clear that Chinese leaders, above all Xi, realized they had just a few days to try to stake out a dominant position before US Navy vessels began reaching the

Spratlys and reinforcements from San Diego reached Yokosuka. At the same time, though, Xi and his top lieutenants sought initially to avoid the unrestrained use of asymmetric tactics, such as cyber-attacks, which could escalate into a clash involving both homelands. Orders appear to have gone out on September 11 for two task forces to make steam, for air forces to begin combat patrols, and for a diversionary fleet in the north.

- From the East Sea Fleet based at Ningbo, four diesel attack submarines, three Type 052D destroyers, nine frigates, two amphibious helicopter carriers, and ten missile patrol craft were dispatched toward the Senkaku/Diaoyu Islands northeast of Taiwan. Their orders were to block any US and Japanese vessels from transiting south of Taiwan into the South China Sea. They were accompanied by twenty armed CCG ships ordered to invade Japan's territorial waters in the Senkakus and thereby draw off Japanese ships.
- The *Liaoning*, China's aircraft carrier, and a small escort group from the East Sea Fleet were sent toward Luzon, in the Philippines, to block the *Gerald Ford* from reaching the South China Sea.
- From the South Sea Fleet based at Zhanjiang, three diesel attack submarines, three Type 052D destroyers, seven frigates, twelve missile patrol craft, and three corvettes were dispatched to the Spratlys. Their mission was to surround and immobilize the *Curtis Wilbur* and the crippled *Bertholf*. Two other diesel attack submarines were sent toward the Strait of Malacca to close passage through to the Indian Ocean, if necessary.
- To prevent the United States from maintaining air cover for its ships, PLAN Type 052D destroyers armed with advanced HQ-9 surface-to-air missiles (SAMs) were ordered to engage any US Navy or Air Force fighters, while Chinese air forces, including the PLAAF and land-based PLANAF fighters, were ordered to make combat air patrols over the Spratlys; US Air Force tankers

were to be targeted off Luzon, so as to make Japan-based fighter coverage impossible.

- As a diversionary tactic, the North Sea Fleet, out of Qingdao, dispatched a flotilla of destroyers, frigates, and corvettes into the East China Sea, toward the Jeju and Korean Straits, hoping to draw off Japan Maritime Self-Defense Force ships (JMSDF) from supporting the US Navy.

The Taiwan Strait Is Lost

First blood in the expanded theater of operations was drawn by the Chinese on September 12. The USS *Stethem* and USS *Patriot*, previously ordered to transit the Taiwan Strait, were caught in a swarm of Chinese fishing craft, Type 22 PLAN missile patrol boats, and Chinese Coast Guard ships that had crossed the median line at a point about halfway through the strait. Slowed to a crawl by the swarm of small craft and alarmed by the threatening tactics from the boats, the *Stethem* felt forced to fire warning shots. This resulted in a missile swarm fired from the small PLAN patrol craft, which apparently had orders to attack the US ships if they gave any justification for doing so, such as firing their guns even in defense. The *Patriot* sustained casualties and serious damage, and the *Stethem*, while also sustaining damage, returned fire, disabling one of the CCG ships and several of the missile boats, and driving off the others. US Air Force F-22s operating out of Kadena (approximately 400 nm away) engaged with older Chinese J-10s and J-11s, which had been sent to harass the American vessels, destroying eight planes before breaking off. The *Stethem* and *Patriot* eventually broke free of the swarm and limped to Kaohsiung, Taiwan. This allowed Beijing to claim on September 13 that Taiwan was now a belligerent and to announce that the Taiwan Strait was closed, send a blockading force to Kaohsiung just outside Taiwan's twelve-mile territorial limit, position two more Type 052D destroyers for antiair missions over the Taiwan Strait, and begin multiple combat aerial patrols around the island. Taiwanese naval ships sent to meet the Chinese were stopped just inside the territorial limit, and the two navies settled for the moment into a watchful stalemate.

The next three days slowed to a dead calm in the region as the various task forces and ships of both sides neared each other. Neither Newsom nor Xi was willing to declare war on the other country, with all the implications that held, but Xi declared a national emergency, and Newsom briefed congressional leaders, who quickly passed a nonbinding resolution declaring support for US forces in Asia and for President Newsom's policy of maintaining a "peaceful and prosperous Indo-Pacific." Despite repeated phone calls between the leaders, neither agreed to pull back forces. Instead, Newsom approved the dispatch to Japan of ten more DDGs and two cruisers from San Diego, though their transit would take at least two weeks. Another two squadrons of F-22s were ordered to Kadena, and two B-2 bombers from Whiteman Air Force Base made a transoceanic flyby over the Senkakus. When Newsom asked for permission to base the F-22s at Clark, widespread anti-US protests broke out in the Philippines, including massive demonstrations that besieged the base; these were organized and directed by Chinese intelligence agents, but they served to paralyze Philippine politics, especially once former president Duterte emerged at the head of the protestors demanding that Manila restore peaceful relations with Beijing.

On September 15, the PLAN South Sea Fleet task force reached the position of the *Curtis Wilbur*, off the Spratlys. The *Bertholf* remained largely inoperable, and the DDG kept watch over the coast guard vessel. Despite warnings to keep a safe maritime distance, the Chinese ships closed in, forcing the DDG to fire warning shots, which were ignored. Being entirely outgunned, the commander of the *Curtis Wilbur* chose to batten down the ship and refrain from further hostilities, hoping to ride out any Chinese attack until relief forces could arrive; the Chinese, who had orders only to isolate the two American ships, formed a barrier around them. In the skies, US tankers had been withdrawn from their refueling stations, as Pacific Air Forces feared losing its limited number of them due to PLA fighters, while the

Philippines' president refused permission for further US air operations to be flown from Clark; this effectively ended US fighter support over the South China Sea.

The Battle of Bashi Channel

The next day, September 16, the aircraft carrier *Liaoning*, which was approximately 175 nm northwest of the Babuyan Islands, just north of Luzon, launched a combination of J-31 and J-15 jets to try to intimidate the *Gerald Ford*, which was to the southeast of Okinawa, approximately 75 nm northeast of the Philippines' Batanes, in the western Pacific Ocean. The geography of eastern Asia's inner seas meant that the most direct route to intercept the American ships would have forced the Chinese to transit past the Japanese-held Ryukyu Islands, making them vulnerable to land-based jets from Okinawa as well as potential antiship missiles launched from islands along the chain. The PLAN vessels instead swung south through the Taiwan Strait, running the risk of encountering lurking US submarines, and then northeast to the Bashi Channel. Nonetheless, the Chinese planes were decisively defeated by a combination of the *Gerald Ford*'s F-35s and F-22s launched from Kadena, on Okinawa, effectively preventing the *Liaoning* and its flotilla from moving forward. However, one Type 055D PLAN destroyer, its newest variant, escorting the *Liaoning* used its HQ-9 SAMs to destroy one F-35 and one F-22, underscoring the danger to US fighters. At the same time, the US escort ships also halted just within visual range of East Sea Fleet vessels on the horizon.

At this point, the clashes threatened to involve land-based forces, which would have escalated the war to a higher, and possibly uncontrollable, level. US Pacific Fleet anticipated the employment of DF-21D antiship ballistic missiles against the *Gerald Ford*, and indeed two missiles were launched from Chinese territory approximately four hours after the aerial engagement. The Americans countered with antimissile SM-6s to knock down the DF-21Ds, which failed; however, both Chinese missiles also missed the *Gerald Ford*. Some in Washington chose to believe the failed missile attack was purposeful, with Beijing trying to send a message that it would knock out the US carrier were it to continue on into the South China Sea. However, in the press of time, voices arguing that Washington needed to send a signal back to Beijing were dismissed. Instead, within three hours of the attempted DF-21 strike, orders came from Hawaii, originating in Washington, that the *Gerald Ford* was to hold position east of the Bashi Channel, located 100 miles north of Luzon and 120 miles south of Taiwan, which essentially formed the border between the Philippine and South China Seas. Now the strategic implications of sending US aircraft carriers into Beijing's "kill zone" were becoming clear. Washington planners were in a quandary, for the *Gerald Ford* remained within range of both DF-21D and DF-26 missiles, but officials were loath to pull the carrier farther back, for fear of being seen as abandoning the conflict; nor did they want to risk an escalation of hostilities by targeting Chinese assets not directly involved in the skirmishing. Again, it appeared that the Chinese had checked the Americans, though without knocking them off the board.

When word reached Taiwan that the *Gerald Ford* had halted, the island's president, from the mainland-leaning Kuomintang (KMT) party, announced on September 17 that Taiwan was henceforth a neutral in the conflict and would accept Chinese naval patrols of its sea-lanes and overflight. He further ordered the two US ships that had taken refuge there to either leave Taiwanese waters or declare they were no longer combatants and remain quarantined in port.

The Chinese Introduce Electronic Warfare

After one day on station, on September 17, the escort ships with the *Gerald Ford*, including the cruiser *Antietam* and three DDGs, continued toward the Spratlys. The PLA Strategic Support Force then began wide-scale electronic warfare measures and cyberattacks on US systems, after hesitant moves to interrupt US systems in the first week of the conflict. It succeeded in repeatedly interrupting GPS and shutting down various US computer and communications systems, including intelligence, surveillance, and reconnaissance (ISR) feeds, through malware. US EA-18G Growler electronic warfare aircraft launched from the *Gerald Ford* and EP-3s from Japan also found their systems jammed, leaving US commanders reliant on incomplete information from satellites and submarines. This significantly slowed the progress of the US flotilla toward the Spratlys and was only partially countered by launching dozens of line-of-sight communications transmitters tethered to medium-altitude balloons from US Navy ships scattered throughout the theater of operations. With the advent of electronic warfare, US policy makers began to fear that a future wave of cyber-attacks would widen the field of conflict to civilian systems, forcing a major US response. For the time being, however, the Chinese hesitated to escalate the crisis horizontally by targeting noncombatants, focusing instead on crippling US operations in the theater of combat.

The Battle of Santiago Island

On September 20, the US flotilla engaged in hostilities with the South Sea Fleet off Santiago Island, near the town of Bolinao on Luzon. The *Gerald Ford* sent F-18s and F-35s for air cover, easily shooting down PLAAF and PLANAF planes from the Spratlys; given the roughly 600-mile distance from PLANAF bases on Hainan Island and PLAAF bases near Guangzhou, and the lack of in-flight aerial refueling, the Chinese were limited to just the three dozen or so fighters on various Spratly bases. Once again, however, HQ-9s launched from Type 052Ds scored hits on US planes, destroying three F-18s. From nearly 100 nm away, two Chinese Type 052C destroyers loosed a volley of six antiship missiles, which scored hits on the *Antietam* and one DDG, disabling both. US naval forces returned fire, sinking one Chinese destroyer and inflicting serious damage on another. The remaining two US DDGs then endured the missile volleys of ten Type 22 missile boats, each of which fired its complement of eight antiship subsonic cruise missiles. While five of the ten Chinese missile boats were destroyed by return American fire, one remaining US DDG was sunk and the other disabled.

The US flotilla from Japan had been stopped several hundred miles north of the Spratlys and the US ships involved in the original melee of September 9. The Chinese then boarded the *Curtis Wilbur* early on the morning of September 21 and scuttled the *Bertholf*, transferring all US military personnel to Mischief Reef for internment. This was a total of 415 sailors and coast guard members, including several dozen seriously wounded.

The Battle of the Senkakus

On September 21–22, Japanese Coast Guard and Japan Maritime Self-Defense Force ships engaged with elements of the PLAN's East Sea Fleet and the People's Armed Forces Maritime Militia (PAFMM). Though PAFMM vessels had reached the Senkakus on September 14, the East Sea Fleet did not release ships to the mission until September 18, after making sure that the *Gerald Ford* had halted at the Batanes in the Bashi Channel. It was, in fact, the sailing away of several East Sea Fleet vessels toward the Senkakus that led the *Gerald Ford*'s escort vessels to continue south toward Santiago Island.

Japanese Coast Guard (JCG) ships had played cat and mouse with PAFMM ships since September 14 in the waters off the Senkakus, but with the arrival of the PLAN ships already on patrol in the East China Sea, the PAFMM vessels boldly moved within two miles or so of the islands. An interdiction by the Japanese turned into a skirmish, but the much heavier-armed PAFMM vessel sank one thousand-ton JCG cutter, with the loss of ten coast guard members. An emergency call was answered by JASDF F-2 fighters, which had been moved to Kadena specifically for antiship missions. The F-2s launched SAM-2 antiship missiles that disabled two PAFMM ships. Three hours later, fighters launched from the *Liaoning*, which had moved north from its position near the Babuyan Islands into the Bashi Channel between the Batanes and Taiwan. These J-15s successfully attacked four JCG cutters with standoff air-to-surface missiles, sinking or disabling them. With JMSDF ships en route to the Senkakus but not yet off station, the JCG withdrew its remaining ships toward Okinawa, leaving the islands undefended except for fighters based at New Ishigaki Airport, which was converted to military use.

The Japanese had another card to play, however, and in the early morning hours of September 22, the *Shoryu* (SS-510), a *Soryu*-class diesel-electric attack submarine that had been lurking southwest of the Senkakus, intercepted the *Liaoning* and loosed four Type 89 guided torpedoes, two of which struck the Chinese aircraft carrier below the water-line. The *Liaoning* was halted and began to list, at which point the *Shoryu* surfaced and launched six Harpoon missiles, four of which found their target, leaving the *Liaoning* out of commission and severely listing to port. Four Chinese attack submarines that had been in Taiwanese waters then hunted down the *Shoryu*, sinking her with all sixty-five hands on board just before midnight on September 23, southeast of Okinawa, where she was making a run for sanctuary.

When intelligence of the disabling of the *Liaoning* reached East Sea Fleet headquarters at Ningbo, the assumption was made that an American submarine had attacked the carrier. In response, orders went out to retaliate by targeting the *Gerald Ford*, which had turned north from the Batanes after receiving word of the battle off the Senkakus. Again, the Chinese launched DF-21D antiship ballistic missiles; unlike on September 16, however, two missiles found their target after ineffective SM-6 countermeasures. The *Gerald Ford* sustained catastrophic damage and severe loss of life, and the ship foundered at nightfall. Japanese and American ships sent out from Okinawa reached the scene late on September 23 and commenced rescue operations, and the USS *John C. Stennis* hove into view the following day.

V. The Choice for Peace: September 23–30, 2025

The successful attacks on the aircraft carriers of both nations were the turning point of the Littoral War. Senior policy makers in both countries realized they were now at the precipice of full-out conflict, where land-based targets and civilian populations could now be targeted. The US preference for containing the conflict in the global commons was at risk of being overtaken by events. Standard operating procedures at US Strategic Command, which controlled America's nuclear arsenal, had moved readiness on September 10 from peacetime Defense Condition (DEFCON) 5 to DEFCON 4, and then on September 12 to DEFCON 3, with enhanced readiness at underground missile silos and the ability to mobilize nuclear-armed bombers on ground alert. The PLA Rocket Force went to high alert on September 11, and a JIN-class nuclear ballistic missile submarine carrying the JL-2 submarine-launched ballistic missile sortied from its base at Longpo on Hainan Island, to join a counterpart already on patrol. When US Strategic Command obtained satellite imagery of the empty submarine wharves on Hainan on September 12, its commander ordered the USS *Louisiana* (SSBN-743) out of Bremerton, Washington, to join the USS *Kentucky* (SSBN-737), already on patrol in the Pacific.

After the Battle of the Senkakus, the expansion of the war to land-based, populated targets became the next logical military step, but one that US political and senior military leaders were loath to take. With the increase in readiness of strategic forces, use of nuclear force itself no longer seemed unthinkable, given the emotionalism likely to break out in both countries at the destruction of the aircraft carriers, the most visible symbols of their military power. More worrisome for operations planners in both countries was the likelihood that the Americans would begin targeting mobile DF-21D and DF-26 launchers on China's mainland to prevent the PLA from using any more antiship ballistic missiles. Such attacks would force the Chinese to begin attacking ground targets in response, possibly in Guam and even Hawaii, as well as in Japan, where US air and naval forces were based. Japanese policy makers braced themselves for a wave of Chinese ballistic missile attacks as a tactic to pressure Tokyo to abandon its American ally.

Unexpectedly, perhaps, the first steps toward a cessation of hostilities were proposed by the Chinese. The Chinese attack on the *Gerald Ford*, in mistaken retaliation for the *Liaoning* disabling, caused a rift in the Chinese leadership. CMC chairman Xi Jinping upbraided the East Sea Fleet leadership for not confirming that the Americans were behind the attack, a point made directly by President Newsom in a nationally televised address on September 23. Xi also concluded that an attack on another US carrier, the *John C. Stennis*, would likely lead the Americans to begin large-scale operations against Chinese land-based missile targets, docks, shipyards, and air bases. With more US ships reaching the theater of battle, it would be harder to control the conflict, and Beijing could wind up losing the gains it had made, namely eliminating the American presence in the South China Sea and taking control of the Taiwan Strait with a Finlandized Taiwan. Xi therefore contacted Newsom on the morning of September 23 and proposed an immediate cease-fire, to be followed by negotiations between military commanders for a permanent halt to combat operations.

Newsom faced a different set of constraints than Xi. With one aircraft carrier gone, the US Navy had only two fully operational carriers left from the total force of nine; it would take weeks to bring two more up to combat readiness and months to get another two ready for deployment. The navy had also deployed the majority of its combat-ready destroyers and submarines, and further losses from missile attacks would begin to seriously degrade the US capability to wage surface war. The US Air Force had outclassed its Chinese opponents, but its number of mission-ready airplanes was declining, as well as its stores of air-to-air missiles. Surging both naval and air units to the region left little in reserve for a longer conflict.

A grim balance had been achieved with the mirror attacks on the aircraft carriers, and Newsom responded positively to Xi's proposal, contingent on the immediate release of all US military personnel held by the Chinese, to which Xi consented, promising that they would be transferred to the Philippines by Chinese ships beginning on September 25. The two agreed that all combat operations would cease at 11:00 Beijing time on September 24, and forces would hold at their positions at the status quo.

The agreement could have been derailed just hours after the two leaders talked, when the USS *Illinois* (SSN-786), a *Virginia*-class nuclear attack submarine, encountered a PLAN South Sea Fleet *Yuan*-class diesel-electric attack submarine off the Riau Archipelago northeast of Singapore. The *Illinois* had picked up the Chinese sub on September 22 and quietly shadowed it for two days before being discovered in turn by its Chinese quarry. Having received information of the submarine attack on the *Liaoning*, the Chinese assumed they were an active target and flooded and opened their torpedo tubes. At that point, the *Illinois* launched a single Mk-48 torpedo that destroyed the Chinese sub. By the time the South Sea Fleet realized their sub was missing on September 29, the inertia of the political agreement between Washington and Beijing was too strong to overcome, and Chinese authorities ordered all forces to adhere to the cease-fire, which had been in effect for four full days.

VI. The Aftermath

The Negotiations and Agreement

Since Congress had not declared war, President Newsom could negotiate and make a settlement directly with Xi Jinping, without having to seek congressional approval. Further, since no territory had been taken by either side, the two leaders agreed to ratify the military status quo at the time of the cease-fire and avoid bringing in diplomats. The commander of US Indo-Pacific Command met the chief of the Joint Staff Department of the PLA's Central Military Commission in Singapore on September 26 and reached an agreement on a permanent cease-fire on September 28.

By the terms of the agreement, each side agreed to inform the other of naval and air activities taking place in the Yellow, East, and South China Seas; the US would notify Beijing of any passage of US naval ships through the South China Sea, while China would undertake to "limit" but not cease its naval activities in the East China Sea to a line extending south from Jeju Island off the southern tip of the Korean Peninsula to approximately 25 degrees north latitude, whence the line would swing southwestward toward Taiwan, bypassing the Senkaku Islands. This would be referred to by both countries as the ECS Median Line.

Further, the US recognized Chinese control over the Spratly and Paracel island chains in the South China Sea, and acknowledged China's "historic interests" in the South China Sea. For its part, the PRC promised never to invade or attack Japan, provided Japan refrained from interfering with peaceful Chinese military activities in the East China Sea. A secret codicil, revealed five years later, contained an American promise to end all military and intelligence aid to Taiwan, effectively killing off the 1979 Taiwan Relations Act.

After the agreement was made public, President Newsom delivered a major address at the Cato Institute think tank in Washington, DC, outlining substantial changes to America's role in the Pacific. He announced a withdrawal of US naval, ground, and air forces from Japan to Guam and Hawaii; the US would leave a token force of one F-16 squadron and two DDGs in Japan but withdraw completely from Okinawa. Enhanced military aid to Japan and full intelligence sharing along the lines of the "Five Eyes" arrangement would be implemented to maintain a strong alliance. In the interests of maintaining peace on the Korean Peninsula, the US Army would maintain a force of 7,000 soldiers—3,500 of them in combat units—down from a prewar total of 28,000, all of them to be located in Busan, on the southern tip of South Korea.

Seeking to reassure America's allies, Newsom reiterated that America's extended deterrence commitments, the so-called nuclear umbrella, would remain in force. He also ordered Defense Secretary Flournoy to submit plans to build up naval and air facilities on Guam and Oahu. Despite public opposition in both locales, land requisition soon expanded the US military's footprint on both islands. In their totality, Newsom's policy shifts caused an uproar among mainstream foreign policy experts, while being applauded on both the progressive left and isolationist right of the political spectrum. The greater geopolitical impact was felt in the emergence of three blocs in the Indo-Pacific.

The Emergence of Three Geopolitical Blocs in East Asia

Within months, or perhaps weeks, after the cease-fire and the announcement of Newsom's new policy, three distinct blocs had begun to form in the region. The first bloc was composed of a rump grouping of US alliances in the region. Japan and Australia remained allied with the United States, though not without significant changes to long-standing security policy. Within six months of Newsom's announcement, Japan had announced the imposition of a national draft for all eighteen- to twenty-five-year-olds for a period of three years; in addition, Tokyo's new National Defense Program Guidelines revealed a $200 billion plan to introduce autonomous systems into all of Japan's combat services, as well as the formation of a cyber warfare command. With only a token US force left in Japan, all US-Japan military exercises were canceled. Press reports by left-wing activist groups suggested that Tokyo had embarked on a secret nuclear weapons program in the northern island of Hokkaido, and that plans were under way to build several nuclear ballistic missile submarines to ensure a survivable counter-strike capability. While left-wing Japanese groups, again supported by Chinese intelligence and United Front operatives, demanded outreach to Beijing, Japan's conservative government reiterated its commitment to the modified alliance with Washington, though public opinion polls indicated that the government might lose its parliamentary majority to the liberal opposition.

Australia announced no change in its posture toward the United States but reiterated calls for full freedom of navigation throughout the Indo-Pacific. Canberra stated that it would be willing to port US Navy ships and expand facilities at the Royal Australian Air Force's Darwin base for the use of US bombers and fighters. Canberra's offer, however, was not immediately acted upon by Washington, which instead announced that it would host Australian units for joint exercises in Hawaii on a semiannual basis. In mid-October, Newsom and the Philippines president announced that the US alliance with the Philippines would be restricted to political cooperation and economic aid, and that the United States would lose access to any Philippine military bases, effectively ending US security guarantees to Manila and canceling annual defense exercises such as Balikatan.

The second bloc, headed by China, re-created a large portion of the traditional Sinic state system. Taiwan moved first, announcing the week after Newsom's address that it had entered a "new era" in cross-strait relations, whereby Beijing had assured Taipei of a "one country-two systems" arrangement that would preserve Taiwan's autonomous status. China would, however, control the island's foreign policy through a new coordination group, and the two capitals announced in October the formation of an exclusive economic partnership, expanding the 2010 Economic Cooperation Framework Agreement. Taipei agreed to begin downsizing its military into a militia designed to maintain public order, act as a coast guard, and monitor airspace over the island. It further agreed to cease all foreign weapons purchases (thereby making irrelevant the secret US promise to China to stop selling arms to Taiwan).

In what became known as the "St. Valentine's Day Massacre," Seoul announced in mid-February 2026 that it was withdrawing from the US-ROK alliance and was entering into a military "friendship pact" with China, whereby Beijing would undertake to ensure peace and stability on the peninsula. The remaining US troops (seven thousand) would be withdrawn by April Fool's Day 2027, and PLAN vessels would be accorded routine porting privileges at Inchon and Busan. It was unclear whether the Newsom administration was aware of Seoul's plans, despite high-level diplomatic talks that had been ongoing since the September cease-fire. This surprise was followed by the promulgation of a formal alliance between North Korea and China, with DPRK forces joining the PLA in joint naval and air exercises, while Seoul and

Pyongyang agreed to establish joint military liaison offices in each capital under the supervision of PLA officers.

Initially, it appeared as though China was the nearly unambiguous victor in the Littoral War, but it soon became clear that Beijing's new allies were largely unwilling and resentful partners who felt they had no other choice but to throw in their lot with China. Taiwanese grassroots groups regularly protested against the alliance with China, despite a crackdown authorized by a new public safety law. More ominously, politicians from both the Democratic Progressive and Kuomintang political parties in Taiwan increasingly saw that Xi Jinping intended to formally annex the island before his retirement in 2032, and they began to plot ways to frustrate Beijing's designs.

Even more resistant were the Koreas, which before long began to discuss the formation of a peninsular unity movement that would allow for a united front to deal with China. Anti-Chinese demonstrations regularly took place in major cities throughout the peninsula, and the two Korean capitals soon learned that they could beg out of joint military exercises with the Chinese by claiming lack of funds, unstable public opinion, or (in the South) looming elections.

The third bloc to emerge out of the Littoral War revived the Cold War–era Nonaligned Movement, declaring a comprehensive neutrality between the US and Chinese blocs, opening itself to trade with both, and—depending on the country—allowing mutual military access to both great powers, though in practice this meant far more access for the PLA than for the US military. The nonaligned bloc was centered on the ten members of the Association of Southeast Asian Nations (ASEAN), headquartered in Jakarta, Indonesia. Some members of ASEAN traditionally had extensive ties with the United States, whether as ally or partner.

While not a formal ally, Singapore nonetheless had had the closest relations with Washington of all Southeast Asian nations prior to the war. In the aftermath, however, Singapore joined its ASEAN partners and moved to distance itself from the United States, announcing that henceforth only noncombat US naval vessels would be allowed porting privileges, while US combat aircraft could no longer land at Changi Air Base. Similarly, the US ally Thailand also chose its ASEAN neighbors. The military-backed junta that had ruled Thailand since its overthrow of yet another popularly elected government in 2022 announced it was suspending cooperation with the US military, while urging both Washington and Moscow to provide further development assistance to help "stabilize" the domestic economy so that parliamentary elections could be scheduled at the "earliest possible date." The Philippines, for its part, welcomed the economic and political aid provided by the revised alliance agreed to with Newsom, but Manila openly sided with ASEAN in proclaiming itself a neutral, having already lost the remainder of its Spratly Islands claims in the weeks after the war, when PLA units took over all contested territory in the chain.

The nonaligned bloc found two champions in India and Russia. Both New Delhi and Moscow took advantage of the trifurcation of East Asia to advance their interests. India became the diplomatic and economic champion of the nonaligned nations, enhancing ties and even proposing maritime partnerships that would see Indian naval vessels escort the merchant ships of Southeast Asian nations. For its part, Russia offered deep discounts on military hardware to all nations pledging to maintain a nonaligned status. Moscow quickly became the major arms dealer in the region and offered Russian armed forces personnel to train nations in their new purchases.

Other global powers, primarily the Europeans, quickly lost the appetite to play any significant role in the Indo-Pacific. Once Beijing announced on October 1 that it would ensure freedom of navigation for all merchant vessels through its "zone of control" in the South China Sea, the European Commission stated that it recognized China's control over the body of water, and would work with the PLAN to file shipping manifests and routes of transit. The British government, which had begun plans to build a new base in Singapore, following on then defense secretary Gavin Williamson's December 2018 announcement, canceled the project and announced that all future planned transits of the HMS *Queen Elizabeth* aircraft carrier through the South and East China Seas would be postponed.

VII. The Lessons

Almost immediately after the announcement of the permanent cease-fire, analysts in the United States began debating the lessons of the war. While few interpretations were universally accepted, several key insights were generally seen as correct.

First, the origins of the war were years in the making. While historians cautioned against assuming that war was inevitable, or that the United States and China were fated to fight, observers agreed that years of deteriorating relations were a precondition to war. As suspicion grew in each country about the other, as working relations became more strained and formal, as the two eyed each other as the major threat each faced, both Washington and Beijing gave up on attempting to establish mechanisms to resolve the growing differences between them. Instead, each increasingly sought to justify actions that increased tensions and suspicion.

American analysts, however, were largely united in seeing China as the aggressor in the years leading up to the war. While the goal of US policy toward China since the 1970s had been to integrate it into the global economic and political system, Beijing increasingly chafed at what it considered to be restrictions on its freedom of action outside its borders. Instead of gaining confidence in dealing with the world, Chinese leaders, and especially Xi Jinping, saw enemies all around China; indeed, as US observers pointed out, in the years before the war, China had disputes with almost all of its neighbors, particularly maritime ones in the East and South China Seas. It was China, moreover, that built up a military designed to target US strengths in the region, precisely at the time when Washington was eager to make China the de facto number two in the global hierarchy. Finally, it was Beijing that intimidated and harassed its neighbors, threatened

Taiwan, took maritime territory when possible, and built and milita-rized island bases in the South China Sea during the 2010s. Ultimately, it was aggressive Chinese actions on September 8–9, 2025, that led to the accidents which precipitated conflict.

Second, all analysts and historians recognized the crucial role of con-tingency in the outbreak of hostilities. Because US and Chinese ships and planes were increasingly in proximity to each other, accidents were more likely to happen, especially given the aggressive nature of Chinese ship drivers and pilots. The 2001 EP-3E incident was a harbinger of the kind of accident that could throw relations into a tailspin. As it turned out, the two unconnected incidents on September 8 were enough to tip the balance toward conflict, given high tensions and the lack of decon-fliction between US and PLA forces in the skies and on the sea. In short, the two nations stumbled into a war neither wanted.

In addition, later on in the conflict, the disabling of the *Liaoning* by a JMSDF attack submarine on September 22 introduced a wild card into combat operations. The Chinese retaliatory attack on the USS *Gerald Ford* had the potential to cause the war to spiral out of con-trol, leading to US attacks on mainland missile launch sites, communi-cations nodes, ports, airfields, and the like. These, in turn, would almost certainly have resulted in Chinese counterattacks on US territory, including Guam and Hawaii, and possibly San Diego. The next step might well have been limited nuclear exchanges (this will be discussed further in the fifth point, below).

Third, probably because the two came into armed conflict acciden-tally, rather than through intent on either side, neither was sure just how far hostilities would develop, nor how far they themselves wanted to go. Rather than activating full war plans, each side initially concentrated on the narrow site of the accidents, combining rescue operations with attempts to clear the other country's forces from the vicinity. Washington hoped that minimum deterrence would initially suffice to send signals to Beijing that US forces would not surrender its position in eastern Asian waters without a fight. For its part, Beijing, though committed to achiev-ing domination in Asia's seas, hesitated to commit to a horizontal

escalation of hostilities to land-based targets, fearing the impact of retaliatory responses on Chinese soil. Severe criticism of Xi Jinping's decision not to launch ballistic missile attacks against US air bases in Japan
discounted his focus on achieving victory solely on the immediate battlefield, as opposed to risking a larger US retaliation for bombing targets
in an allied country. This initial hesitancy on both sides led to a gradual
widening of conflict, but each escalation was linked directly to the specific action that preceded it. This kept the scale of the conflict limited in
its early days, which in turn shaped the operational response (see a
fuller discussion of limited war aims in the fifth point, below).

Fourth, the actual course of combat operations largely followed the
insights of geopolitical analysts Halford Mackinder and Nicholas John
Spykman.[42] Both Mackinder and Spykman stressed the crucial importance of the "rimlands": the littoral and adjacent maritime space, which
Spykman called the "marginal seas." The rimlands are the vital areas
that must be controlled, given their importance in populations, industrial production, and access to the continental interior and its resources.
However, to control the rimlands, the inner seas must be dominated
by one power. In other words, it is in the marginal or inner seas that
the struggle for mastery takes place, between what Mackinder called
the "inner crescent" of the littoral mainland and the "outer crescent"
of the peninsular littoral (in this case, formed by Japan, Taiwan, the
Philippines, and other nations of Southeast Asia).

US and Chinese combat operations focused on winning the war in
the marginal seas, along the littorals, and not on expanding combat
either to the continent (in the case of the United States) or to third
countries like Japan (in the case of China). Naval forces were concentrated at key choke points or along vital sea lines of communication,
such as the Miyako and Jeju Straits, which formed the hinges between
the East and South China Seas. Taiwan also played a central geopolitical role here, and its declaration of neutrality was a major strategic
gain for China. Similarly, the Battles of the Batanes, Ryukyus, and
Santiago Island all underscored the importance of the littorals and
strategic transit points.

Both US and Chinese forces faced constraints due to distance in the theater of operations. US naval forces in the region were inadequate to prosecute combat operations without help, but the amount of steaming time from (a) Japan to the Spratlys, (b) Hawaii to Japan, and (c) San Diego to Japan meant that US forces were stretched too thin to fight effectively in the South China Sea. Moreover, US land-based and naval air forces could not operate at enough range to maintain persistent presence over the battle sites in the South China Sea. They were dominant in all air-to-air encounters when they were located within stand-off missile range, such as at the Battle of the Batanes and Santiago Island, but were vulnerable to SAMs fired from PLAN destroyers. The subsequent disabling of the *Gerald Ford* and the threat to aerial tankers, however, forced US forces to limit air cover after the initial days of battle.

On the other hand, the Chinese naval forces benefited from proximity to bases on the mainland and Hainan, as well as in the Paracel and Spratly Islands. Yet Chinese air forces were bested by their US opponents, and China also lost effective air cover after the early days of the war. Chinese military officials did not hesitate to use land-based missiles, especially DF-21D ASBMs against large US targets, and effectively used swarm missile attacks from smaller Type 22 missile patrol boats in both the Taiwan Strait and off Santiago Island.

Given the relatively brief duration of the war and its limitation to force-on-force battles in the littorals, neither side faced severe logistical constraints, such as lack of ordnance or fuel. American land-based and naval air forces did face a drawdown of ordnance, due to the relatively limited carrying capacity of F-35s in stealth mode. Along with routine mechanical problems, this would have wound up further limiting the effectiveness of US air operations had the conflict continued for several more weeks.

Fifth, crucially, neither Washington nor Beijing was willing to risk or felt prepared for a full war. Rather, even after the loss of their aircraft carriers, both sides showed restraint during combat operations, as noted in the third point, above. The key moment of restraint for the US was to avoid attacks on the Chinese mainland, especially missile sites, after the launching of DF-21Ds on two occasions against the *Gerald Ford*. Similarly, the Chinese did not target US air and naval bases on Okinawa, Guam, Hawaii, or the Japanese main island of Honshu, even when the US Indo-Pacific Command began moving assets from those bases to the area of the campaign. Most surprisingly to US war planners, the PLA conducted relatively limited electronic warfare operations, perhaps out of fear that expansion of electronic warfare to the US mainland would result in similar attacks and significant disruption at home; moreover, US workarounds, primarily the ship-launched balloon communications network, partially blunted the effectiveness of China's initial electronic warfare salvoes. No satisfactory explanation was ever offered for the Chinese restraint, but suspicions remained rife that Xi Jinping was not willing to risk any domestic disruption that could mutate into anti-CCP movements, especially if the Americans could be checkmated early in the conflict.

Instead, each side limited itself to force-on-force encounters in the littoral seas and skies, confident of its ability to cripple the forward forces of the other and thereby impose an unacceptable cost in making the other commit further military assets. The United States did surge forces from Japan, Hawaii, and San Diego, but the Japan-based forces were checked at sea, while the Chinese decided to propose a cease-fire before US naval forces surged from Hawaii and San Diego could reach the combat zones. From a political perspective, Beijing was willing to cease combat operations to consolidate its significant gains, while the United States accepted its strategic losses and did not want to widen the war, which could have resulted in further defeats, especially once the effectiveness of the Chinese DF-21D and swarm missile attacks was proven. Instead, Washington decided that a reduced military presence in the region, centered on its alliances with Japan and Australia, was a better outcome than betting on the fortunes of war.

With each combatant willing, therefore, to limit future operations to preserve gains or prevent further loss, the political conditions were created for a geopolitical settlement that resulted in the emergence of the three blocs discussed in the previous section. Beijing concluded that its victory provided momentum whereby it could continue to squeeze the rump American alliance network and steadily put pressure on the nonaligned bloc. Publicly, Chinese officials repeatedly maintained that Beijing considered the diplomatic solution as merely "temporary," and that China would not rule out further action to follow up on its gains, but it failed to put into motion any plans to take advantage of its success. Moreover, as discussed, Beijing soon discovered that its unwilling allies required the investment of Chinese political, economic, and military capital, which restricted Beijing's freedom of action postbellum.

The United States limited its strategic goals to protecting Japan and ensuring that it could operate in part of East Asia's marginal seas (namely, the eastern portion of the East China Sea) as well as beyond the outer crescent of Japan. This allowed for the possibility of power projection into the inner seas and littorals in a future crisis, but turned the US largely into an offshore balancer, with its forces concentrated in Hawaii and on Guam. That made its remaining alliances, with Japan and Australia, inherently weaker than before the war.

The end result was a trifurcation of the Indo-Pacific into three geopolitical blocs, two of which—the Chinese and American—were mutually antagonistic, while the third, nonaligned block maneuvered for advantage between the other two. A cold peace settled on East Asia, reducing, though not eliminating, intraregional trade, while multilateral diplomatic mechanisms such as those sponsored by ASEAN became arenas for rhetorical combat between the blocs. A sharp drop in Sino-US trade rocked both countries, with the United States entering a recession that lasted three years, while reports of widespread demonstrations in China hinted at pervasive domestic unrest. Trade slowly stabilized between the two, but some of the nonaligned countries, particularly India, Vietnam, and Malaysia, retooled their economies to supplant China in the global supply chain, leading to a boost in their exports to America and Europe.

As the cold peace settled on the region, the Chinese and American blocs settled down into a prolonged contest for influence in Asia. Beijing continued its military buildup, though at a slower pace than during the

2000s and 2010s, given its economic slowdown. American defense planners increased their reliance on unmanned systems, hypersonics, underwater systems, and cyberwar capabilities. Both increased their espionage activities and conducted a regular military cat-and-mouse game in the skies and on the waters of the region. As of this writing, the two antagonists have so far avoided outright conflict and a repeat of the Littoral War, perhaps as much through luck as through a wariness on both sides to stumble once again into armed conflict.

Notes

1. Robert Ross, "The 1995–96 Taiwan Strait Confrontation: Coercion, Credibility, and the Use of Force," *International Security* 24, no. 2 (Fall 2000): 87.
2. "Cox Report, 1999," USC US-China Institute, https://china.usc.edu/cox -report-1999; "APT1: Exposing One of China's Cyber Espionage Units," Mandiant, https://www.fireeye.com/content/dam/fireeye-www/services /pdfs/mandiant-apt1-report.pdf.
3. "Remarks by President Obama and President Xi Jinping of the People's Republic of China after Bilateral Meeting," White House Office of the Press Secretary, June 8, 2013, https://obamawhitehouse.archives.gov /the-press-office/2013/06/08/remarks-president-obama-and-president -xi-jinping-peoples-republic-china-.
4. Tom Phillips, "Barack Obama 'Deliberately Snubbed' by Chinese in Chaotic Arrival at G20," *The Guardian*, September 4, 2016.
5. Hillary Rodham Clinton, "Remarks at Press Availability," July 23, 2010, US Department of State, https://2009-2017.state.gov/secretary/20092013 clinton/rm/2010/07/145095.htm.
6. "Pivot to the Pacific? The Obama Administration's 'Rebalancing' toward Asia," Congressional Research Service, March 28, 2012, https://fas.org /sgp/crs/natsec/R42448.pdf; Johnathan Marcus, "Leon Panetta: US to Deploy 60% of Navy Fleet to Pacific," *BBC News*, June 2, 2012.
7. Edward Wong, "Chinese Military Seeks to Extend Its Naval Power," *New York Times*, April 23, 2010.

8. Jane Perlez, "American and Chinese Navy Ships Nearly Collided in South China Sea," *New York Times*, December 14, 2013; Elisabeth Rosenthal and David Sanger, "US Plane in China after It Collides with Chinese Jet," *New York Times*, April 2, 2001.

9. Lolita Baldor, "Report: China Has Reclaimed 3,200 Acres in South China Sea," *Associated Press*, May 13, 2016.

10. Jane Perlez, "Tribunal Rejects Beijing's Claims in South China Sea," *New York Times*, July 12, 2016.

11. Sam LaGrone, "China Upset over 'Unprofessional' U.S. South China Sea Freedom of Navigation Operation," *USNI News*, January 31, 2016.

12. The National Security Strategy can be found at https://www.whitehouse.gov/wp-content/uploads/2017/12/NSS-Final-12-18-2017-0905-2.pdf.

13. "'Prepare for War': China's President Xi Jinping Tells Advisers of South China Sea," *New Zealand Herald*, October 28, 2018.

14. This section owes much to Bernard D. Cole, "The People's Liberation Army in 2020–30: Focused on Regional Issues," in *The Chinese People's Liberation Army in 2025*, ed. Roy Kamphausen and David Lai (Carlisle, PA: US Army War College Press, 2015), 165–206. See also Rick Joe, "Predicting the Chinese Navy of 2030," *The Diplomat*, February 15, 2019.

15. Cole, "The People's Liberation Army," 183–86.

16. Extrapolated from projected figures. See Department of Defense, "Annual Report to Congress: Military and Security Developments Involving the People's Republic of China 2018," May 16, 2018, 33, https://media.defense.gov/2018/Aug/16/2001955282/-1/-1/1/2018-CHINA-MILITARY-POWER-REPORT.PDF.

17. Department of Defense, "Annual Report to Congress," 70.

18. Based on current US Navy force levels. See "The United States Seventh Fleet," Commander, US 7th Fleet website, https://www.c7f.navy.mil/About-Us/Facts-Sheet.

19. "About the United States Third Fleet," Commander, US 3rd Fleet website, https://www.c3f.navy.mil/About-Us/Fact-Sheets/Article/638101/about-us.

20. Extrapolated from current US Air Force deployment figures. See "Pacific Air Forces," October 9, 2015, US Air Force website, https://www.af.mil/About-Us/Fact-Sheets/Display/Article/104483/pacific-air-forces.

21. See Kerry K. Gershaneck and James E. Fanell, "How China Began World War III in the South China Sea," *National Interest*, March 26, 2019.

22. Martin Petty, "Exclusive: At Strategic Shoal, China Asserts Power Through Control, And Concessions," *Reuters*, April 9, 2017, https:// www.reuters.com/article/us-southchinasea-china-philippines-exclu /exclusive-at-strategic-shoal-china-asserts-power-through-control-and -concessions-idUSKBN17B124.

23. "Mutual Defense Treaty between the United States and the Republic of the Philippines; August 30, 1951," available at the Yale Law School Lillian Goldman Law Library website, http://avalon.law.yale.edu/20th_century /phil001.asp.

24. Barbara Starr, Ryan Browne, and Brad Lendon, "Chinese Warship in 'Unsafe' Encounter with US Destroyer, Amid Rising US-China Tensions," *CNN Politics*, October 1, 2018.

25. Willy Lo-Lap Lam, "Xi Jinping Warns against the 'Black Swans' and 'Gray Rhinos' of a Possible Color Revolution," *China Brief*, February 20, 2019, https://jamestown.org/program/china-brief-early-warning-xi-jin ping-warns-against-the-black-swans-and-gray-rhinos-of-a-possible -color-revolution.

26. Barbara Demick, "In a Disputed Reef, Philippines Sees Face of Chinese Domination," *Los Angeles Times*, May 14, 2013.

27. Khan Vu, "Vietnam Protests to China over South China Sea Boat Sinking," *Reuters*, March 21, 2019, https://www.reuters.com/article/us -vietnam-southchinasea/vietnam-protests-to-china-over-south-china -sea-boat-sinking-idUSKCN1R307O.

28. Gordon Lubold and Jeremy Page, "U.S. Ship Sails near Disputed South China Sea Islands in Challenge to Beijing," *Wall Street Journal*, January 7, 2019.

29. Bart Elias and Ian Rinehart, "China's Air Defense Identification Zone (ADIZ)," Congressional Research Service, January 30, 2015, https://fas .org/sgp/crs/row/R43894.pdf.

30. Rosenthal and Sanger, "US Plane in China after It Collides with Chinese Jet."

31. Michael Fabey, "U.S. Navy's EP-3 Replacement Plan Still Raises Concerns," *Aerospace Daily and Defense Report*, May 12, 2016.

32. Starr, Browne, and Lendon, "Chinese Warship in 'Unsafe' Encounter."

33. Mari Yamaguchi, "Japan Shows Video of Alleged Radar Lock-On by SKorea Warship," *ABC News*, December 28, 2018.

34. "Littoral Combat Ship (LCS)," Department of Defense's Director, Operational Test and Evaluation, https://www.dote.osd.mil/pub/reports/FY2017/pdf/navy/2017lcs.pdf.
35. "An Accounting of China's Deployments to the Spratly Islands," Asia Maritime Transparency Initiative, May 9, 2018, https://amti.csis.org/accounting-chinas-deployments-spratly-islands.
36. On US base vulnerability, see Tanner Greer, "US Bases in Japan Are Sitting Ducks," *Foreign Policy*, September 4, 2019, https://foreignpolicy.com/2019/09/04/american-bases-in-japan-are-sitting-ducks/; see also Oriana Skylar Mastro and Ian Easton, *Risk and Resiliency: China's Emerging Air Base Strike Threat*, Project 2049 Institute, November 8, 2017, https://project2049.net/2017/11/08/risk-and-resiliency-chinas-emerging-air-base-strike-threat/; Thomas Shugart and Javier Gonzalez, *First Strike: China's Missile Threat to US Bases in Asia*, Center for a New American Security, June 2017, https://s3.amazonaws.com/files.cnas.org/documents/CNASReport-FirstStrike-Final.pdf?mtime=20170626140814.
37. Elizabeth McLaughlin and Luis Martinez, "US B-52 Flies over Disputed Islands in the South China Sea," *ABC News*, March 5, 2019.
38. I would like to thank Toshi Yoshihara for highlighting this point to me and introducing the concept of "minimum deterrence" from Donald Kagan.
39. "Anti-Japan Protests across China over Islands Dispute," *BBC News*, August 19, 2012.
40. See Gerry Shih and Emily Rauhala, "Angry over Campus Speech by Uighur Activist, Chinese Students in Canada Contact Their Consulate, Film Presentation," *Washington Post*, February 2, 2019. On the United Front Work Department, see "China's Overseas United Front Work," U.S.-China Economic and Security Review Commission, August 24, 2018, https://www.uscc.gov/sites/default/files/Research/China%27s%20Overseas%20United%20Front%20Work%20-%20Background%20and%20Implications%20for%20US_final_0.pdf.
41. Chris Buckley and Chris Horton, "Xi Jinping Warns Taiwan That Unification Is the Goal and Force Is an Option," *New York Times*, Jan 1, 2019.
42. Halford Mackinder, "The Geographical Pivot of History," in *Geographical Journal* 23, no. 4 (April 1904): 421–37; Nicholas John Spykman, *The Geography of the Peace* (New York: Harcourt, Brace, 1944).

ABOUT THE AUTHOR

Michael R. Auslin is the inaugural Payson J. Treat Distinguished Research Fellow in Contemporary Asia at the Hoover Institution, Stanford University. He is also a senior fellow at the Foreign Policy Research Institute and a fellow of the Royal Historical Society. Prior to joining Hoover, he was an associate professor of history at Yale University, a resident scholar at the American Enterprise Institute, and a visiting professor at Tokyo University. His books include *The End of the Asian Century: War, Stagnation, and the Risks to the World's Most Dynamic Region*; *Pacific Cosmopolitans: A Cultural History of U.S.-Japan Relations*; and *Negotiating with Imperialism: The Unequal Treaties and the Culture of Japanese Diplomacy*. He has been a regular contributor to the *Wall Street Journal* and *National Review*, and has written articles and essays for *The Atlantic, Financial Times, Foreign Affairs, Politico*, and *The Spectator*, among other publications. He was a Fulbright scholar and was named a Young Global Leader by the World Economic Forum, among other honors, and serves as the vice chair of the Wilton Park USA Foundation.

Payson J. Treat, for whom Auslin's current Hoover position is named, held the first professorship in "Far Eastern history" at any American university, a post created for him at Stanford in 1906.

INDEX

Abe, Shinzo, 95, 107, 109, 135, 137
  foreign policy of, 112–13, 114, 115, 116,
    126, 128
Adams, Henry, 102
ADB. *See* Asian Development Bank
aerial warfare, 11–12
AIIB. *See* Asia Infrastructure Investment
  Bank
airlines
  China's conflict over Taiwan indepen-
    dence and global, 21–22, 41
  US, 21–22
Akihito (Heisei emperor), 100, 104
ARIA. *See* Asia Reassurance Initiative
  Act of 2018
Article 9 (Japanese constitution), 114–115
ASEAN. *See* Association of Southeast
  Asian Nations
Asia
  dim prospects for stability and growth
    in, 4
  Japanese foreign policy and, 95
  key trends shaping, 1
  Sino-American relations and, 121–22,
    123–24, 130, 165, 224–25
  Sino-Japanese relations and, 3, 122,
    123–24, 126, 127, 130–44
  Soviet Union and, 174
  US Indo-Pacific strategy and, 149–50
  US-Japan relations and, 131, 139, 141

  See also East Asia; Indo-Pacific region;
    US-Asian relations; *specific topics*
Asia Infrastructure Investment Bank
  (AIIB), 132–33
Asia Reassurance Initiative Act of 2018
  (ARIA), 176–77
Asian Development Bank (ADB), 131–33
Asian economic sphere
  China and, 132–35, 142, 144
  financial architecture, 132–33
  institutions, agreements, development
    and aid, 131–34
  Japan and, 131–35, 142, 144
  Sino-Japanese competition and, 132–35,
    142
  US economy and, 161
  US Indo-Pacific strategy and, 161
Asian national development
  Chinese model, 139–43
  Japanese model, 139–43, 146n25
  Sino-Japanese competition and,
    139–43
Asian security sphere
  post World War II, 136
  Sino-Japanese competition and, 136–39,
    166
  US Indo-Pacific strategy and, 177–78
Asiatic Mediterranean, 1–2, 9
  China's threat to, 13, 14
  control of, 11

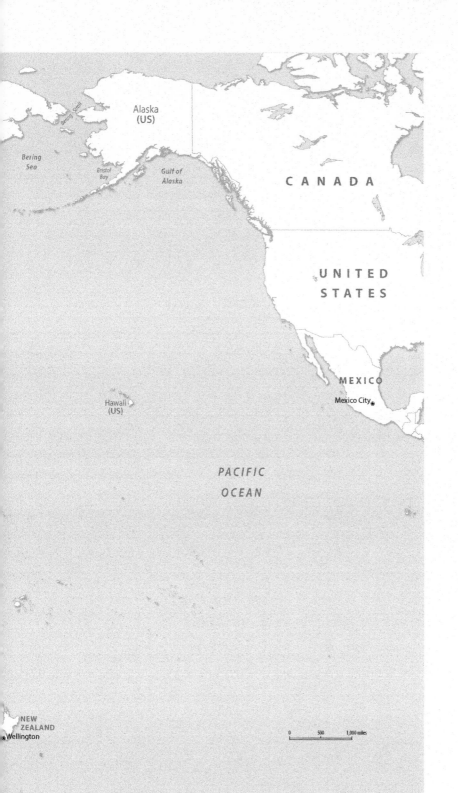